Microsoft® Office
Publisher 2007
ILLUSTRATED

INTRODUCTORY

Microsoft® Office Publisher 2007

ILLUSTRATED

INTRODUCTORY

Elizabeth Eisner Reding

THOMSON

COURSE TECHNOLOGY™

Australia • Canada • Mexico • Singapore • Spain • United Kingdom • United States

THOMSON

COURSE TECHNOLOGY™

Microsoft® Office Publisher 2007—Illustrated Introductory
Elizabeth Eisner Reding

Senior Acquisitions Editor:
Marjorie Hunt

Senior Product Manager:
Christina Kling Garrett

Product Manager:
Jane Hosie-Bounar, Dana Burnham

Associate Product Manager:
Rebecca Padrick

Editorial Assistant:
Michelle Camisa

Associate Director of Product Strategy and Communications:
Joy Stark

Marketing Coordinator:
Jennifer Hankin

Developmental Editor:
Ann Fisher

Production Editor:
Catherine G. DiMassa

Proofreader:
Gail Marks

Indexer:
Sharon Hilgenberg

QA Manuscript Reviewers:
Danielle Shaw, Susan Whalen

Cover Designers:
Elizabeth Paquin, Kathleen Fivel

Cover Artist:
Mark Hunt

Composition:
GEX Publishing Services

About This Book

Welcome to *Microsoft Office Publisher 2007—Illustrated Introductory*! Since the first edition of this book was published, millions of students have used various texts in the *Illustrated* series to learn many software applications. We are proud to bring you the latest edition of this book.

As we set out to write this book, our goals were to develop a textbook that:

- meets the needs of students who want to learn how to create professional-looking custom publications
- provides real-life exercises and examples
- serves as a reference tool
- makes your job as an educator easier, by providing resources above and beyond the textbook to help you teach your course.

Our popular, streamlined format is based on advice from instructional designers and customers. This flexible design presents each lesson on a two-page spread, with step-by-step instructions on the left, and screen illustrations on the right. This signature style, coupled with high-caliber content, provides a comprehensive yet manageable introduction to Microsoft Office Publisher 2007 — it is a teaching package for the instructor and a learning experience for the student.

Author Acknowledgments

A book may look like only a few people worked on it, but in reality, it takes scores of dedicated professionals to take it from a table of contents to a printed package. It's just not possible to thank every person involved in this project, but I will take this opportunity to mention a few key members of the team: Marjorie Hunt, the Executive Editor who made this team a reality; Ann Fisher, the Development Editor, Product Manager, and constant companion; Jane Hosie-Bounar and Dana Burnham, the (Inside) Product Managers, Rebecca Padrick, the Associate Product Manager who put together the Instructor Resources, Cathie DiMassa, the Production Editor and manager of all aspects of the production process; Susan Whalen and Danielle Shaw, the QA testers who were able to debug these lessons with style and class; and Michael Reding, my husband, whose unending patience and support is a constant joy.

Preface

Welcome to *Microsoft Office Publisher 2007—Illustrated Introductory*. If this is your first experience with the Illustrated series, you'll see that this book has a unique design: each skill is presented on two facing pages, with steps on the left and screens on the right. The layout makes it easy to digest a skill without having to read a lot of text and flip pages to see an illustration.

This book is an ideal learning tool for a wide range of learners—the "rookies" will find the clean design easy to follow and focused with only essential information presented, and the "hot-shots" will appreciate being able to move quickly through the lessons to find the information they need without reading a lot of text. The design also makes this a great reference after the course is over! See the illustration on the right to learn more about the pedagogical and design elements of a typical lesson.

What's New in This Edition

We've made many changes and enhancements to this edition to make it the best ever. Here are some highlights of what's new:

- **Redesigned Unit Opener Page** — The first page of each unit now includes a listing of all the Data Files that are needed for the unit.

- **Real Life Independent Challenge** — The new Real Life Independent Challenge exercises offer students the opportunity to create projects that are meaningful to their lives, such as a resume, a personal budget, or a database to keep track of classes, books, and professors.

- **Content Improvements** — All of the content in the book has been updated to cover Publisher 2007 and also to address instructor feedback. See the Instructor Resources CD for details on specific content changes for each application section.

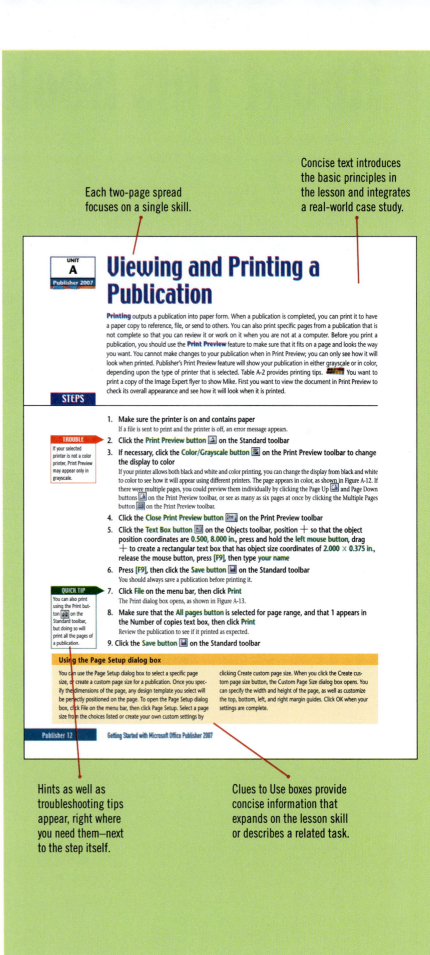

Each two-page spread focuses on a single skill.

Concise text introduces the basic principles in the lesson and integrates a real-world case study.

Hints as well as troubleshooting tips appear, right where you need them—next to the step itself.

Clues to Use boxes provide concise information that expands on the lesson skill or describes a related task.

Assignments

The lessons feature Image Expert, a small, fictional advertising agency that works with a wide range of clients to improve their appearance through the use of print media. The assignments on the light purple pages at the end of each unit increase in difficulty. Additional case studies provide a variety of interesting and relevant exercises for students to practice skills. Assignments include:

- **Concepts Reviews** consist of multiple choice, matching, and screen identification questions.

- **Skills Reviews** provide additional hands-on, step-by-step reinforcement.

- **Independent Challenges** are case projects requiring critical thinking and application of the unit skills. The Independent Challenges increase in difficulty, with the first one in each unit being the easiest. Independent Challenges 2 and 3 become increasingly open-ended, requiring more independent problem solving.

- **Real Life Independent Challenges** are practical exercises in which students create documents to help them with their every day lives.

- **Advanced Challenge Exercises** set within the Independent Challenges provide optional steps for more advanced students.

- **Visual Workshops** are practical, self-graded capstone projects that require independent problem solving.

Every lesson features large, full-color representations of what the screen should look like as students complete the numbered steps.

Application tabs indicate which section of the book you are in.

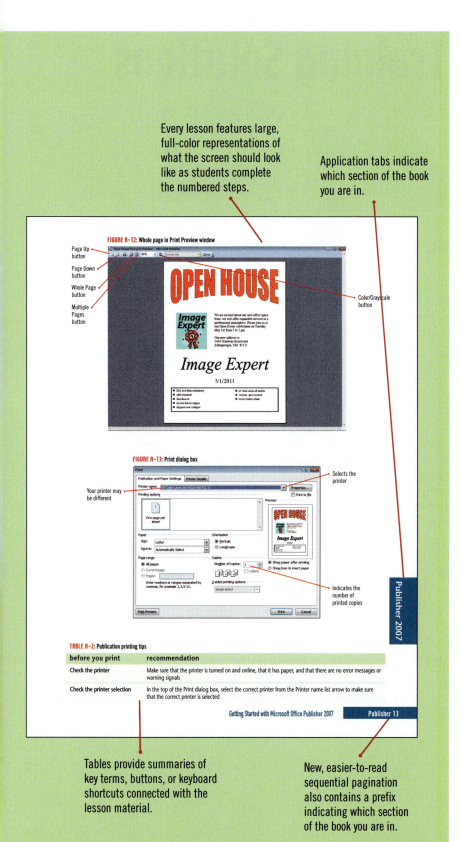

Tables provide summaries of key terms, buttons, or keyboard shortcuts connected with the lesson material.

New, easier-to-read sequential pagination also contains a prefix indicating which section of the book you are in.

Assessment & Training Solutions

SAM 2007

SAM 2007 helps bridge the gap between the classroom and the real world by allowing students to train and test on important computer skills in an active, hands-on environment.

SAM 2007's easy-to-use system includes powerful interactive exams, training, or projects on critical applications such as Word, Excel, Access, PowerPoint, Outlook, Windows, Internet Explorer, and much more. SAM simulates the application environment, allowing students to demonstrate their knowledge and think through the skills by performing real-world tasks.

Designed to be used with the Illustrated series, SAM 2007 includes built-in page references so students can print helpful study guides that match the Illustrated textbooks used in class. Powerful administrative options allow instructors to schedule exams and assignments, secure tests, and run reports with almost limitless flexibility.

Student Edition Labs

Our Web-based interactive labs help students master hundreds of computer concepts, including input and output devices, file management and desktop applications, computer ethics, virus protection, and much more. Featuring up-to-the-minute content, eye-popping graphics, and rich animation, the highly interactive Student Edition Labs offer students an alternative way to learn through dynamic observation, step-by-step practice, and challenging review questions. Also available on CD at an additional cost.

A Guided Tour of Microsoft Office 2007, Windows Vista Edition

This CD of movie tutorials helps students get exposed to the new features of Microsoft Office 2007 quickly. Dynamic and engaging author Corinne Hoisington presents the highlights of the new features of Word, Excel, Access, and PowerPoint plus a bonus movie tutorial on Windows Vista. This CD is a great supplement to this book, offering a fun overview of the software to inspire students and show them what is possible.

Instructor Resources

The Instructor Resources CD is Thomson Course Technology's way of putting the resources and information needed to teach and learn effectively into your hands. With an integrated array of teaching and learning tools that offer you and your students a broad range of technology-based instructional options, we believe this CD represents the highest quality and most cutting edge resources available to instructors today. Many of these resources are available at *www.course.com*. The resources available with this book are:

- **Instructor's Manual**—Available as an electronic file, the Instructor's Manual includes detailed lecture topics with teaching tips for each unit.

- **Sample Syllabus**—Prepare and customize your course easily using this sample course outline.

- **PowerPoint Presentations**—Each unit has a corresponding PowerPoint presentation that you can use in lecture, distribute to your students, or customize to suit your course.

- **Figure Files**—The figures in the text are provided on the Instructor Resources CD to help you illustrate key topics or concepts. You can create traditional overhead transparencies by printing the figure files. Or you can create electronic slide shows by using the figures in a presentation program such as PowerPoint.

- **Solutions to Exercises**—Solutions to Exercises contains every file students are asked to create or modify in the lessons and end-of-unit material. Also provided in this section is a document outlining the solutions for the end-of-unit Concepts Review, Skills Review, and Independent Challenges. An Annotated Solution File and Grading Rubric accompany each file and can be used together for quick and easy grading.

- **Data Files for Students**—To complete most of the units in this book, your students will need Data Files. You can post the Data Files on a file server for students to copy. The Data Files are available on the Instructor Resources CD, the Review Pack, and can also be downloaded from *www.course.com*. In this edition, we have included a lesson on downloading the Data Files for this book on page xix.

Instruct students to use the Data Files List included on the Review Pack and the Instructor Resources CD. This list gives instructions on copying and organizing files.

- **ExamView**—ExamView is a powerful testing software package that allows you to create and administer printed, computer (LAN-based), and Internet exams. ExamView includes hundreds of questions that correspond to the topics covered in this text, enabling students to generate detailed study guides that include page references for further review. The computer-based and Internet testing components allow students to take exams at their computers, and also saves you time by grading each exam automatically.

CourseCasts—Learning on the Go. Always Available...Always Relevant.

Want to keep up with the latest technology trends relevant to you? Visit our site to find a library of podcasts, CourseCasts, featuring a "CourseCast of the Week," and download them to your mp3 player at *http://coursecasts.course.com*.

Our fast-paced world is driven by technology. You know because you're an active participant—always on the go, always keeping up with technological trends, and always learning new ways to embrace technology to power your life.

Ken Baldauf, a faculty member of the Florida State University Computer Science Department, is responsible for teaching technology classes to thousands of FSU students each year. He knows what you know; he knows what you want to learn. He's also an expert in the latest technology and will sort through and aggregate the most pertinent news and information so you can spend your time enjoying technology, rather than trying to figure it out.

Visit us at *http://coursecasts.course.com* to learn on the go!

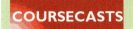

Brief Contents

Contents

Read This Before You Begin

Frequently Asked Questions

What are Data Files?

A Data File is a partially completed Publisher publication, or another type of file that you use to complete the steps in the units and exercises to create the final document that you submit to your instructor. Each unit opener page lists the Data Files that you need for that unit.

Where are the Data Files?

Your instructor will provide the Data Files to you or direct you to a location on a network drive from which you can download them. Alternatively, you can follow the instructions on the next page to download the Data Files from this book's Web page.

What software was used to write and test this book?

This book was written and tested using a typical installation of Microsoft Office 2007 installed on a computer with a typical installation of Microsoft Windows Vista Home Premium Edition, with Aero turned off. If you are using Windows XP, please see "Important Notes for Windows XP Users" on the next page.

The browser used for any steps that require a browser is Windows Internet Explorer 7.

Do I need to be connected to the Internet to complete the steps and exercises in this book?

Some of the exercises in this book assume that your computer is connected to the Internet. If you are not connected to the Internet, see your instructor for information on how to complete the exercises.

What do I do if my screen is different from the figures shown in this book?

This book was written and tested on computers with monitors set at a resolution of 1024 × 768. If your screen shows more or less information than the figures in the book, your monitor is probably set at a higher or lower resolution. If you don't see something on your screen, you might have to scroll down or up to see the object identified in the figures.

Important Notes for Windows XP Users

The screenshots in this book show Publisher 2007 running on Windows Vista. However, if you are using Microsoft Windows XP, you can still use this book because Publisher 2007 runs virtually the same on both platforms. There are a few differences that you will encounter if you are using Windows XP. Read this section to understand the differences.

Dialog boxes

If you are a Windows XP user, dialog boxes shown in this book will look slightly different than what you see on your screen. Dialog boxes for Windows XP have a blue title bar, instead of a gray title bar. However, beyond this difference in appearance, the options in the dialog boxes across platforms are the same.

Alternate Steps for Windows XP Users

Nearly all of the steps in this book work exactly the same for Windows XP users. However, there are a few tasks that will require you to complete slightly different steps. This section provides alternate steps for a few specific skills.

Starting a program

1. Click the **Start button** on the taskbar
2. Point to **All Programs**, point to **Microsoft Office**, then **Microsoft Office Publisher 2007**

FIGURE 3: Starting a program

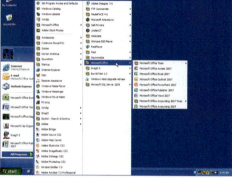

Saving a file for the first time

1. Click **File**, then click **Save As**
2. Type a name for your file in the File name text box
3. Click the **Save in list arrow**, then navigate to the drive and folder where you store your Data Files
4. Click **Save**

FIGURE 4: Save As dialog box

Opening a file

1. Click **File**, then click **Open**
2. Click the **Look in list arrow**, then navigate to the drive and folder where you store your Data Files
3. Click the file you want to open
4. Click **Open**

FIGURE 5: Open dialog box

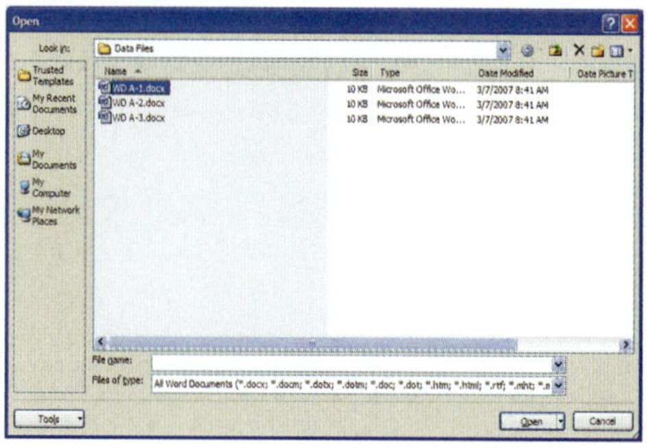

Downloading Data Files for This Book

In order to complete many of the lesson steps and exercises in this book, you are asked to open and save Data Files. A **Data File** is a partially completed Publisher publication, or another type of file that you use as a starting point to complete the steps in the units and exercises. The benefit of using a Data File is that it saves you the time and effort needed to create a file; you can simply open a Data File, save it with a new name (so the original file remains intact), then make changes to it to complete lesson steps or an exercise. Your instructor will provide the Data Files to you or direct you to a location on a network drive from which you can download them. Alternatively, you can follow the instructions in this lesson to download the Data Files from this book's Web page.

1. Start Internet Explorer, type www.course.com in the address bar, then press [Enter]

2. When the Course.com Web site opens, click the Student Downloads link

3. On the Student Downloads page, click in the Search text box, type this book's ISBN: 9781423905288, then click Go

QUICK TIP
You can also click Student Downloads on the right side of the product page.

4. When the page opens for this textbook, in the left navigation bar, click the Download Student Files link, then, on the Student Downloads page, click the Data Files link

5. If the File Download – Security Warning dialog box opens, click Save. (If no dialog box appears, skip this step and go to Step 6)

TROUBLE
If a dialog box opens telling you that the download is complete, click Close.

6. If the Save As dialog box opens, click the Save in list arrow at the top of the dialog box, select a folder on your USB drive or hard disk to download the file to, then click Save

7. Close Internet Explorer and then open My Computer (Windows XP) or Computer (Windows Vista) or Windows Explorer and display the contents of the drive and folder to which you downloaded the file

8. Double-click the file 905288.exe in the drive or folder, then, if the Open File – Security Warning dialog box opens, click Run

QUICK TIP
By default, the files will extract to C:\CourseTechnology\

9. In the WinZip Self-Extractor window, navigate to the drive and folder where you want to unzip the files to, then click Unzip

10. When the WinZip Self-Extractor displays a dialog box listing the number of files that have unzipped successfully, click OK, click Close in the WinZip Self-Extractor dialog box, then close Windows Explorer, My Computer, or Computer

You are now ready to open the required files.

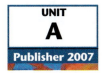

Getting Started with Microsoft Office Publisher 2007

Files You Will Need:

PUB A-1.pub

PUB A-2.pub

PUB A-3.pub

PUB A-4.pub

PUB A-5.pub

Microsoft Office Publisher 2007 is a popular desktop publishing program that uses the Windows operating system. In this unit, you learn how to start Publisher and work in the Publisher program window. You also learn how to open and save existing files, enter text in a publication, view and print a publication, use the extensive Help system, and change Business Information. You work at Image Expert, a small advertising agency, as an assistant to Mike Mendoza, an account executive. Mike asks you to create a flyer announcing the location of the agency's new office. You decide to use Publisher to create this publication.

OBJECTIVES

Define publication software

Start Publisher 2007

View the Publisher window

Open and save a publication

Enter text in a text box

View and print a publication

Get Help and change Business Information

Close a publication and exit Publisher

Capstone Project: Study Abroad Flyer

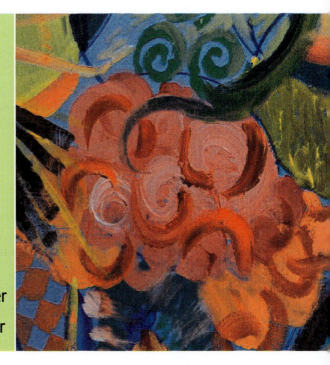

Defining Publication Software

Publisher is a **desktop publishing program**, a software program that lets you combine text and graphics, as well as worksheets and charts created in other programs, to produce typeset-quality documents for output on a computer printer, or for commercial printing. A document created in Publisher is called a **publication**. Table A-1 describes the types of publications you can create. You want to learn how to use Publisher so that you can generate a professional-looking flyer quickly and easily.

The benefits of using Publisher include the ability to:

- **Create professional publications**

  Publisher comes with a generous collection of templates, designs that let you choose the type of publication you want to develop, help you decide on its appearance, then suggest text and graphic image placement to complete the publication. Once you choose a template from the Publication Types list, you can easily modify it to meet specific needs, using options in the Format Publication task pane.

- **Use clip art**

  Artwork not only makes any publication appear more vibrant and interesting, but also helps to reflect and reinforce your ideas with visual images. Publisher comes with more than 150,000 pieces of artwork that can be incorporated into publications. In addition, other illustrations, sound files, video clips, and photographs can be imported into **Microsoft Clip Organizer**, the artwork library that all Office 2007 applications share.

- **Create logos**

  Most organizations use a recognizable symbol, shape, color, or combination of these to attach to their name. This distinctive artwork, called a **logo**, can be created using Publisher's Design Gallery, or by designing your own artwork and text. Figure A-1 illustrates a sample flyer created in Publisher that contains a logo formed by combining clip art and text.

- **Make your work look consistent**

  Publisher has many tools to help you create consistent publications that have similar design elements. You can use **designs** to create different types of stylized publications. When creating work from scratch, you might, for example, want to designate an area on the page that always displays the same information, such as a company name or mission statement. Using rulers and layout guides, you can create grids to help position graphics and text on a page. You can also save a publication as a **template**, a specially formatted publication of your own design with placeholder text that serves as a master for other, similar publications.

- **Work with multiple pages**

  Publisher makes it easy to work with multi-page publications. Pages can be added, deleted, and moved within a publication. Text that flows from one page to another can be connected with continued on and continued from notices, sometimes called 'jump lines'.

- **Emphasize special text**

  Even great writing can be less than compelling if all the text looks the same. Using varied text styles to express different meanings and convey messages can add interest and help guide the reader's eye. You can use headlines to grab readers and lead them to stories of specific significance. You can use a sidebar to make a short statement more noticeable, or a pull quote to make an important point stand out and grab a reader's attention. Altering the appearance of text by making it bold, italicized, or underlined can emphasize the significance of text.

- **Publish to the Internet**

  Publisher contains design elements specifically for Web sites, making it easy to include links and graphics. Page backgrounds and animated GIFs add color and motion to your pages. The Publish to the Web command helps you add common Web features to a print document, and makes your Web site available to a local network drive, an intranet, or an Internet Service Provider for worldwide viewing.

FIGURE A-1: Sample flyer

Logo consists of text and graphic images

TABLE A-1: Common publications you can create in Publisher

publication type	example
Informational	Brochures, signs, calendars, forms
Periodical	Newsletters, catalogs
Promotional	Advertisements, flyers, press releases
Stationery	Letterhead, labels, business cards, envelopes, postcards, invitations
Specialty	Banners, airplanes, origami, resumes, award certificates, gift certificates

Publisher 2007

Design Matters

Creating branded publications

Branded publications are those that have a similar look to them giving your company instant recognition. It may be as simple as putting your company logo on everything, or using a specific color in a special design. Common examples of branding are seen in the Nike swoosh and the Motorola 'M'. When you use templates that have the same patterns, such as the Arrows and Brocade designs, or your own design, all your print and Web materials will have a similar look. This similar look will be associated with your company or 'brand'.

Starting Publisher 2007

To start Publisher, you click the Start button on the taskbar to access the Start menu. A slightly different procedure might be required for computers on a network, and those that use utility programs to enhance Windows. If you need assistance, ask your instructor or technical support person for help. When you start Publisher, the program displays a list of publication types and file options in the left pane, and a workspace in the right pane. The workspace may also display samples of publication types when you click a link in the left pane. Before you can create the publication, you need to start Publisher and open a new document.

STEPS

1. **Locate the Start button 🔵 on the taskbar**
   The Start button is on the left side of the taskbar and is used to start programs on your computer.

2. **Click 🔵**
   Microsoft Office Publisher is located in the All Programs group, located near the bottom of the Start menu.

3. **Point to All Programs**
   All of the programs on your computer, including Microsoft Office Publisher, can be found in this area of the Start menu. Your All Programs menu might look different, depending on which programs are installed on your computer.

> **TROUBLE**
> If you don't see the Microsoft Office Publisher 2007 icon, look in a folder called Microsoft Office or Office 2007, or ask your instructor or technical support person

4. **Click Microsoft Office**
   A submenu opens, listing all the Microsoft Office programs installed on your computer. You can see the Microsoft Office Publisher 2007 icon 🔲 and the icons of other programs.

5. **Click the Microsoft Office Publisher 2007 program icon 🔲, as shown in Figure A-2**
   The Microsoft Publisher window opens with the Publication Types list on the left side of the screen. You can start a new publication by choosing a publication category in the Publication Types list, then clicking a template design in the workspace. You can also start a new blank publication by clicking the Blank Page Sizes category or open an existing publication (by clicking the From File link in the Recent Publications section).

6. **Position ⬚ over Blank Page Sizes in the Popular Publication Types workspace, but do not click**
   The pointer changes to 🖑 when positioned over Blank Page Sizes.

7. **Click Blank Page Sizes in the Popular Publication Types workspace**
   You can choose from a variety of page widths and dimensions

> **QUICK TIP**
> for help.
> You can also double-click your choice instead of single-clicking your choice,

8. **Click Letter (Portrait) 8.5 x 11" as shown in Figure A-3, then click Create**
   A blank full-page publication appears in the workspace.

9. **Click the Close button ⊠ in the Format Publication task pane, then click the Close button ⊠ in any floating toolbars, if necessary**

FIGURE A-2: Start menu and All Programs menu

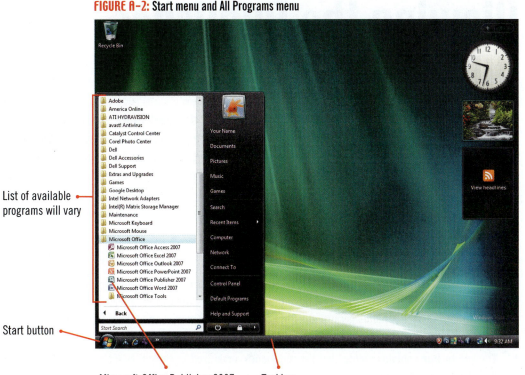

List of available programs will vary

Start button

Microsoft Office Publisher 2007 program icon

Taskbar

FIGURE A-3: Blank page sizes

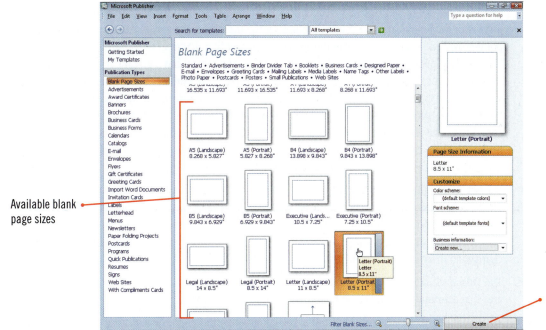

Available blank page sizes

Click to create publication

Publisher 2007

Creating a New Publication

When you first open Publisher, the Microsoft Publisher window opens with the "Getting Started" category selected along the left side of the window. This window has three sections: Publication Types, the workspace, and Recent Publications. The Publication Types section is simply a list of categories for publication types, such as newsletters. The workspace section displays all of the available template designs based upon which category is selected in the Publication Types list and the Recent Publications section allows you to open a recently used file, or to search for an existing publication. Once you make a selection, you will be asked to choose a style or page size and paper width. Click Create in the lower-right corner and your new publication will open.

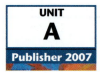

Viewing the Publisher Window

The area where a new or existing publication appears is called the **workspace**, which includes both the publication page and the scratch area. The workspace is where you actually work on a publication, and view your work. The workspace is bordered above and on the left by horizontal and vertical rulers that help you position text and graphics in your publications. The workspace is also bordered by horizontal and vertical scroll bars that allow you to view different areas of the workspace. You decide to take some time to get familiar with the Publisher workspace and its elements before working on the flyer. Compare the descriptions below to Figure A-4.

STEPS

- The **title bar** is at the top of the window, and displays the program name (Microsoft Publisher), the type of publication (Print or Web), and the filename of the open publication. In Figure A-4, the filename is Publication1, a default name, because the file has not yet been named and saved. The title bar also contains a Control menu box, a Close button, and resizing buttons.

- The **menu bar** contains menus that list commands, organized in categories such as View and Format. In Publisher, you can choose a menu command by clicking it with the mouse, or by pressing [Alt] plus the underlined letter in the menu name. Some menu commands contain a right-pointing arrow indicating that there are submenus with additional options. The Publisher Help feature can also be accessed by typing a question in the box on the right of the menu bar.

QUICK TIP

Any floating (non-docked) toolbar can be closed by clicking the Close button ✕ in its upper-right corner.

- The **toolbars** contain buttons for frequently used Publisher commands. The **Standard toolbar** is located just below the menu bar and contains buttons for the most frequently used Publisher commands. Place the pointer over each button to display the ScreenTip, a label that describes what each button does. To select a button, click it with the left mouse button. The face of any button has a graphic representation of its function; for instance, the Print button has a printer on its face. The **Objects toolbar** is on the left side of the screen next to the vertical ruler, and contains buttons used to insert the most frequently used objects (text boxes, clip art, geometric shapes) into publications. The **Formatting toolbar** appears just above the horizontal ruler and contains buttons for often used text formatting commands such as bold, italics, or underlining. Toolbars can be opened or closed by clicking View on the menu bar, pointing to Toolbars, and clicking to select or deselect the particular toolbar.

- **Rulers** let you precisely measure the size of objects, as well as place objects in exact locations on a page. They can be moved from the edge of the workspace to more convenient positions. Your rulers may have different beginning and ending numbers, depending on the size of your monitor, the resolution of your display, and the positioning of the page on the workspace. The units of measurement displayed in rulers can be changed to show inches, centimeters, picas, or points.

- The workspace contains the currently displayed page and the scratch area. The **scratch area** is the gray area that surrounds the publication page, and can be used to store objects.

- The **status bar** is located at the bottom of the Publisher window. On the left side of the status bar are **page navigation icons**, which show you the number of pages in a publication, and are used to navigate from page to page. Click the icon for the page you want to view. In a multi-page publication, an icon is displayed for each page; the icon for the current page appears in light blue. The right side of the status bar shows the object status, which includes the size and position of selected objects.

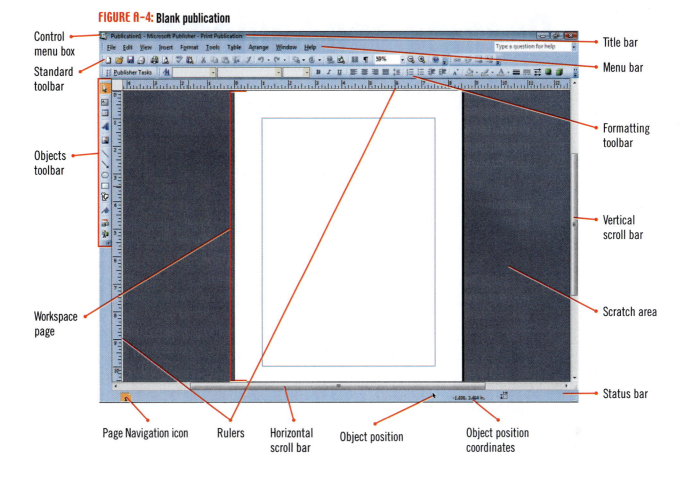

FIGURE A-4: Blank publication

Control menu box

Standard toolbar

Objects toolbar

Workspace page

Page Navigation icon

Rulers

Horizontal scroll bar

Object position

Object position coordinates

Title bar

Menu bar

Formatting toolbar

Vertical scroll bar

Scratch area

Status bar

Using task panes

The **task pane** is an area of the Publisher window that is used to organize design templates, color schemes, font schemes, and other layout tools in a visual gallery, which appears alongside your publication. In addition to the Format Publication task pane, seen in Figure A-5, you can use task panes for a variety of activities such as creating a new publication, editing business information, choosing font schemes, selecting a publication design, working with styles and formatting, and even doing a mail merge. You can turn the Task Pane feature on or off using the View menu on the menu bar. You can move back and forth between open task panes by clicking the Forward or Back buttons in the upper-left corner of the task pane. You can see more task pane options by clicking the Other Task Panes list arrow in the task pane title bar. You can also close the task pane by clicking the Close button in the upper-right corner of the task pane.

FIGURE A-5: Format Publication task pane

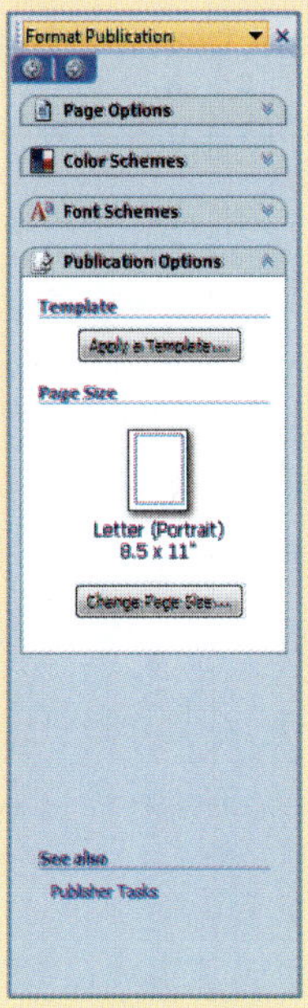

Publisher 2007

Opening and Saving a Publication

Often a project is completed in stages: you start working on a publication, save it, and then stop to do other work or take a break. Later, you open the publication and resume working on it. Sometimes you open a file and save it under another name, either because you want to create a new publication by modifying one that already exists, or because you want to make changes to the document while preserving a copy of the original for safekeeping. Throughout this book, you will be instructed to open a file from the drive and folder where you store your Data Files, use the Save As command to create a copy of the file with a new name, then modify the new file by following the lesson steps. Saving the files with new names keeps your original Data Files intact in case you have to start the lesson over again, or you wish to repeat an exercise. Mike started the Image Expert flyer and gives you the file so that you can complete the document. You are ready to open the file and create a copy of it with a new name so that you can safely make changes.

STEPS

1. **Click the Open button 📂 on the Standard toolbar**
    The Open Publication dialog box opens. A dialog box is a window that opens when more information is needed to carry out a command. A list of the available folders and publications appears. The files that you need for these lessons are located where you store your Data Files.

2. **Navigate to the drive and folder where you store your Data Files**
    A list of the Data Files appears, as shown in Figure A-6.

3. **Click PUB A-1.pub, then click Open**
    The file PUB A-1 opens. You could also double-click the filename in the Open Publication dialog box to open the file.

4. **Click File on the menu bar, then click Save As**
    The Save As dialog box opens.

    > **TROUBLE**
    > If you receive a message that the printer cannot be initialized, click OK to change to your default printer.

5. **Make sure that the drive and folder where you store your Data Files appears in the Folders list.**
    You should save all your files in the drive and folder where you store your Data Files unless instructed otherwise.

6. **Select the current filename in the File name text box if necessary, then type Open House Flyer**
    See Figure A-7.

    > **QUICK TIP**
    > Use the Save As command to create a new publication from an existing one. Use the save command to store any changes made to an existing file on your disk.

7. **Click Save**
    The Save As dialog box closes, the file PUB A-1.pub closes, and a duplicate file named Open House Flyer.pub is now open, as shown in Figure A-8. Changes made to Open House Flyer will not be reflected in the file PUB A-1.pub. To save the publication in the future, you can click File on the menu bar, then click Save, or click the Save button 💾 on the Standard toolbar.

FIGURE A-6: Open Publication dialog box

Views list arrow

Previous Locations list arrow

FIGURE A-7: Save As dialog box

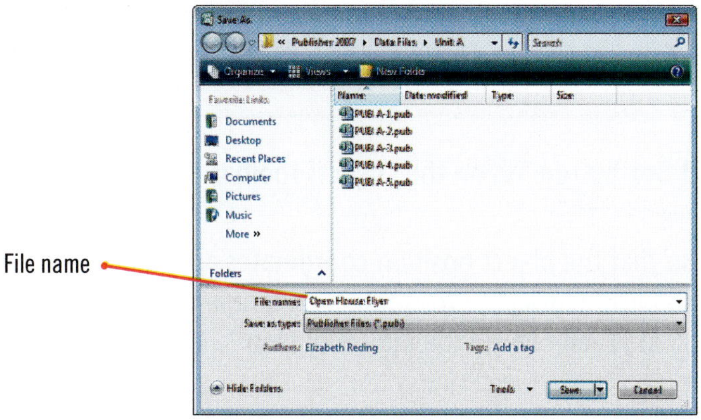

File name

FIGURE A-8: Open House Flyer publication

Publication name appears in title bar

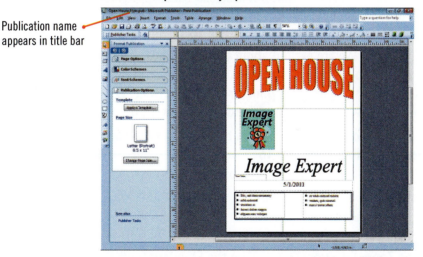

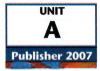
Entering Text in a Text Box

In word processing, text is entered directly on a page and is the main element of a document. In desktop publishing, text forms part of the publication, along with images and graphic design elements. A **text box** is an object that can be resized and repositioned on a page. Once you type or paste text in a text box, you can easily manipulate the object relative to the graphics and other objects on a page, to achieve the best overall layout. **Point size** is the unit of measurement for fonts, and the space between paragraphs and text characters. There are 72 points in an inch. Because stories often continue onto another page, you can connect two or more text boxes, so the text flows logically from one page to the next. You can select a text box by clicking anywhere within it. When selected, small hollow circles called **handles** appear at eight points around its perimeter. A publication also includes **placeholders**, which help you envision what type of information to include and where. **Ruler guides** are green horizontal and vertical lines that appear on the screen to help you position objects on a page, but do not print in the publication. You want to include the address of the new office space in the flyer, so you decide to create a text box to the right of the Image Expert logo to contain this information. You'll use ruler guides to position the text box just where you want it.

STEPS

1. **Click the Text Box button ▣ on the Objects toolbar**
   The pointer changes to ➕.

2. **Position ➕ so that the object position coordinates are 3.500, 4.000 in., press and hold the left mouse button, drag ➕ to create a rectangle that has object size coordinates of 4.000 × 2.750 in., then release the mouse button**
   As you drag the text box, the coordinates on the status bar display the position of the pointer and object size. The ruler guides also help you position and size the text box correctly. When you release the mouse button, the text box appears as a selected object surrounded by handles, with the insertion point blinking in the upper-left corner, as shown in Figure A-9. Additional buttons appear on the Standard and Formatting toolbars when the text box is selected. This means that Publisher is ready for you to type text, and has made the relevant tools available to you.

   QUICK TIP

   You can also zoom in using the View menu or the Zoom In 🔍 button on the Standard toolbar.

3. **Press [F9], type We are excited about our new office space. Here, we will offer expanded services in a professional atmosphere. Please join us at our Open House celebration on Tuesday, May 1st, from 1 to 5 p.m., press [Enter] twice, type Our new address is:, press [Enter], type 3444 Tramway Boulevard, press [Enter], then type Albuquerque, NM 87111**

   TROUBLE

   Wavy red lines under typed text indicate words that may be misspelled. Press [Backspace] or [Delete] to correct any typed spelling errors.

4. **Press [Ctrl][A] to select all the text in the box, click the Font Size list arrow ▣ on the Formatting toolbar, then click 16**
   Enlarging the font size makes the text stand out so it is easier to read.

5. **Click anywhere on the scratch area**
   Clicking outside the text box deselects it. You could also press [Esc] twice to deselect the text box. Compare your screen to Figure A-10.

   QUICK TIP

   You can also zoom out using the View menu or the Zoom Out 🔍 button on the Standard toolbar.

6. **Click the Zoom list arrow 100% ▾ on the Standard toolbar, then click Whole Page**
   The magnification adjusts so that the entire page is in view on the screen.

7. **Click the Save button 💾 on the Standard toolbar**
   It is a good idea to save your work early and often in the creation process, especially before making significant changes to the publication, or before printing.

Text Box button

Object width
appears on ruler

Text box

Placeholder text

Insertion point

Handles

Object position
coordinates

Object size

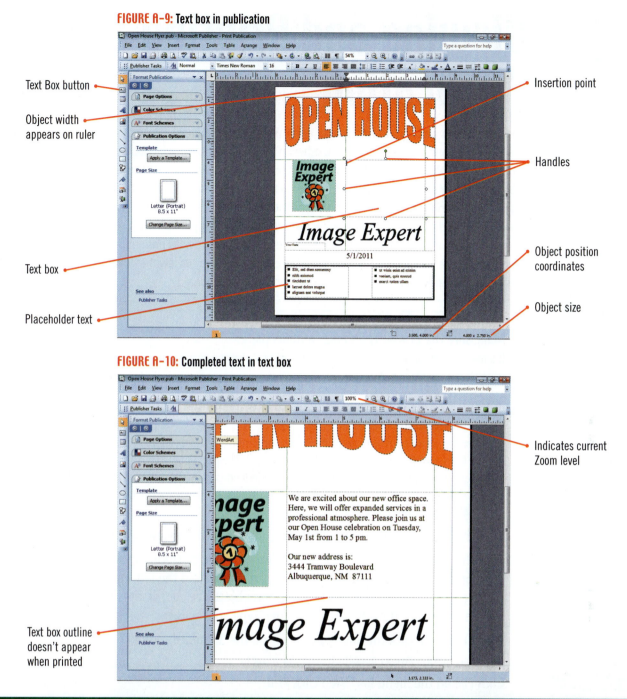

We are excited about our new office space. Here, we will offer expanded services in a professional atmosphere. Please join us at our Open House celebration on Tuesday, May 1st from 1 to 5 pm.

Our new address is:
3444 Tramway Boulevard
Albuquerque, NM 87111

Indicates current
Zoom level

Text box outline
doesn't appear
when printed

Design Matters

Understanding objects

Objects are elements such as tables, text boxes, geometric shapes, clip art, and picture frames that can be resized, moved, joined, or organized so that one object appears to be in front of another. In addition, text boxes can be wrapped around other objects. The advantage to using text boxes is that the contents within the box can be easily moved anywhere within a publication. Figure A-11 shows text wrapped around a graphic image.

FIGURE A-11: Text wrapped around a picture

to market your product or service, and also create credibility and build your organization's identity among peers, members, employees, or vendors.

First, determine the audience of the newsletter. This could be anyone who might benefit from the information it contains, for

You might consider purchasing a mailing list from a company.

If you explore the Publisher catalog, you will find many publications that match the style of your newsletter.

Next, establish how much time and money you can spend on your newsletter.

Viewing and Printing a Publication

Printing outputs a publication into paper form. When a publication is completed, you can print it to have a paper copy to reference, file, or send to others. You can also print specific pages from a publication that is not complete so that you can review it or work on it when you are not at a computer. Before you print a publication, you should use the **Print Preview** feature to make sure that it fits on a page and looks the way you want. You cannot make changes to your publication when in Print Preview; you can only see how it will look when printed. Publisher's Print Preview feature will show your publication in either grayscale or in color, depending upon the type of printer that is selected. Table A-2 provides printing tips. You want to print a copy of the Image Expert flyer to show Mike. First you want to view the document in Print Preview to check its overall appearance and see how it will look when it is printed.

STEPS

1. **Make sure the printer is on and contains paper**
   If a file is sent to print and the printer is off, an error message appears.

TROUBLE

If your selected printer is not a color printer, Print Preview may appear only in grayscale.

2. **Click the Print Preview button 🔍 on the Standard toolbar**

3. **If necessary, click the Color/Grayscale button 🖼 on the Print Preview toolbar to change the display to color**
   If your printer allows both black and white and color printing, you can change the display from black and white to color to see how it will appear using different printers. The page appears in color, as shown in Figure A-12. If there were multiple pages, you could preview them individually by clicking the Page Up 🔼 and Page Down buttons 🔽 on the Print Preview toolbar, or see as many as six pages at once by clicking the Multiple Pages button 🔲 on the Print Preview toolbar.

4. **Click the Close Print Preview button Close on the Print Preview toolbar**

5. **Click the Text Box button 🔲 on the Objects toolbar, position + so that the object position coordinates are 0.500, 8.000 in., press and hold the left mouse button, drag + to create a rectangular text box that has object size coordinates of 2.000 × 0.375 in., release the mouse button, press [F9], then type your name**

6. **Press [F9], then click the Save button 💾 on the Standard toolbar**
   You should always save a publication before printing it.

QUICK TIP

You can also print using the Print button 🖨 on the Standard toolbar, but doing so will print all the pages of a publication.

7. **Click File on the menu bar, then click Print**
   The Print dialog box opens, as shown in Figure A-13.

8. **Make sure that the All pages button is selected for page range, and that 1 appears in the Number of copies text box, then click Print**
   Review the publication to see if it printed as expected.

9. **Click the Save button 💾 on the Standard toolbar**

Using the Page Setup dialog box

You can use the Page Setup dialog box to select a specific page size, or create a custom page size for a publication. Once you specify the dimensions of the page, any design template you select will be perfectly positioned on the page. To open the Page Setup dialog box, click File on the menu bar, then click Page Setup. Select a page size from the choices listed or create your own custom settings by clicking Create custom page size. When you click the Create custom page size button, the Custom Page Size dialog box opens. You can specify the width and height of the page, as well as customize the top, bottom, left, and right margin guides. Click OK when your settings are complete.

Page Up button

Page Down button

Whole Page button

Multiple Pages button

Color/Grayscale button

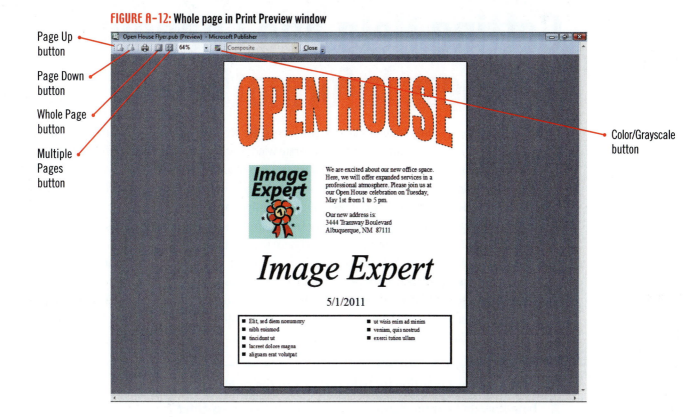

FIGURE A-13: Print dialog box

Your printer may be different

Selects the printer

Indicates the number of printed copies

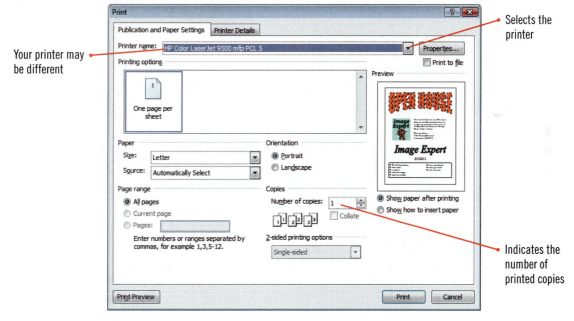

TABLE A-2: Publication printing tips

before you print	recommendation
Check the printer	Make sure that the printer is turned on and online, that it has paper, and that there are no error messages or warning signals
Check the printer selection	In the top of the Print dialog box, select the correct printer from the Printer name list arrow to make sure that the correct printer is selected

Publisher 2007

Getting Help and Changing Business Information

Publisher offers extensive **Help** features that give you immediate access to definitions, explanations, and useful tips. When open, the Help window floats in a separate window that displays over the workspace and contains links to information that assist you in your work. The window can be resized or moved for your purposes, and can remain on the screen so you can refer to it as you work. You can access Help any time while Publisher is open. Because you probably create publications for yourself, or your business or organization, Publisher makes it easy for you to store frequently used information about these entities. This feature, called **Business Information Sets**, means that you won't have to enter this information each time. You can store an unlimited number of Business Information Sets: for your business, another organization, and your home or family members. The information in the default business set can easily be changed to other information sets that you have created. You decide to use Help to find out about Business Information and how it can be modified. You want to find out how to create a Business Information Set for Image Expert that you can use to easily insert company information into publications.

STEPS

1. Click the Type a question for help text box to the right of the menu bar

2. Type How do I change Business Information?, then press Enter
   The Publisher Help window opens displaying topics about business information, as shown in Figure A-14.

3. Click Create, change, or remove business information data in the list of results, scroll down, click Change information within a business information set in the next window, then read about making modifications

4. Close the Publisher Help window

5. Click Edit on the menu bar, then click Business Information
   Any Business Information set can be modified, and the changes can be used in future publications.

6. Press [Tab] three times to select the name in the Individual name text box, type Your Name, press [Tab], then refer to Figure A-15 to enter the rest of the information in the Business Information dialog box including job title, phone numbers, and e-mail

7. Select the contents of the Business Information set name text box, type Secondary Business Information Set
   The information in the dialog box is for the current secondary business.

8. Click Save, then click Update Publication after confirming that the information you entered is correct
   Clicking Update Publication confirms your changes to the information set.

> **QUICK TIP**
>
> You can print the information in any Help window by clicking the Print button on the Publisher Help window toolbar.

> **QUICK TIP**
>
> You can also edit Business Information by clicking the Other Task Panes list arrow, then clicking Business Information. Click the list arrow next to the information you want to edit, then click Change Business Information.

Search topic

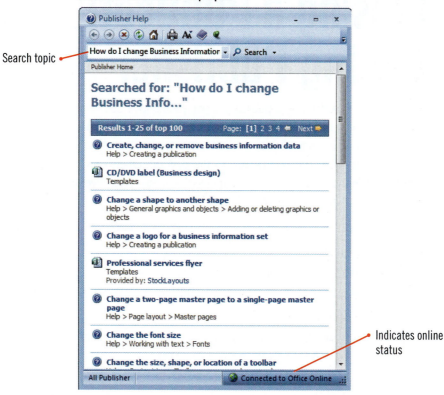

Indicates online status

FIGURE A-15: Create New Business Information Set dialog box

Information displayed is for the Secondary Business information set

Saves current information

Closing a Publication and Exiting Publisher

When you finish working on a publication, you should save the file and close it. Closing a file puts away a publication so you can no longer work on it, but leaves Publisher running so you can work on other publications. When you complete all your work in Publisher, you want to exit the program. Exiting puts away any open publication files and returns you to the desktop, where you can choose to run another program. You finished adding the information to the Image Expert flyer and need to attend a meeting, so you close the publication and then exit Publisher.

STEPS

1. **Click File on the menu bar**
   The File menu opens. See Figure A-16.

2. **Click Close, then click Yes if a dialog box opens asking if you want to save your changes**

3. **Click File on the menu bar, then click Exit**
   You could also double-click the program control menu box to exit the program. Publisher closes, and computer memory is freed up for other computing tasks.

Opening a file with a single click

You can quickly open a recently used publication with a single click using the Recent Publications list. The Recent Publications list appears at the bottom of the File menu and displays a list of recently used Publisher files. To open a file in this list, simply click the name of the file you want.

FIGURE A-16: Closing a publication using the File menu

Close command

Exit command

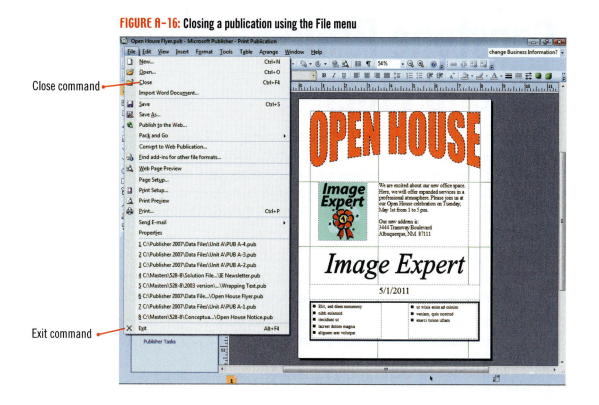

Microsoft Office Publisher World Wide Web site

You can get even more information about Microsoft Publisher by accessing the Microsoft Office Publisher Web site. This site is updated frequently, and offers tips, upgrades, sales promotions, and information on new developments in Publisher. By clicking on the blue underlined links, you'll be able to find additional information on the Microsoft product line. Figure A-17 shows the Web site for Microsoft Office Publisher. It may look different on your screen, because the site changes often. To find even more information, you can search the Internet using your favorite search engine for any sites about Microsoft Publisher. To visit the Publisher Web site, click the Help menu, then click Microsoft Office Online. When the Web site opens, click Products, then the Publisher link.)

FIGURE A-17: Microsoft Office Publisher 2007 Web site

Site address

Links to other Web pages

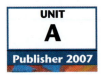
Capstone Project: Study Abroad Flyer

You have learned the basic skills necessary to modify an existing publication. You can open a file and save it under a different name. You know how to create a text box, insert text, zoom, and increase the font size to add emphasis. Once your work is complete, you can preview the flyer in both black and white and in color, then print it. ⬛ Using a template, Mike started a flyer for the Community College Council that advertises a one-credit course in Mexico. He asks you to complete the project by adding contact information and then reviewing and printing the document.

STEPS

1. Start Publisher, click **File** on the menu bar, click **Open**, open **PUB A-2.pub** from the drive and folder where you store your Data Files, then save the publication as **Study Abroad Flyer**

2. Close the task pane if necessary, click the **Text Box button** 🔲 on the Objects toolbar, then use ➕ to create a rectangular text box from 1 1/4" H/9" V to 5 1/2" H/10" V

3. Press **[F9]** to zoom in to the text box

4. Type **For more information, contact:**, press **[Enter]**, type **your name**, press **[Enter]**, then type **Extension 5750**

5. Press **[Ctrl][A]**, click the **Font Size list arrow** [10 ▾] on the Formatting toolbar, then click **16**

    Compare your publication to Figure A-18.

6. Press **[Esc]** twice, press **[F9]** to zoom out, then click the **Save button** 💾 on the Standard toolbar

    The overall design of the publication looks good.

7. Click the **Print Preview button** 🔍 on the Standard toolbar

    The publication appears on the screen as it will appear printed. You cannot see the outlines of text boxes, or other non-printing characters.

8. Click the **Color/Grayscale button** 🖼 on the Print Preview toolbar, if necessary

    The view changes from black and white to color. Compare your publication to Figure A-19.

9. Close the Print Preview window, click the **Print button** 🖨 on the Standard toolbar, then exit Publisher

FIGURE A-18: Contact information inserted in Study Abroad Flyer

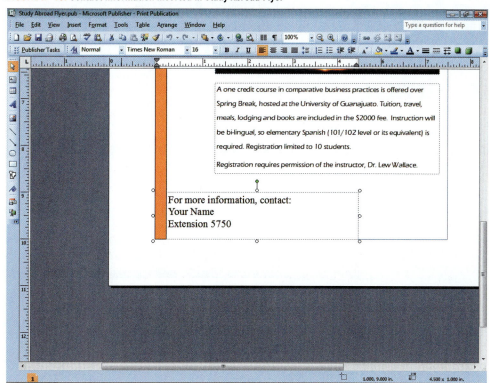

FIGURE A-19: Print Preview of Study Abroad flyer

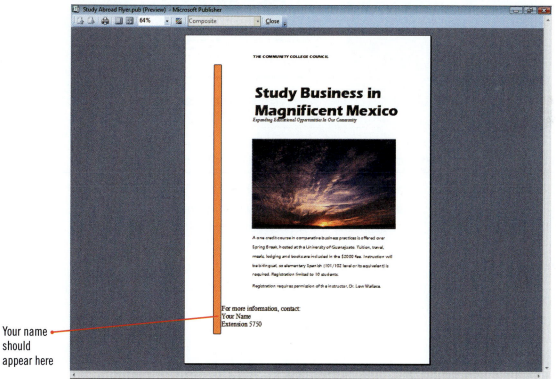

Your name
should
appear here

Practice

If you have a SAM user profile, you may have access to hands-on instruction, practice, and assessment of the skills covered in this unit. Log in to your SAM account (http://sam2007.course.com/) to launch any assigned training activities or exams that relate to the skills covered in this unit.

▼ CONCEPTS REVIEW

Label each of the elements in the Publisher window shown in Figure A-20.

FIGURE A-20

Match each of the terms or buttons with the statement that describes its function.

7. **Handles**

8. ![save icon]

9. **Text box**

10. ![print icon]

11. **Status bar**

12. ![open icon]

a. Used to save a publication to a disk

b. Small hollow circles surrounding an object

c. Shows size and position of selected object

d. Contains typed text

e. Opens an existing publication

f. Prints every page in the publication

Select the best answer from the list of choices.

13. **A document created in Publisher is called a:**
    a. Publication.
    b. Notebook.
    c. Booklet.
    d. Brochure.

14. **Which of the following is considered an object?**
    a. Text box
    b. Pictures
    c. Tables
    d. All of the above

15. **Which key is pressed to zoom into a selected area?**
    a. [F8]
    b. [F9]
    c. [F6]
    d. [F2]

16. **A template is:**
    a. A distinctive shape in a publication.
    b. A short statement placed off to the side to grab a reader's attention.
    c. An online artwork organizer.
    d. A publication that serves as a master for other publications.

17. **Which of the following statements about text boxes is false?**
    a. They can be connected to other frames.
    b. They can be resized.
    c. They aren't very useful.
    d. They can be moved.

18. **Which button is used to create a text box?**
    a. ▦
    b. ▣
    c. Times New Roman ▾
    d. 10 ▾

19. **Which type of information is not included in the Business Information set?**
    a. Address
    b. Tagline or motto
    c. Type of Business
    d. Job position or title

20. **Each of the following is found in the status bar, except:**
    a. A selected object's position.
    b. The name of the current publication.
    c. Page icons.
    d. A selected object's size.

21. **Which feature is used to magnify the view?**
    a. Magnify
    b. Amplify
    c. Enlarge
    d. Zoom In

▼ SKILLS REVIEW

1. **Define publication software.**
   a. Identify five advantages of using a desktop publishing program.
   b. Name three Publisher features that you can use to create a publication.

2. **Start Publisher 2007.**
   a. Start Publisher.
   b. Open a new blank publication of any size.

3. **View the Publisher window.**
   a. Identify as many elements in the Publisher window as you can without looking back in the unit.
   b. Which toolbars are always visible?

4. **Open and save a publication.**
   a. Open PUB A-3.pub. If you get a message to initialize the default printer, click OK.
   b. Save the publication as **Sample Business Card** in the drive and folder where you store your Data Files.
   c. Click the Format Publication task pane Close button, if necessary.

Publisher 2007

5. **Enter text in a text box.**

   a. Create a text box with the size coordinates 2.000 × 0.500 in. for your name, using Figure A-21 as an example. The top-left corner should be placed at 1.250, 0.500 in. (ruler guides were inserted to make this placement easier). Type your name using a 16 point font size or larger.

   b. Create a text box with the size coordinates 2.000 × 0.750 in. for your address, using Figure A-21 as a guide. The top-left corner should be placed at 1.250, 1.250 in. Substitute your contact information for the text shown using a 10-point text size.

   c. Save the publication.

FIGURE A-21

6. **View and print a publication.**

   a. Zoom out.

   b. Zoom in.

   c. Use the Print button to print one copy of the publication.

7. **Get Help and change Business Information.**

   a. Click the Type a question for help text box.

   b. Find information on creating a text box. (*Hint*: Use keywords "text box," then read several of the search result topics.)

   c. Click the Print button in the Publisher Help window to print the information you find.

   d. Close the Publisher Help window.

   e. Open the Business Information dialog box.

   f. Select the Secondary Business information set.

   g. Change the area codes in the telephone numbers listed from 555 to 505.

   h. Save and close the Business Information dialog box.

8. **Close the publication and exit Publisher.**

   a. Save and close your publication.

   b. Exit Publisher.

▼ INDEPENDENT CHALLENGE 1

The Publisher Help feature provides definitions, explanations, procedures, and other helpful information. You need to add a page to a brochure you are working on for your new client, Mangez!, a French importer of baked goods and cheeses. Open any existing publication, and find out how to add a page to a publication. Print out the information.

Advanced Challenge Exercise

■ Using the Type a question for help text box, find out how you can display the Measurement toolbar, then print this information.

▼ INDEPENDENT CHALLENGE 2

Publisher can be used in many ways in business and education. If you were teaching a class, how could you use Publisher to your advantage as a teaching aid?

   a. Think of three types of publications you could create with Publisher that would be effective in a classroom.

   b. Sketch a sample of each publication.

▼ INDEPENDENT CHALLENGE 2 (CONTINUED)

c. Open a blank publication for each sample. Using text boxes, re-create your sketches. (These publications do not need to be fancy; they can just contain text boxes.) Your three publications should be named **Suggestion 1**, **Suggestion 2**, and **Suggestion 3**.

d. In a separate blank publication, use text boxes to explain why each of your suggestions would be an effective use of Publisher. Name this publication **Explanations**.

e. Be sure to include your name in a text box in each publication, then print each one.

f. Save and close the publications, then exit Publisher.

▼ INDEPENDENT CHALLENGE 3

You are selected as the Image Expert Employee of the Month. You're being honored because you always come up with creative ways of accomplishing tasks. When you are given your award, you are asked for ways to improve the certificate. To complete the certificate, more explanatory text about the recipient is needed.

a. Start Publisher, if necessary, open PUB A-4.pub, then save it as **Image Expert Award** in the drive and folder where you store your Data Files.

b. If necessary, close the task pane.

c. Zoom in or out as needed. In the space above the Name of Recipient placeholder, insert a text box that contains an explanation of why you deserve this award.

d. Replace the Name of Recipient placeholder with your name.

e. Print the final publication.

f. Save your work, then compare it to the sample shown in Figure A-22.

FIGURE A-22

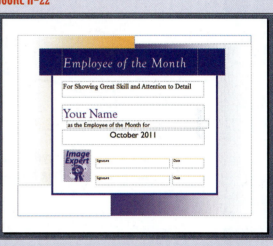

Advanced Challenge Exercise

- Open the task pane, then switch to the Font Schemes task pane.
- Browse through the list of schemes, then click a font scheme of your choice. Observe the change in the publication.
- Change the color scheme, save the modified publication as **Image Expert Award ACE**, then print a copy.

g. Close the publication, then exit Publisher.

▼ REAL LIFE INDEPENDENT CHALLENGE

The World Wide Web is a rich resource for individuals and businesses. You examine the possibility of starting your own desktop publishing business. The advantages include: flexible hours, low start-up costs, having an outlet for artistic impulses, the ability to conduct business remotely over the Internet, contact with other business people, and being your own boss. On the negative side, you have no formal education in design. You decide to look on the Internet to learn something about design.

a. Start Publisher, if necessary, then open a new blank publication.

b. Save the publication as **Graphic Ideas** in the drive and folder where you store your Data Files.

c. Connect to the Internet, then use a search engine to find information on design basics.

d. Click the topics listed to find articles on design basics.

e. Create text boxes in the blank publication and type brief descriptions of some of your findings.

f. Disconnect from the Internet, if necessary.

g. Complete your publication. Be sure to include a title and your name.

h. Print the publication, then exit Publisher.

▼ VISUAL WORKSHOP

Open PUB A-5.pub from the drive and folder where you store your Data Files, and add the text shown in Figure A-23 using the skills you learned in this unit. The font size in the text box is 14 points. Save the publication as **Image Expert Gift Card** where you store your Data Files. Be sure to include your name. Print the publication.

FIGURE A-23

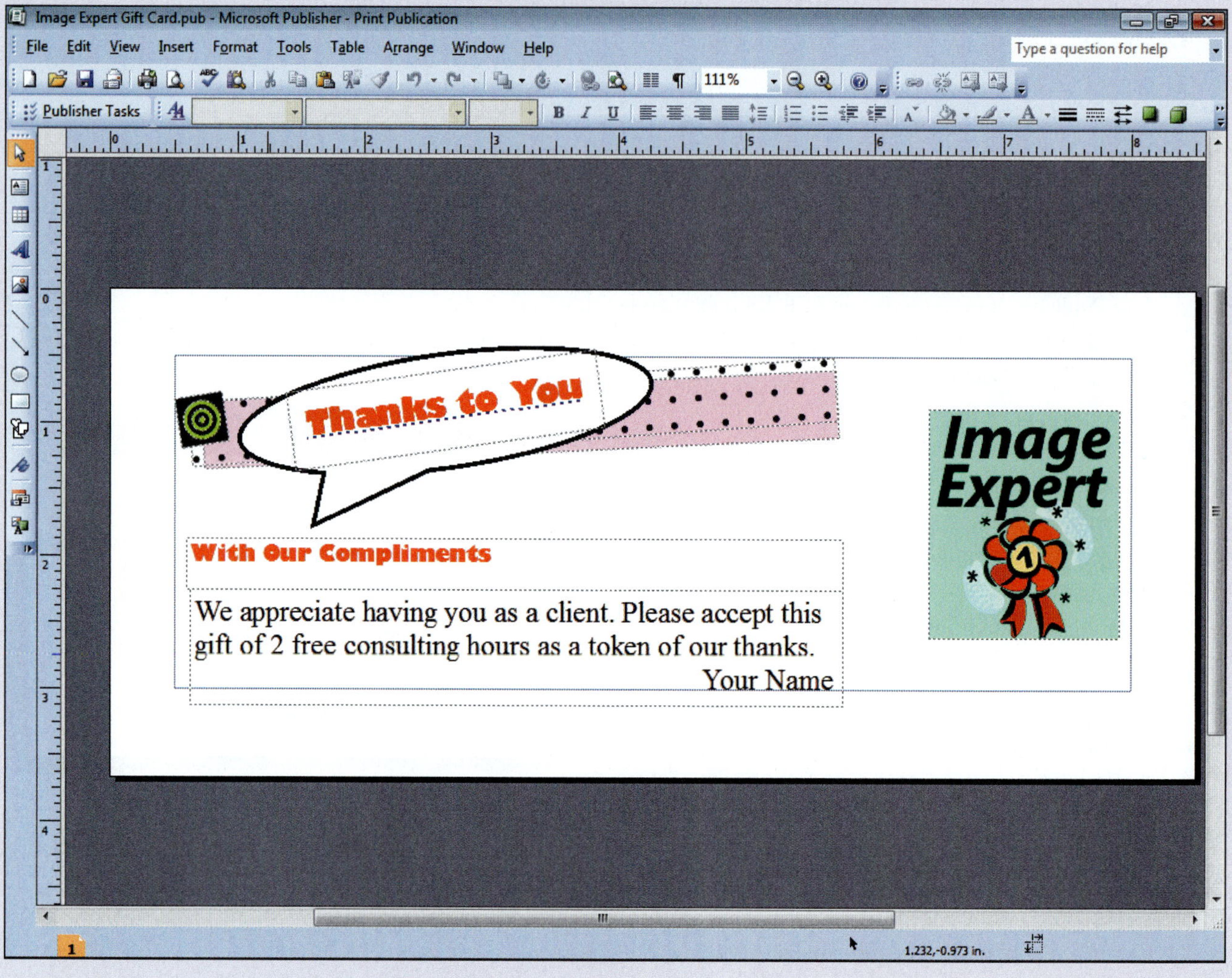

Creating a Publication

Now that you are familiar with the Publisher window and understand how to open and save a file, you are ready to create your own publication. It is important to think about the purpose and objectives of your publication, as well as your design goals, so that you can make effective layout decisions. Once you establish the message and layout of your publication, you must add text and graphics, as well as ensure objects are in the correct places. Mike Mendoza, your boss at Image Expert, has assigned you the task of designing a company newsletter. You decide to use Publisher to create this publication.

OBJECTIVES

Plan a publication

Design a publication

Create a publication using a template

Replace existing text

Add a graphic image

Add a sidebar

Use the Design Gallery

Group objects

Capstone Project: College Brochure

Planning a Publication

To create an effective publication, you should start with a planning session. Planning a publication involves at least three steps: determining what you want to achieve, deciding what information to include, and figuring out how to best present it. Knowing the goals of your publication helps you determine what form it should take. Keeping in mind the content of the message and your audience helps you to decide how the publication should be written, and how it should look. While there are many ways to plan a publication, it's best to start by determining its purpose. See Figure B-1. ▓▓▓ Your assignment is to create a one-page newsletter. Before starting, you answer these questions: Who is the audience? What is the message? What form should the message take?

DETAILS

Answering the following questions is the key to planning a successful publication:

- ### What is the purpose of the publication?

  Are you trying to inform, motivate, sell, inspire confidence, raise morale, solicit a vote, or solicit a contribution of time or money?

  In your discussions with Mike and other managers at Image Expert, you learn that the purpose of the company newsletter is to inform employees of news within the company and to publicize business and personal achievements.

- ### What type of response do you want?

  Do you intend this to be a one-way communication, or do you want feedback? If you do want feedback, what form should it take? Do you want volunteers, attendance at an event, and/or inquiries for additional information via phone or e-mail? For example, do you want visits to a Web site; registrations; contracts signed and returned; payments by check, cash or credit card; RSVPs, etc.?

  The Image Expert newsletter is intended to make employees feel important and included. It is primarily a one-way communication.

- ### What are you going to do with the responses you receive?

  If you solicit inquiries for additional information via mail or e-mail, but don't prepare a polite, informative response to send, you risk alienating your audience. If you solicit information, but neglect to gather it, interpret it, or fail to use it, you wasted time and effort, and lost an opportunity.

- ### Who is the target audience?

  The more narrowly you can define the characteristics of your target audience, the more you can tailor the content and appearance of the message to appeal to that group. For instance, a colorful comic book publication would be right for trying to educate fourth graders, but not appropriate for informing cardiologists of newly identified risk factors for heart disease.

  Some of the possible ways to identify a group are by age, gender, geography, reading level, educational background, first language, hobbies, nationality, ethnicity, religion, culture, political affiliation, employment, income level, taste in music and art, home ownership, and health or ill health.

  The Image Expert newsletter has a narrow audience. It will be read by employees and clients of the company. While their demographics vary, all share an interest in the Image Expert agency and its core service, advertising.

Design Matters

Developing design sense

Designing publications is a skill that can be learned through thoughtful practice and critical observation. Just as artists gather ideas from trips to museums, and musicians gather ideas from attending concerts, you can sharpen your design skills by looking at publications created by others. Start with a visit to a library or a magazine stand, observing the overall design of the publications.

Gauge your overall reaction to a publication, and judge for yourself what you find appealing and what you find distracting or offensive. Concentrate on how your eye moves across a page. What combinations of design elements (balance, color, consistency, contrast, and white space) are you drawn to, and what do you find unappealing?

FIGURE B-1: Planning process

Including the facts

Probably the most daunting part of creating a new publication is the notion of what information is essential, and what is not. Space, of course, is a factor, but you should consider the following criteria:

- What information will the reader want? What questions is the reader likely to have? Your text should answer questions, not raise them.
- How much time does the reader have? Make sure the content is easy to read and scan, and that text is presented in 'bite-sized' chunks.

- Are there others in your organization who can provide guidance and ideas as you complete the planning stage?

There are many aspects to consider, and you should certainly get a consensus from your teammates. Take the time to hold one or more brain-storming sessions with all who will be involved in the development of the publication. It's easier to incorporate valuable feedback before beginning the design process, and saves time in the long run.

Designing a Publication

Just as form follows function in the old adage, planning should always precede design. The elements of design—unity, balance, color, consistency, contrast, and white space—should be combined to support the objectives of the publication. This is why design follows planning, because it must support the goals identified in the planning stages. After planning, you know that you want the newsletter to catch the eye of potential readers, be easy to read, and look professional to clients. You decide to include the company logo to identify the newsletter as belonging to Image Expert, and you want to call attention to specific text to be sure it is seen and understood. You also want the newsletter to display a tasteful sense of humor, so that it entertains readers and keeps them looking forward to the next issue.

DETAILS

- ### View the document as a whole
  The publication needs enough contrast and variety to be interesting, but must be consistent and logical so the reader can find the meaning without confusion or unnecessary effort.

- ### Use placeholders for text and graphics to create an effective layout
  Placeholder text and graphics are objects that are inserted into a publication to illustrate how the finished product will appear when replaced with more significant materials at a later time. Publisher uses placeholder text boxes and graphics extensively in its templates, to demonstrate how the combined design elements in a finished publication will look.

- ### Use graphics to add interest and present ideas
  Use of artwork not only adds interest, but also is a means to communicate ideas and feelings that can reinforce text in a publication.

- ### Use white space liberally
  White space, also known as negative space, describes the open space between design elements. It can exist between elements of text (letters or paragraphs), in between and surrounding graphics, and between all other objects on the page. It is crucial for establishing spatial relations between visual items, and actually guides the reader's eye from one point to another. Without sufficient white space, text is unreadable, graphics lose emphasis, and there is no balance between the elements on a page. White space tells you where one section ends and another begins.

- ### Prominently feature the company logo
  The Image Expert logo appears on all its print material—letterhead, envelopes, business cards, and advertisements—to reinforce the identity of the company. It boosts morale for employees and associates to see the logo displayed with pride, and enhances clients' perception of the firm.

- ### Emphasize certain text
  Some text on a page should stand out. See Figure B-2. For example, **sidebars** are text related to the story but not vital to it. They are placed adjacent to the story to add emphasis and pique the interest of readers. Usually sidebars have a different background color, font, or point size to set them apart from the story.

Masthead

Volume and issue number

Graphic image

Sidebar is a related story with formatting to add emphasis

Pull quote text is taken from an article

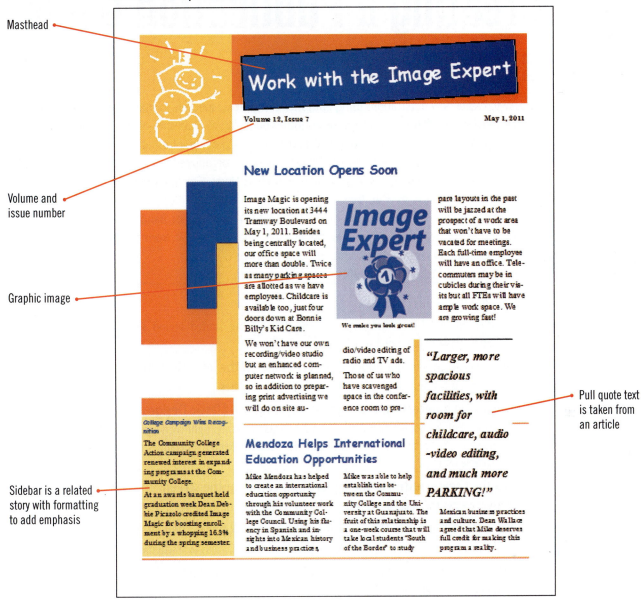

Design Matters

Recognizing bad design

Thoughtful practice and critical observation are the keys to learning good design. But how can you recognize bad design? First, look at a publication from the reader's point of view, and try to identify what is of interest in the publication. If you don't spot something of interest right away, do you think the typical reader is going to pursue it or set it aside? Nothing discourages a reader more than long columns of dull gray type, unless it is long columns of dull gray type that are hard to read. Ornate type that might look stylish on the sample sheet in a well-lighted print shop may be very hard to read elsewhere. Is the artwork carefully chosen and well placed to generate interest, or is the publication too cluttered with fluff that will only distract the reader from the information you are trying to present? In a nutshell, "bad" design is anything that fails to capture or sustain a reader's interest.

Publisher 2007

Creating a Publication Using a Template

It's easy to create new publications using Publisher **templates**, specially formatted publications containing placeholder text, that serve as a master for other publications. Publisher offers an enormous amount of publication templates that serve different audiences and provide information in different ways. The Publication Types section of the Microsoft Publisher window organizes templates by category. The categories range from common types of publications, such as Flyers, Calendars, and Envelopes, to the not-so-common types, such as Gift Certificates and Paper Folding Projects. Each category is further organized by design schemes such as Arrows, Bounce, Brocade, Color Band, Marker, and so on. The choices you select help create the initial publication, and you take it from there.   You use a Publisher template to create a newsletter.

STEPS

TROUBLE

If Publisher is already open but you do not see the Microsoft Publisher window with all of the templates, click File on the menu bar, then click New. Clicking the New button on the Standard toolbar will not open the Microsoft Publisher window.

1. **Start Publisher**
    The Microsoft Publisher window opens with the Getting Started option selected, displaying Popular Publication Types in the center pane.

2. **Click Newsletters in the Publication Types list on the left side of the screen**
    The Newletters category displays different newsletter templates.

3. **Scroll down if necessary, then click Borders (in the Classic Designs subcategory)**
    A thumbnail of the Borders newsletter layout appears in the top right corner of the window, with options for customizing it, as shown in Figure B-3. You can keep the default settings or choose from the available options.

4. **Click the Create button in the lower-right corner of the screen**
    Publisher creates the publication and displays it on the screen.

5. **Click Color Schemes in the Format Publication task pane, then click Office**
    The existing color scheme is immediately replaced with the Office color scheme, as shown in Figure B-4.

6. **Click the Close button on the Format Publication task pane**
    You now have a clear view of the newsletter in the workspace.

7. **Click the Save button 🖫 on the Standard toolbar, navigate to the drive and folder where you store your Data Files, select the text in the File name text box if it is not highlighted, type IE Newsletter, then click Save**

Design Matters

Using templates

Have you ever stared at a blank piece of paper or a blank screen and just didn't know where to begin? You can use a template as a starting point, particularly if you are just beginning in design. Just browsing through the templates can spark your creativity and get you started down the path to creating your own masterpieces. Believe it or not, there are occasions when even the best designers use templates. You can use a template if you just need a routine expense form or an invoice, if your client can't afford a "one-of-a-kind design," or just to save time. The important thing to remember about using a template is to choose one that is appropriate to the publication. A bad choice will require too many alterations and the advantages of using a template will be lost.

FIGURE B-3: Choosing the Borders Newsletter template

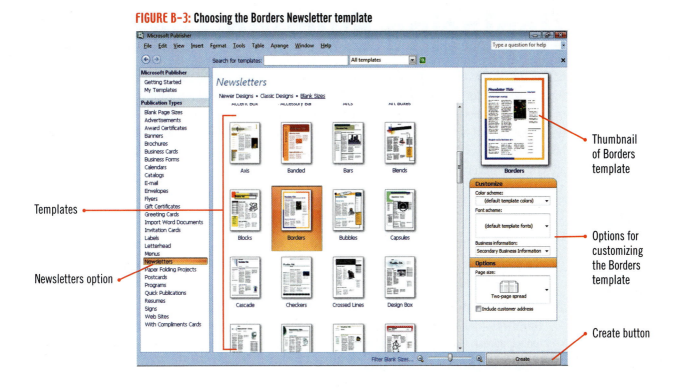

Templates

Newsletters option

Thumbnail of Borders template

Options for customizing the Borders template

Create button

FIGURE B-4: Newsletter with the Office color scheme

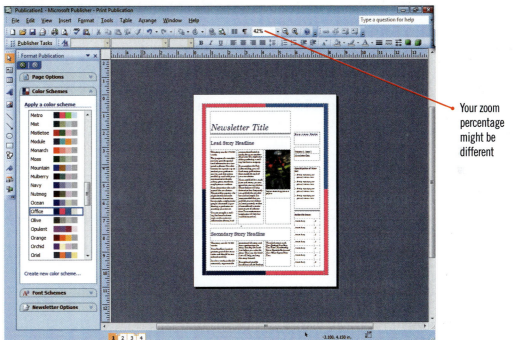

Your zoom percentage might be different

Understanding template options

The Microsoft Publisher window is a visual directory that contains more than 1600 different templates, which are organized into categories in the Publication Types section of the window. Each category offers a variety of choices. Brochures, for example, are available in many different styles and layout schemes. Labels can be created for computer disks, binders, audiocassettes, videocassettes, and CD case liners. Publications created using templates can be easily modified.

Replacing Existing Text

One of the benefits of using templates is that your new document contains preformatted placeholders that suggest content for your publication. In order to replace these placeholders with your own content, you must first select the existing text in a text box. You can then either type directly in the text box, or insert a document created with a word processor, such as Microsoft Word. You need to replace the placeholders in the newsletter with text for the Image Expert newsletter. Mike Mendoza has provided you with a Word 2007 document to use for the lead story.

STEPS

QUICK TIP

You can zoom in or out whenever you need to. Zooming doesn't affect the printed publication in any way.

1. **Press [F9]**

   Zooming into the selected text can help you get a closer look at specific objects. You can zoom by clicking the Zoom list arrow `100%` ▾, which always displays the Zoom factor, or clicking the Zoom In 🔍 and Zoom Out 🔍 buttons.

2. **Click the Lead Story Headline text at 2" H / 2", as shown in Figure B-5**

   Handles surround the selected text box, and its position and size appear on the status bar. The Formatting toolbar appears below the Standard toolbar.

QUICK TIP

Press [Ctrl][A] if you need to select the entire contents of a text box.

3. **Type New Location Opens Soon**

   The placeholder text is deleted with the first keystroke of the new text.

4. **Click the placeholder text in the column below the new heading to select it**

   Clicking placeholder text selects all the text.

5. **Click Insert on the menu bar, click Text File, locate the drive and folder where you store your Data Files, click PUB B-1.docx, then click OK**

   You might have to use the scroll buttons to see the new text. Compare your newsletter to Figure B-6. Instead of using the menu bar to insert text from a document file, you could right-click placeholder text, point to Change Text, then click Text File.

6. **Press [F9], then click the Save button 💾 on the Standard toolbar**

FIGURE B-5: Selected text box

Handles surround selected text box

Lead story headline placeholder text

Lead story placeholder text

Placeholder graphic

Upper-left corner coordinates of the selected text box

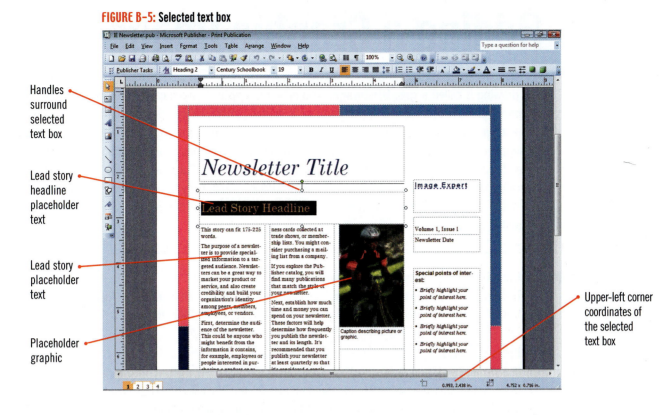

FIGURE B-6: Word document text in newsletter

Word document replaces placeholder text

Dimensions of the selected text box

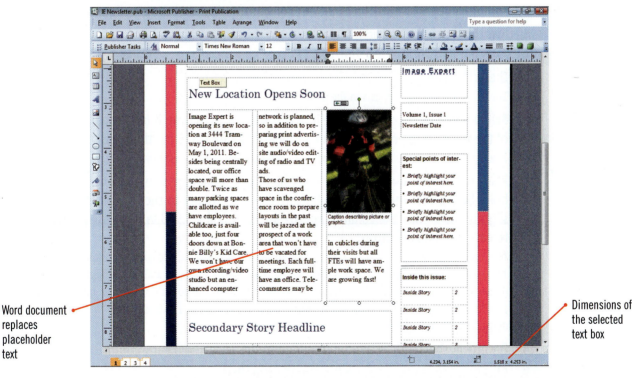

Resizing a frame

A frame—whether it is a text box or contains an object—can be resized. Once a frame is selected, you can change its size by placing the mouse pointer over a handle, then dragging the handle. The pointer may change to ⟷, ↕, ⤢, or ⬉ depending on which handle you place the pointer on. If, for example, the Text in Overflow button **A ▪▪▪** appears at the end of a selected frame, it may be possible to resize the frame, enabling the text to fit.

Adding a Graphic Image

Artwork can express feelings and ideas that words just can't capture. A picture, a piece of clip art, a graph, or a drawing is called a **graphic image**, or simply a **graphic**. Artwork can also be scanned into your computer, created using drawing programs or a digital camera, or purchased separately on a disk or online. **Clip art** is a term for graphic images that can be used free of charge or for a fee. Clip art is usually supplied on a disk or over the Web. Publisher comes with thousands of pieces of clip art. Table B-1 lists some of the common graphic image formats that can be used with Publisher. You have decided to include the Image Expert logo in the newsletter. Luckily, you already have this image in electronic format. You decide to place this logo near the graphic image placeholder of the bicyclist, so first you need to delete that placeholder.

STEPS

QUICK TIP

Use the ruler and the horizontal and vertical coordinates, like the ones given in Step 1, to help you locate the correct placeholders throughout this unit.

1. **Click the graphic image placeholder at 5" H / 5" V**

   Handles surround both the placeholder clip art and the caption beneath it, indicating that both are selected. Underneath the selection is the Ungroup Objects button 🔳, which indicates that you selected objects that were purposely grouped together so that they can be treated as one unit.

2. **Press [Delete]**

   The graphic image and caption text box placeholders disappear, and the text box expands to replace them. If the graphic image were inserted here without first deleting the placeholder, it would replace the current graphic. It would be the same size as the current one, and in the same location.

3. **Click Insert on the menu bar, point to Picture, then click From File**

   The Insert Picture dialog box opens.

4. **Navigate to the drive and folder where you store your Data Files**

QUICK TIP

You can change the view in the Insert Picture dialog box to Extra Large Icons so that it shows you a sample of the images available in the folder.

5. **Click the Views list arrow, click Extra Large Icons, click IE logo.tif as shown in Figure B-7, then click Insert**

   The Image Expert logo appears in the publication.

6. **Select the IE logo graphic image if necessary, use ⭣ to drag it until the upper-left corner of the image is approximately at coordinates 4.250, 3.875 in., then press [F9]**

   The repositioned image is near the upper-left portion of the column, as shown in Figure B-8.

7. **Place the pointer over the lower-right handle of the image so it turns to ⬊, press and hold [Shift], click the left mouse button, drag ╋ up and to the left until the image is slightly wider than the column (approximately 1.668 x 1.938 in.), release [Shift], then release the mouse button**

   The top-left corner of the image is now at coordinates 4.250, 3.875 in., and has dimensions of approximately 1.6 x 1.9 in., as shown in Figure B-9. Placing the pointer over a handle and then dragging the frame edge resizes an image. As you drag the pointer, the status bar reflects the object's size and position, using the ruler coordinates. To preserve an image's scale while increasing or decreasing its size, press and hold [Shift] while dragging the frame edge.

8. **Press [F9], then click away from the logo to deselect it**

9. **Click the Save button 🖫 on the Standard toolbar**

FIGURE B-7: Insert Picture dialog box

Available graphic images appear here

Preview of selected file

Displays recognized picture file formats

FIGURE B-8: Repositioned graphic image

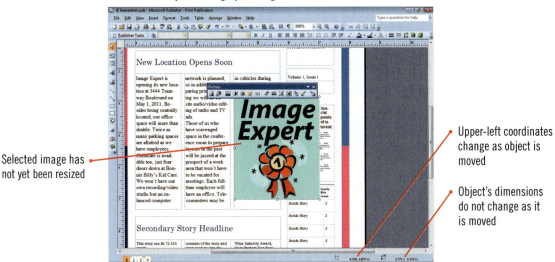

Selected image has not yet been resized

Upper-left coordinates change as object is moved

Object's dimensions do not change as it is moved

FIGURE B-9: Resized graphic image

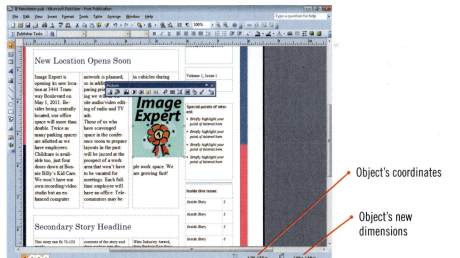

Object's coordinates

Object's new dimensions

TABLE B-1: Common graphic image formats

graphic image	extension	graphic image	extension
Bitmap	.BMP	Tagged Image File Format	.TIF
PC Paintbrush	.PCX	JPEG Picture Format	.JPG or .JPEG
Graphics Interchange Format	.GIF	Windows Metafile	.WMF
Encapsulated PostScript	.EPS	CorelDraw	.CDR

Adding a Sidebar

Information not vital to a publication can make interesting reading when placed in a sidebar. A **sidebar** is a short news story containing supplementary information. You can place it alongside or below a feature story. It can use the same font size as regular body text, but it may look better in a larger size or a different font. Adding a border or shading can help to emphasize sidebars. You want to add a brief story to the newsletter about the success of a recent Image Expert ad campaign. You decide to use the sidebar placeholder in the third column to insert this existing text. You also want to experiment with some formatting effects, to draw greater attention to the sidebar.

1. **Click inside the sidebar placeholder, as shown in Figure B-10, then press [Ctrl][A] to select all the text**
    Handles appear around the sidebar.

2. **Press [F9], click Insert on the menu bar, click Text File, change the View to Medium Icons if necessary, click PUB B-2.docx from the drive and folder where you store your Data Files, then click OK**
    The new text appears in the text box. Notice the changes to the formatting. The text from the inserted Word document is not italicized, and the font size changed to fit the text in the frame. The heading is bold, and is now in the Arial font.

3. **Press [Esc] to deselect both the text and the text box, leaving the sidebar selected**

4. **Click the Shadow Style button ▣ on the Formatting toolbar, click Shadow Style 1 ▤, then press [Esc] to deselect the frame**
    Compare your work to Figure B-11. A gray shadow is behind the white background containing the text.

5. **Click the scratch area to deselect the sidebar**
    The sidebar is deselected.

6. **Click the Save button ▤ on the Standard toolbar**

7. **Press [F9]**
    Looking at the full-page image, you can see that all the text fits nicely inside the frame.

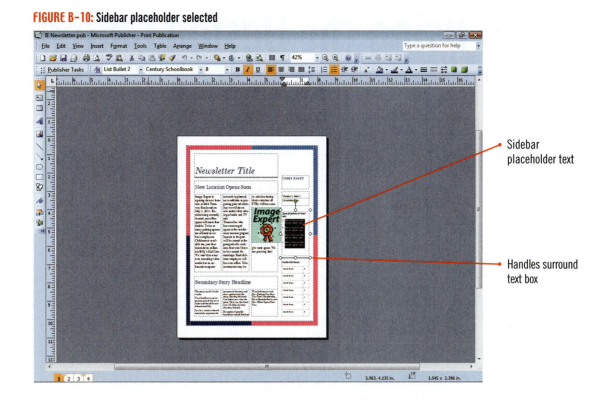

Sidebar placeholder text

Handles surround text box

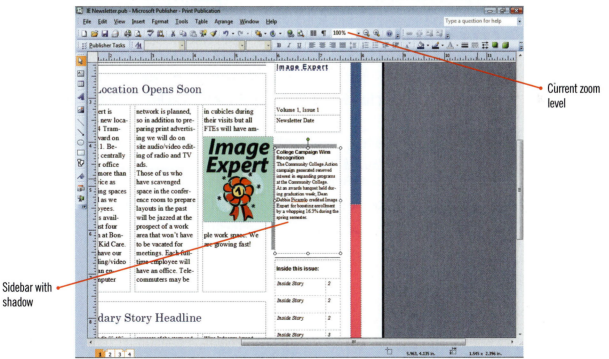

Current zoom level

Sidebar with shadow

Using the Design Gallery

The Design Gallery contains a wide variety of preformatted design objects you can insert to assemble a publication quickly. These include ads, calendars, coupons, logos, mastheads, pull quotes and more. A **pull quote** is an excerpt pulled from the text and set next to it, usually in a different typeface. The purpose of a pull quote is to draw attention to the story from which it is quoted. Pull quotes should be short enough to read easily, but long enough to capture interest. They should be on the same page as the story and placed close to it. The wording is not always an exact quote from the article, but should be an accurate reflection of the content. You want to insert a pull quote near the article on the company's new location. Because the Image Expert newsletter is a one-page publication, you do not need a Table of Contents, so you decide to replace that placeholder with the pull quote.

STEPS

QUICK TIP
Whenever possible, whole number coordinates are provided to help locate an object.

1. Click the Table of Contents at 7" H / 7" V, click Edit on the menu bar, then click Delete Object

2. Click the Design Gallery Object button 🖾 on the Objects toolbar
   The Design Gallery opens. The Design Gallery is organized into categories that help you select the type of object you want to add to a publication, and the specific design.

3. Click the Pull Quotes Category, click Borders in the Current design subcategory, then click Insert Object
   You select the Borders pull quote because you want the pull quote to have a plain design. It is often best to use less ornate design elements, to avoid distracting the reader. The pull quote placeholder appears on the first page of the publication, as shown in Figure B-12.

4. Place the pointer over the upper-left edge of the pull quote so it changes to ⬆, drag the upper-left corner to 5 3/4" H / 7.0" V in., then press [F9]
   The pull quote sits just below the sidebar. Compare your pull quote text box to Figure B-13.

5. Click the pull quote text to select it, then type "Twice as many parking spaces are allotted as we have employees. Childcare is also available."
   When the pull quote is selected, the horizontal ruler becomes active, just as with any text box.

6. Use the lower-right handle to resize the pull quote so its lower-right handle is at 7 3/4" H / 9 3/4" V

7. Click the pull quote text, press [Ctrl][A] to select the text, click Format on the menu bar, point to AutoFit Text, then click Best Fit
   Compare your pull quote to Figure B-14.

8. Press [F9], then click the scratch area to deselect the pull quote

9. Click the Save button 🖫 on the Standard toolbar

FIGURE B-12: Pull quote added

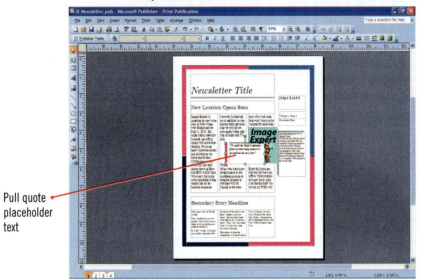

Pull quote
placeholder
text

FIGURE B-13: Repositioned pull quote

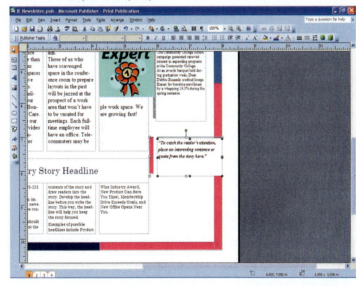

FIGURE B-14: Pull quote after AutoFit

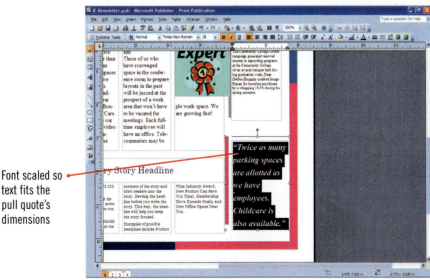

Font scaled so
text fits the
pull quote's
dimensions

Grouping Objects

Once many objects are positioned on a page, you may find that you want to move one or more of them. Moving a single object is as simple as selecting it, then dragging it to a new location. But it gets more complicated when more than one object is involved, and you want them to retain their relative positions. **Grouping**, or defining several objects as one object, is an easy way to move multiple items. Later, you can always ungroup them, turning the combined objects back into individual objects, for individual modifications. You want to place a caption under the Image Expert logo. To change the size of the caption text box, you need to ungroup the objects, make the modifications, then regroup the logo and caption.

STEPS

1. Click the Image Expert logo, press [F9], then press [Esc]

2. Click the Text Box button on the Objects toolbar, draw a text box for a caption that slightly overlaps the bottom of the object (suggested starting point: 4.250, 5.781 in., with dimensions of approximately 1.500 x 0.250 in.)

3. Type We make you look great! in the text box, press [Ctrl][A], click the Bold button **B** on the Formatting toolbar, click Format on the menu bar, point to AutoFit Text, then click Best Fit

   The new caption appears beneath the logo and is now in a Century Schoolbook font.

4. With the text box still selected, press and hold [Shift], click the Image Expert logo, then release [Shift]

   The Group Objects button appears beneath the two selected objects, as shown in Figure B-15. Notice that both objects have handles surrounding them.

5. Click, position over the object, drag the upper-left corner of the object up to 4.250, 3.25 in., then deselect the object

   The handles change to a single set of handles surrounding both the combined objects.

6. Scroll up to the text box above the Volume and Issue number, click inside the text box, press [Ctrl][A], type Your Name, then press [Esc] twice

7. Press [F9], then click the Save button on the Standard toolbar

   Compare your newsletter to Figure B-16.

8. Click File on the menu bar, click Print, click the Current page option button, then click OK

   A copy of the publication is printed.

9. Click File on the menu bar, then click Exit

FIGURE B-15: Preparing to group objects

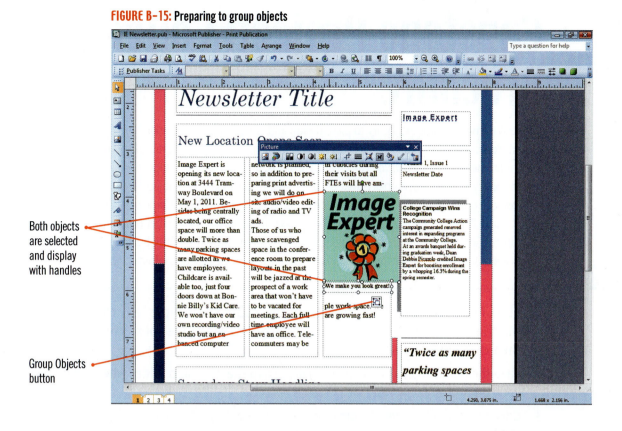

Both objects are selected and display with handles

Group Objects button

FIGURE B-16: Publication with grouped and repositioned objects

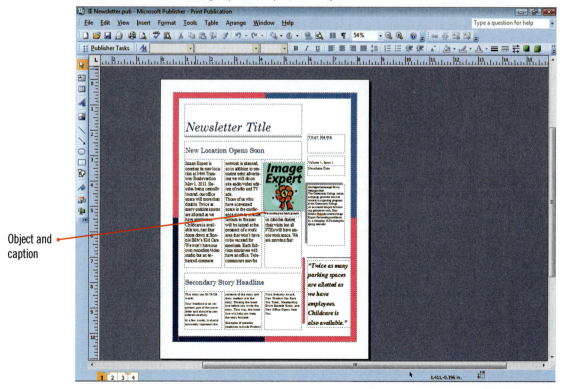

Object and caption

Capstone Project: College Brochure

You have learned the skills necessary to plan, design and create a new publication, and open an existing publication. You can save an existing publication or a template with a new descriptive name of your choice. Using buttons on the Objects toolbar, you can create a text box, and add graphic images and sidebars, and using the Design Gallery, you can insert objects that enhance your publication. Once objects are placed in your publication, you can group them so they can be treated as a single object. Camelback Community College is one of Image Expert's local clients. You have been asked to create a brochure that promotes their courses. For the purposes of drafting the design, you decide to use the Image Expert Business Information Set as placeholder text. Once it has been approved, you can update it with the college's information.

STEPS

1. Start Publisher, click **Brochures** from the Publication Types list, click **Blends** in the Classic Designs Informational subcategory, change the color scheme to **Sunrise**, then click **Create**

2. Save the publication as **Camelback Brochure** to the drive and folder where you store your Data Files

3. Click the **Product/Service Information placeholder**, type **Camelback University**, press **[Esc]** twice, then close the Format Publication task pane

4. Click the placeholder beneath the Camelback University text box, press **[Ctrl][A]** to select the text, then type **An Education You Can Use!**

5. Click the **Design Gallery Object button** 📇 on the Objects toolbar, click the **Pull Quotes** category, click **Blends**, then click **Insert Object**
   See Figure B-17.

6. With the pull quote still selected, press **[Shift]**, click the object at **5.000, 5.250 in.**, then click the **Group Objects button** 📇
   The objects are grouped, as shown in Figure B-18.

7. Position the pointer over the grouped object, when the pointer changes to ⬚⬚ click and drag the grouped objects until the coordinates are **4" H / 2" V**, then release the mouse button
   The grouped objects are now on the center panel of the brochure.

8. Click the **placeholder text** in the pull quote, replace it with **Your Name**, press **[Ctrl][A]**, click **Format** on the menu bar, point to **AutoFit Text**, click **Best Fit**, then press **[Esc]** three times
   Compare your publication with Figure B-19.

9. Save the publication, print the first page, then exit Publisher

FIGURE B-17: Inserted Design Gallery object

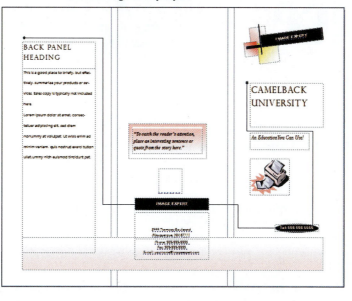

FIGURE B-18: Grouped objects

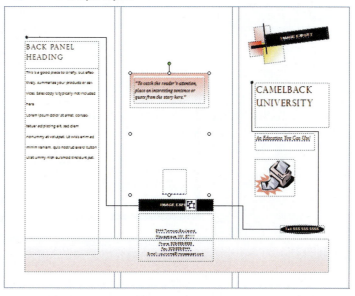

FIGURE B-19: Objects moved and text replaced

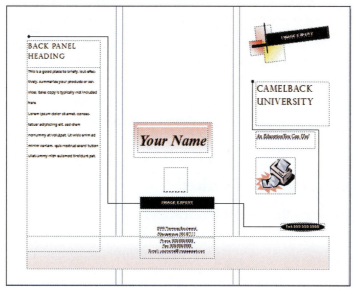

Practice

▼ CONCEPTS REVIEW

Label each of the elements of the Publisher window shown in Figure B-20.

FIGURE B-20

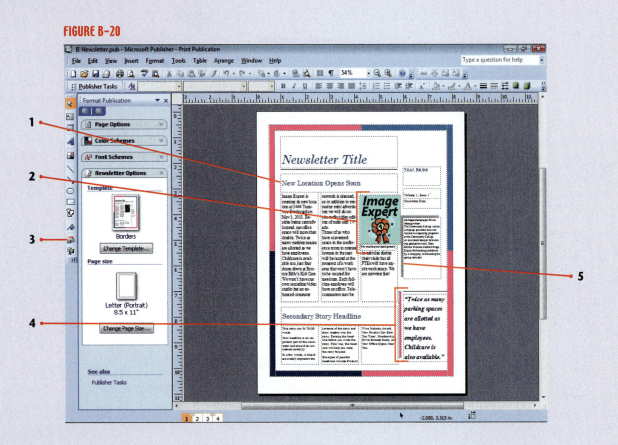

Match each of the terms or buttons with the statement that describes its function.

6.
7.
8. **Publication Types**
9.
10. **Design Gallery**
11. **Graphic image**

a. Can be used to create an ad or logo, for example
b. A directory of categorized templates
c. Resizes a frame vertically
d. Creates a text box
e. Artwork stored in an electronic file
f. Displays different shadows

Select the best answer from the list of choices.

12. **Which menu is used to access the AutoFit text feature?**
   a. Edit
   b. Format
   c. Tools
   d. Arrange

13. **Which button is the Design Gallery Object button?**
    a.
    c.
    b.
    d.

14. **Paraphrased information that invites you to read a story is called a:**
    a. Placeholder.
    c. Pull quote.
    b. Sidebar.
    d. Side quote.

15. **Group objects by holding and pressing [Shift], clicking each object, then clicking:**
    a.
    c.
    b. Tools on the menu bar, then Group Objects.
    d. Objects on the menu bar, then Group.

16. **Maintain the scale of an image while resizing a graphic image by pressing:**
    a. [Esc].
    c. [Alt].
    b. [Shift].
    d. The right mouse button.

17. **Which of the following statements about graphic images is false?**
    a. Scanned artwork can be used in Publisher.
    b. Artwork created in drawing programs can be used in Publisher.
    c. You can use only the artwork that comes with Publisher.
    d. You can use any electronic artwork in Publisher, as long as it's saved in a format that Publisher recognizes.

18. **Which of the following statements about a pull quote is false?**
    a. It should entice you to read the article.
    b. It should be short and easy to read.
    c. It does not have to be identical to the text in the article.
    d. It should be on a different page from the actual text.

19. **Which pointer is used to change the location of an object?**
    a.
    c.
    b.
    d.

20. **Which of the following extensions does not indicate a common graphic image format?**
    a. .GFX
    c. .CDR
    b. .TIF
    d. .GIF

▼ SKILLS REVIEW

1. **Planning a publication.**
    a. Name the three steps involved in planning a publication.
    b. Identify the questions you should ask as part of planning a publication.

2. **Designing a publication.**
    a. Name as many elements of design, such as consistency, as you can.
    b. Identify at least three guidelines of good design, such as viewing the document as a whole.

3. **Create a publication using a template.**
    a. Start Publisher, then select Newsletters from Publication Types list.
    b. Create a publication that has the following options: Marble design, two-page spread, and does not include the customer address. Use the Business Information Set you created in Unit A, or enter information for address, phone number, and other pertinent information.
    c. Change to the Monarch color scheme. In the Page Options section of the task pane, change to two columns. (*Hint*: You can change the number of columns by clicking Page Options in the task pane, then clicking the 2 Columns option.)
    d. Save this publication as **Mock-up Newsletter** to the drive and folder where you store your Data Files.

4. **Replace existing text.**
    a. Close the task pane.
    b. Click the Lead Story Headline placeholder, then zoom in.
    c. Replace the placeholder text with the following text: **Making the Most of Your Workspace**
    d. Select the lead story text, then delete it.

    e. Insert the Word file **PUB B-3.docx** from the location where you store your Data Files.

    f. Read the article, zoom out, then save the publication.

5. Add a graphic image.

    a. Select the graphic image placeholder and its caption, then delete them.

    b. Insert the picture file **IE logo.tif** from the drive and folder where you store your Data Files.

    c. Press and hold [Shift], resize the image to approximately 2.050 × 2.375 in., then reposition it so that the upper-left corner is at 6" H /5" V, then save the publication.

6. Add a sidebar.

    a. Select the sidebar placeholder in the left column above the Table of Contents (Inside this issue), then select all text within it.

    b. Zoom in to view the Special Points of Interest placeholder text in the sidebar, then delete the text.

    c. Insert the Word file **PUB B-4.docx** from the drive and folder where you store your Data Files.

    d. View and read the sidebar, zoom out so you can see the entire publication, then deselect the sidebar.

    e. Save the publication.

7. Use the Design Gallery.

    a. Click the Design Gallery Object button on the Objects toolbar, then click Pull Quotes.

    b. Add the Marble pull quote, then zoom in to view the pull quote.

    c. Move the pull quote so the upper-right corner is at the right margin and the top of the pull quote meets the bottom of the text box containing the Image Expert logo.

    d. Replace the placeholder with: **"Work shouldn't hurt. If you feel pain while sitting at your workstation, stop what you are doing."**

    e. Select AutoFit Text on the Format menu, then click Best Fit.

    f. Zoom out so you can see the entire publication, deselect the pull quote, zoom in, then save the publication.

8. Group objects.

    a. Press and hold [Shift], then select both the volume and newsletter date text boxes in the right column.

    b. Group the two selected objects.

    c. Move the grouped object so the top-left corner of the combined object is at 0.500, 3.000 in.

    d. Ungroup the objects, deselect the objects, then replace the Newsletter Date text with **Your Name**.

    e. Save your work, print the first page of the publication, then exit Publisher.

▼ INDEPENDENT CHALLENGE 1

You volunteered to help the local Rotary Club design a flyer for its upcoming fund-raiser, a Fun Run. The organization is trying to raise money for victims of earthquakes in Central America. The funds will go toward medicine, building materials, food, clothing, and transportation costs for the material and some volunteers.

    a. Start Publisher if necessary, then create a flyer using the Charity Bazaar Fundraiser flyer design.

    b. Save the publication as **Fun Run Flyer** in the folder where you store your Data Files.

    c. Change the Color Scheme to Monarch, then accept the default options.

    d. Modify the Charity Bazaar text placeholder to say **Rotary Fun Run**, replace the five bulleted items with five of your own good reasons to attend this event, then include your name somewhere on the flyer.

    e. Make up the necessary information, such as the location of the fundraiser, the address of the Rotary Club, and the date and time of the event, to make sure all the text in the flyer relates to the Fun Run event.

Advanced Challenge Exercises

    ■ Try resizing at least two of the frames within the flyer.

    ■ See how the pointers change during resizing, and how the text reflows.

    f. Save and print the publication, then close the publication and exit Publisher.

▼ INDEPENDENT CHALLENGE 2

You are a regular at the Come and Get It Luncheonette. They ask you to help create a menu for their new take-out division. Use a template to create this menu, and replace the existing text with your own.

a. Start Publisher if necessary, then create a take-out menu by choosing the Gingham Take-Out Menu.

b. Change the Color Scheme to Plum, and accept the default options.

c. Save the publication to the drive and folder where you store your Data Files as **Take-Out Menu**.

d. Modify the placeholder company name and information for the Come and Get It Luncheonette.

e. Replace the placeholder text under the restaurant's name with a description of the food served at this establishment.

f. Include your name as the contact person for take-out orders.

g. Make sure all the text in the flyer relates to the take-out menu.

h. Make up at least two menu items. (*Hint*: Click the Page 2 icon to access the second page.)

i. Group two objects on the menu and move them.

j. Save the publication, print the publication, then exit Publisher.

▼ INDEPENDENT CHALLENGE 3

The tenants in your rental property just gave you 30 days notice, so you must find new tenants. You need to create a sign in which you can describe the house in order to attract new tenants.

a. Start Publisher if necessary, then use the For Rent Sign template in the Signs category of the Publication Types list.

b. Save the publication to the drive and folder where you store your Data Files as **For Rent Sign**.

c. Replace the bulleted items with your descriptions of the house for rent.

d. Modify the telephone number placeholder using your number or a ficticious number.

e. Create a text box under the telephone number that says **Call Your Name for more information**.

f. Select the text containing your name, then make the font size 18 points. (*Hint*: Resize the text box to fit the text if necessary, and resize the telephone number text box if you think it improves the overall design.)

Advanced Challenge Exercises

■ Use a command on the Format Publication task pane to change the publication design to a different For Rent sign. Make sure you add any elements necessary so that the new design contains the same information.

g. Save the publication, print the publication, then exit Publisher.

▼ REAL LIFE INDEPENDENT CHALLENGE

You are asked to create a Web page for your school's Publisher class. You will use the Publication Types list in the Microsoft Publisher window. This site should discuss what topics are covered in the class.

a. Connect to the Internet and go to your school's Web site.

b. Print out the home page and the page for the department offering this Publisher course. You can use these materials as a reference throughout this project.

c. Start Publisher if necessary, then use the Publication Types list to create a Web site for your Publisher class.

d. The Web page should consist of one page, using a style, color scheme, and background that complement the school's existing Web site.

e. Save your publication as **Publisher Class Web Page** to the drive and folder where you store your Data Files.

f. Create a text box for contact information, if necessary. Add a telephone number and a fax number, and add Your Name as part of a ficticious e-mail address.

g. Replace the text placeholders with your own text, based on the topics that are covered in this class. (*Hint*: Consult your class syllabus and the materials you printed from your school's Web site.)

h. Save and print your publication, then exit Publisher.

▼ VISUAL WORKSHOP

Use the Publication Types list to create the informational postcard shown below. Save the publication as **IE Postcard** to the drive and folder where you store your Data Files. Use the Borders Informational Postcard layout, the quarter-page format, and accept other defaults. Add the IE logo graphic image, apply the Wildflower color scheme, and replace the placeholder text and add new text in text boxes, as necessary, using Figure B-21 as a guide. Add your name to an existing text box in the publication, then save your work and print the page.

FIGURE B-21

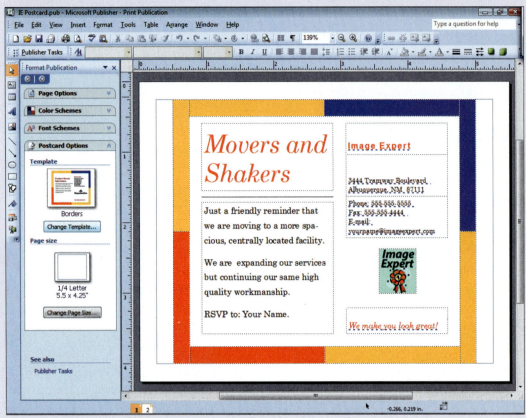

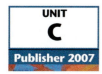
Working with Text

Files You Will Need:

PUB C-1.docx
PUB C-2.docx
PUB C-3.docx

Publisher has many powerful tools to help you design and lay out text with confidence. You can use layout guides and rulers to assure that your layout is accurate and consistent. You can check spelling and apply formatting so that the finished text looks professional. And you can add objects such as tables to organize text more effectively.  Your current assignment is to design a flyer that will be used to promote an upcoming Image Expert Professional Design Seminar. You want the flyer to be colorful and informative, and to grab people's attention.

OBJECTIVES

Use layout guides

Use ruler guides

Format a text box

Add bullets and numbering

Check spelling

Modify a Design Gallery Object

Paint formats

Add a table

Capstone Project: College Brochure

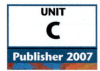

Using Layout Guides

Elements in a well-designed publication achieve a balanced and consistent look. This balance and consistency occurs only with careful planning and design. **Layout guides** include **margin guides** and **grid guides** which are horizontal and vertical lines visible only on the screen. Guides help you accurately position objects on a page and across pages in a publication. Margin guides encompass the top, bottom, left and right sides of a publication, whereas grid guides appear as column and row guides. Both types of guides can be defined in the Layout Guides dialog box. For example, you can choose a number of column and row grid guides for your publication and you can define the distance for each margin guide from the four edges of the page. Your assignment is to create a flyer for an upcoming design seminar. You decide to use a template, then set up the layout guides to help plan for future placement of objects in the publication. You also want to experiment with a different color scheme.

STEPS

1. Start Publisher, click **Flyers** in the Publication Types list, click **Bars** in the Classic Designs Informational group, then click **Create**

   A new publication based on this template opens, and the Format Publication task pane opens as well with the Flyer Options section expanded.

2. Click **Color Schemes**, click **Orchid**, then click the **Close button** on the Format Publication task pane

   The task pane is not necessary for the remainder of your work on this design.

3. Save the publication as **Design Seminar Flyer** to the drive and folder where you store your Data Files

4. Right-click the **graphic placeholder** containing the photograph, then click **Delete Object**

5. Right-click the text box at **5" H / 7" V**, then click **Delete Object**

   The image and text box are deleted from the flyer. When selecting an object, you can click anywhere within its borders, but coordinates are provided here to make it easy to locate each specific object.

6. Click **Arrange** on the menu bar, then click **Layout Guides**

   The Layout Guides dialog box opens. You use the Layout Guides dialog box to change the margin dimensions.

7. If necessary, click the **Margin Guides tab**, then verify that the Left, Right, and Top margins are each set at **0.5"**, and the Bottom margin is set at **0.66"**, as shown in Figure C-1

   The top and bottom margins are small enough to allow lots of information to be placed on each page. Layout guides create a grid to help you line up design elements, such as images and text boxes, on the page.

8. Click the **Grid Guides tab**, click the **Columns up arrow** until **3** appears in the text box, click the **Rows up arrow** until **3** appears in the text box, click the **Add center guide between columns and rows check box** as shown in Figure C-2, then click **OK**

   The pink lines represent the column guides, and the blue lines represent the column guide margins. The guides appear on the screen, as shown in Figure C-3, but do not print on the page.

9. Click the **Save button** 🖫 on the Standard toolbar

FIGURE C-1: Margin Guides tab of Layout Guides dialog box

Creates right- and left-hand pages

Margin Settings

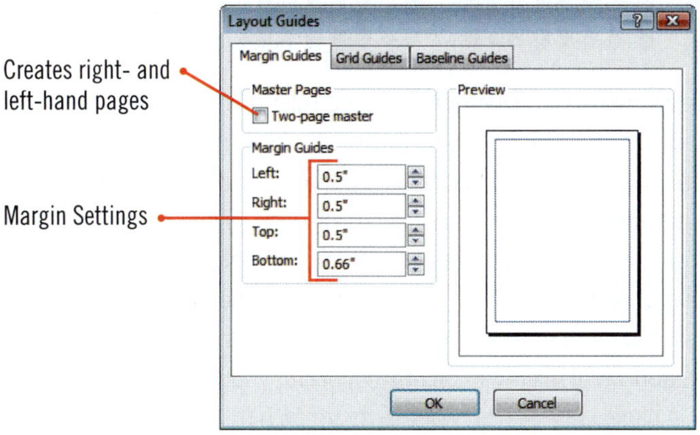

FIGURE C-2: Grid Guides tab of Layout Guides dialog box

Changes the number of columns and rows

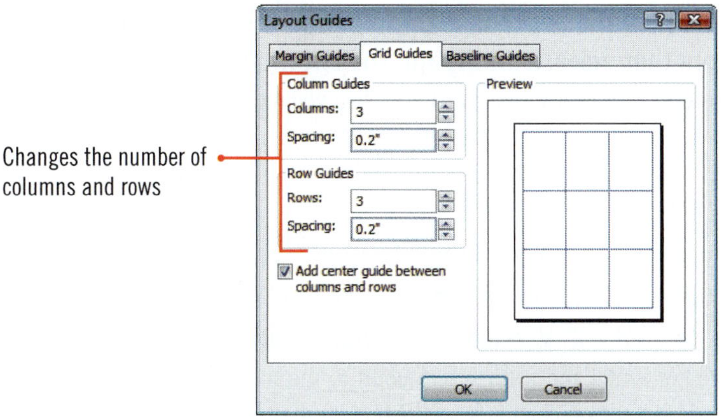

FIGURE C-3: Layout guides in publication

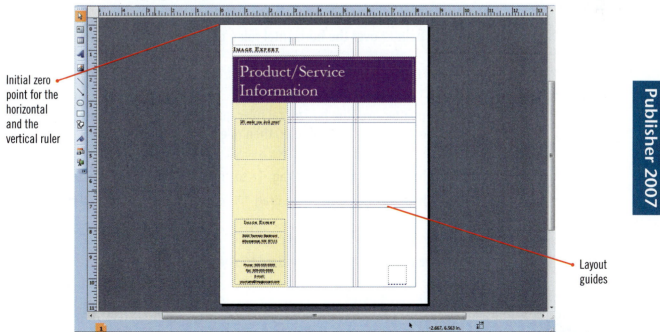

Initial zero point for the horizontal and the vertical ruler

Layout guides

Publisher 2007

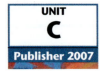

Using Ruler Guides

Publisher lets you create individual page guides, called ruler guides. These are useful when you have set layout guides for a specific page type, but want to lay out elements differently on one particular page. **Ruler guides** work just like layout guides but appear in the foreground of an individual page or selection of pages, whereas layout guides appear on the background of each page, or selected pages, in the publication. Functionally, layout guides and ruler guides are the same, and neither prints on the publication. Ruler guides are green horizontal and vertical lines that are dragged from the rulers into the workspace, and can make it easy to position a text box or graphic image in a specific location. The location of zero, the **zero point**, on both the vertical and horizontal rulers can be moved, giving you the flexibility to make precise measurements from any point on the page. You want to move each ruler's zero point so you can measure distances from a specific point on a page, and add ruler guides to make it easier to position a graphic image on the first page. First, you move the vertical ruler closer to the page.

STEPS

1. **Position ⬚ over the vertical ruler, press and hold [Shift], when the pointer changes to ⟺, press and hold the left mouse button, drag the vertical ruler to the left edge of the publication, then release [Shift] and the left mouse button**

   The ruler is repositioned, as shown in Figure C-4. When you move a ruler, the zero point does not change; the ruler simply moves closer, making it easier to locate positions. You don't need to move the horizontal ruler because it sits just above the top of the page. Currently, the horizontal and vertical zero point is set at the top-left edge of the page.

2. **Position ⬚ over the Move Both Rulers button ⬚ (at the intersection of the horizontal and vertical rulers) when the pointer changes to ⬚ press and hold [Shift], right-click ⬚, drag ⬚, to ½" H / ½" V, release the mouse button, then release [Shift]**

   You changed the horizontal and vertical zero point to the start of the left and top margins. This makes it easy to determine exact measurements from the top-left margin.

3. **Position ⬚ at the top-left corner of the margin guides**

   The coordinates in the object position on the status bar are 0.000, 0.000 in.

4. **Position the pointer anywhere over the vertical ruler, drag +⦀+ to 3" H, then release the mouse button**

   A green vertical ruler guide appears on the screen at the 3" horizontal mark.

5. **Position the pointer over the horizontal ruler, drag ⯐ to 3" V, then release the mouse button**

   After looking at the new horizontal ruler guide, you realize its position is too high for the text box you plan to add.

6. **Position the pointer over the horizontal ruler guide at 3" until it changes to ⯐, drag the ruler guide to 3¾" on the vertical ruler, then release the mouse button**

   The ruler guides will be helpful when a text box is added.

7. **Place ⬚ on the vertical ruler, then drag +⦀+ to create a vertical ruler guide at 5½" H**

8. **Place ⬚ on the horizontal ruler, then drag ⯐ to create three horizontal ruler guides: at 6¼" V, 7" V, and 8¾" V**

   Compare your ruler guides to those shown in Figure C-5.

9. **Click the Save button ⬚ on the Standard toolbar**

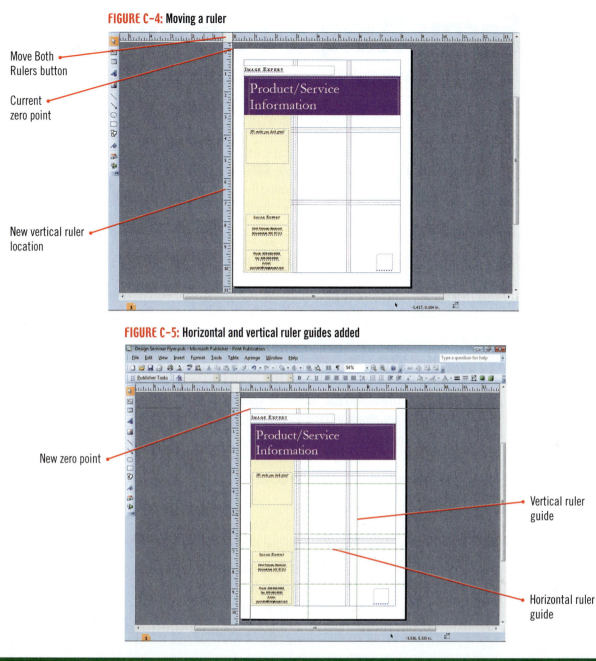

FIGURE C-4: Moving a ruler

Move Both
Rulers button

Current
zero point

New vertical ruler
location

FIGURE C-5: Horizontal and vertical ruler guides added

New zero point

Vertical ruler
guide

Horizontal ruler
guide

Design Matters

Choosing measurement tools

Publisher provides different ways to measure the dimensions and positions of objects. The Object Position and Object Size coordinates on the status bar are always visible, but it can be difficult to place and size objects using them. The **Measurement toolbar** is a direct way to precisely position and size objects to one 1/1000 of an inch accuracy. To open the Measurement toolbar, shown in Figure C-6, click View on the menu bar, point to Toolbars, then click Measurement. This toolbar lets you control horizontal position, vertical position, width, height, rotation, tracking, text scaling, kerning, and line spacing. Another option for positioning items is the Format dialog box for a selected object, such as a text box, picture, etc. This dialog box has tabs that let you position and size the item, but requires you to shift from one tab of the dialog box to another. The horizontal and vertical rulers have the advantage of being the closest tools to the publication, and they are moveable so they can be even closer.

FIGURE C-6: Measurement toolbar

Measurement		
x	0.1"	
y	3.208"	
	2.05"	
	1.617"	
∠	0.0	
	100%	
	100%	
	0pt	
	1sp	

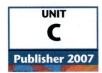

Formatting a Text Box

Once you add a text box to a page, you can move or resize it. You can add and format a border in any available color or line width you choose. The Formatting toolbar contains buttons for the commands most commonly used to improve a text box's appearance. When adding a text box or other object to a page, ruler guides can be helpful—either by providing a visual reference, or by literally pulling objects so they align exactly. To create this magnetic effect, you turn on the Snap To command. This feature pulls whatever you're trying to line up toward the ruler, guide, or object. You want to add a text box that describes how to best use logos. You decide to place the text box using the ruler guides and Snap To feature, and then enhance it with formatting attributes. To begin, you move the vertical ruler out of the way.

STEPS

1. **Position the pointer over the vertical ruler, press and hold [Shift], when the pointer changes to ⟺, drag the vertical ruler to the left edge of the workspace, then release [Shift]**
   The vertical ruler is now out of the way.

2. **Click the flyer heading placeholder text at 1" H / 1" V, type Professional Design Seminar, then press [Esc] three times**
   The new heading appears in the text box, and the text box is deselected.

3. **Click Arrange on the menu bar, point to Snap, then click To Ruler Marks and To Guides if these options *do not* already have a check mark**
   A check mark next to a menu option indicates that it is selected, or activated. Clicking the option again turns it off.

4. **Click the Text Box button 🔲 on the Objects toolbar**
   The pointer changes to + .

5. **Drag + from approximately 3" H / 3¾" V to 5" H / 6¼" V**
   The text box automatically snaps to the ruler and layout guides.

   > **TROUBLE**
   > A text box must be selected before you can modify it.

6. **Right-click the text box, click Format Text Box, click the Line Color list arrow, then click the Accent1 (Violet) (second from left) color box**
   A sample of the color appears in the Format Text Box dialog box, as shown in Figure C-7. Because you selected a color scheme in the Format Publication task pane, those colors are presented on this palette to help you retain design consistency in the publication. You could click More Colors from the Line Color drop down list if you wanted to work outside the color scheme.

7. **Click the Weight up arrow until 4 pt appears in the text box, then click OK**
   The text box that you placed on the page using the ruler guides appears with the thick violet border, as shown in Figure C-8.

8. **Click the Save button 🔲 on the Standard toolbar**

FIGURE C-7: Format Text Box dialog box

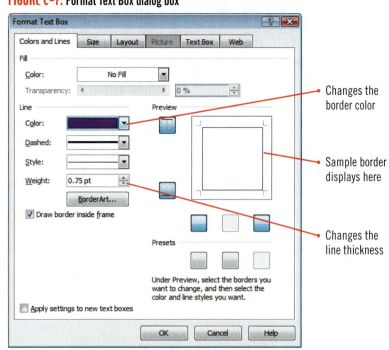

Changes the border color

Sample border displays here

Changes the line thickness

FIGURE C-8: Text box with thick, violet border

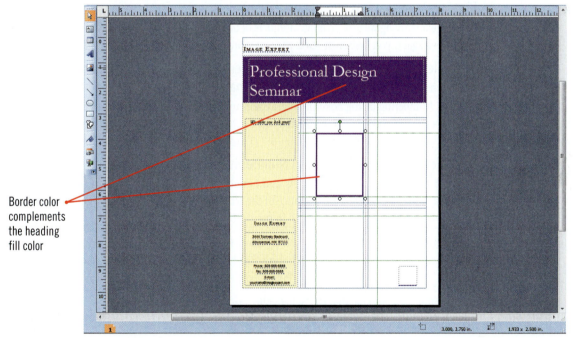

Border color complements the heading fill color

Publisher 2007

Design Matters

Making use of margins

When you think of **margins**, you probably think of the space surrounding the four edges of a page. The term also applies to the space that surrounds any boundary, so each design object, including columns, tables, and text boxes, have their own margins. Margins are often used to create **white space**, the designer's term for space on a page that is not covered with printed or graphic material. The addition of white space is critical for clarity because without it the page looks cluttered and is difficult to read.

Adding Bullets and Numbering

When you need to display information in a list, you can add emphasis to the items by formatting them with bullets or numbers. A **numbered list** is generally used to present items that occur in a particular sequence, while items in a **bulleted list** can be in any order. Both numbered and bulleted list formats can be applied either before or after the text is typed. You can switch back and forth between numbers and bullets, trying different styles of numbers and bullets until you arrive at the right format. You want the information in the text box to be large enough to read, and you've decided to add a numbered list in the text box you just created. You may not like the way the numbered list looks, but you can easily change this to a bulleted list.

STEPS

1. Make sure that the text box with the violet border is still selected, then press [F9]

2. Click the Font Size list arrow `10` on the Formatting toolbar, click 16, type Why use a logo?, then press [Enter]

   Although it is not mandatory, the heading, which is not part of the numbered list, is entered first.

3. Click the Numbering button on the Formatting toolbar

   1. appears in the text box.

4. Type Customers look for it., press [Enter], type It distinguishes your firm from others., press [Enter], then type It is a marketing element.

   Compare your text with Figure C-9. To apply numbers or bullets to existing text, or to change from numbers to bullets, or back again, you first must select the text you want to format.

5. Drag I to select the text from Customers to element. so that the three numbered sentences are selected, click Format on the menu bar, then click Bullets and Numbering

   The Bullets and Numbering dialog box opens and the Numbering tab displays. You can change the appearance of a numbered list, convert it to a bulleted list, or change the appearance of the bullets by using this dialog box.

6. Click the Bullets tab in the Bullets and Numbering dialog box

   Available bullet options appear in the Bullets and Numbering dialog box, as shown in Figure C-10. To enhance any list, you can change the appearance of the bullets. Publisher lets you use a variety of characters as bullets, as well as change the size (measured in points) of the bullets.

7. Click the diamond bullet, click OK, then press [Esc] twice

   Compare your work with Figure C-11. The numbered list has been converted to a bulleted list.

8. Press [F9]

   You can see the full page, and see that the bulleted list fits nicely on the page.

9. Click the Save button on the Standard toolbar

Design Matters

Using Bullets or Numbers: Which is correct?

The general rule to follow for using bullets or numbers is that numbers should be used when it is necessary for steps to be followed in a specific sequence. Bullets are appropriate when the order in which steps are carried out is not important. For example, use numbers when giving instructions for backing your car out of the garage; use bullets when describing the things you need to do before hosting a dinner party.

FIGURE C-9: Numbered list in a text box

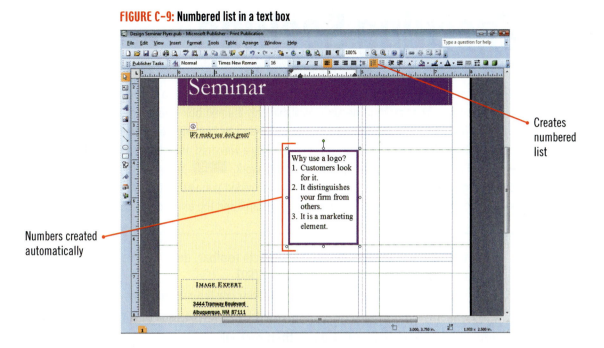

Creates numbered list

Numbers created automatically

FIGURE C-10: Bullets and Numbering dialog box

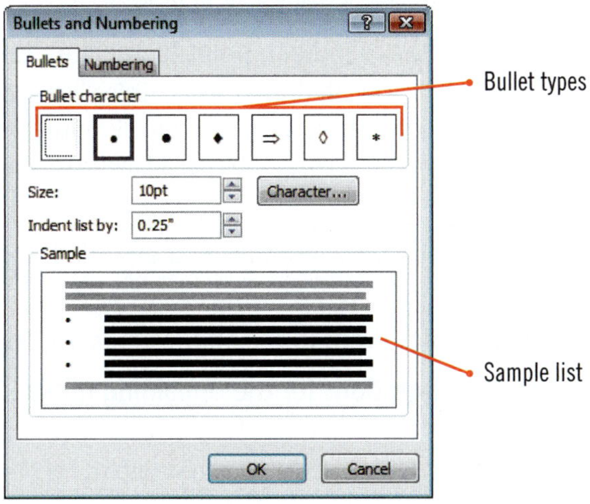

Bullet types

Sample list

FIGURE C-11: Numbered list changed to a bulleted list

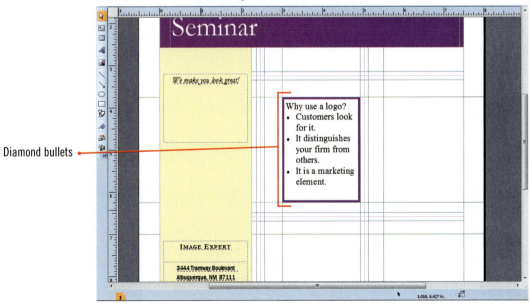

Diamond bullets

Checking Spelling

Spelling errors can ruin the most beautifully designed and well-written publication by distracting the reader from the message. Fortunately, using the **Spelling Checker** helps you to correct misspelled words before the reader sees them. The Spelling Checker is available only if a text box is selected. You can then check spelling using the Tools menu, or by right-clicking text, pointing to Proofing Tools, then clicking Spelling. Spelling errors are shown immediately as you type, indicated by a wavy red underline. You can add words that are not recognized by the Office/Publisher dictionary as you work. 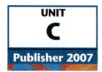 You need to add information to the flyer about the guest speaker for the seminar. Mike has provided you with a text file containing this information. Once you create a text box for this information, you can insert the text file and check for any spelling errors.

STEPS

1. **Click the Text Box button ⊞ on the Objects toolbar, drag ╋ from 5½" H / 3¾" V to the margin guide at 7½" H / 6¼" V, then press [F9]**

   The text box appears on the page. Text placed in a text box is sometimes referred to as a **story**.

2. **Click Insert on the menu bar, click Text File, locate the drive and folder where you store your Data Files, click PUB C-1.docx, then click OK**

   The text stored in the document file PUB C-1 is inserted into the text box, as shown in Figure C-12. This text contains misspelled words that you want to correct.

3. **Click Tools on the menu bar, point to Spelling, then click Spelling**

   The Check Spelling: English (United States) dialog box opens, as shown in Figure C-13. The first incorrect word found is "prievious." Publisher checks its dictionary to determine a word's spelling and places a suggestion in the Change to text box, so you don't have to click a suggestion.

4. **Click Change**

   The Spelling feature advances to the next misspelled word, "ebent." This word is incorrect and should be "event."

5. **If necessary, click event in the Suggestions list, then click Change**

6. **Accept the suggestions for the remaining misspelled words: gaols, Leeder, prestigous, and Desing**

   The Spelling feature finished checking the text box.

7. **Click No in the dialog box prompting you to check other text boxes in your publication, click OK, then press [Esc] twice**

   Compare your corrected text to Figure C-14.

8. **Press [F9], then click the Save button ⊟ on the Standard toolbar**

FIGURE C-12: Spelling errors in text

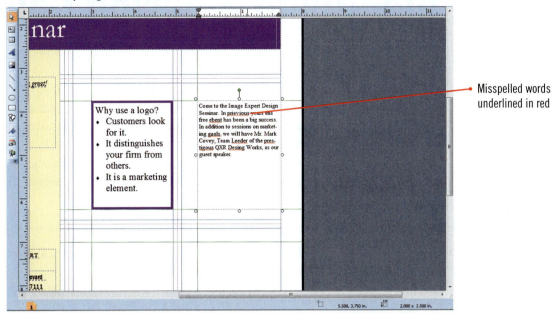

Misspelled words underlined in red

FIGURE C-13: Check Spelling dialog box

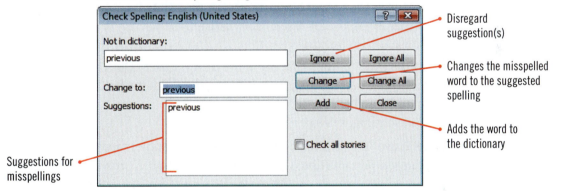

Disregard suggestion(s)

Changes the misspelled word to the suggested spelling

Adds the word to the dictionary

Suggestions for misspellings

FIGURE C-14: Corrected spelling

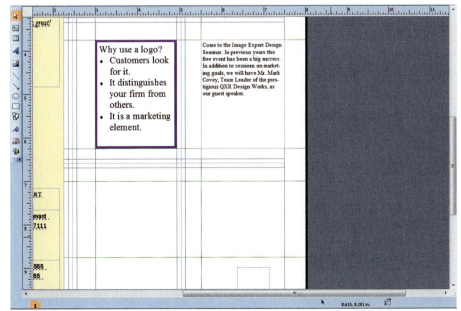

Modifying a Design Gallery Object

In addition to all the choices you can make using the Publication Types list, you can also insert and modify individual objects from the Design Gallery. These **Design Gallery Objects** contain text or graphic images and can be edited for size, shape, and content. You can modify a Design Gallery Object by adding text or resizing the object to enhance the meaning of your text or draw attention to it. 🎨 You want to draw attention to the information about the guest speaker, so you decide to add a Design Gallery Object just above this information. First, you add a ruler guide to help place this new object.

1. **Position** ⌖ **over the horizontal ruler, drag** ⬍ **to 3" on the vertical ruler, then release the mouse button**

   You can add ruler guides at any time during the design process to make positioning objects easier.

2. **Click the Design Gallery Object button** 🖼 **on the Objects toolbar, click Attention Getters in the Categories list, click the Corner Starburst Attention Getter, then click Insert Object**

   The new object is placed somewhere on the page and can be moved to a better location.

3. **Place** ⌖ **over the Corner Starburst object, drag the object to 5½" H / 3" V, then press [F9]**

   Text within a Design Gallery Object can be modified, and you can use the AutoFit Text feature to fill the text box.

4. **Select the text Attention Grabber in the Design Gallery Object text box, type Special, press [Enter], type Guest Speaker, press [Ctrl][A], then click the Bold button** 𝐁 **on the Formatting toolbar**

   Compare your work with Figure C-15.

5. **Place** ⌖ **over the selected object's right-center handle, then drag** ⬌ **to 7½" H**

   Compare your work with Figure C-16. The width of the Attention Getter is now consistent with the width of the text.

6. **Click the Save button** 💾 **on the Standard toolbar**

FIGURE C-15: Design Gallery Object positioned and new text inserted

Bold button

Design Gallery
Object

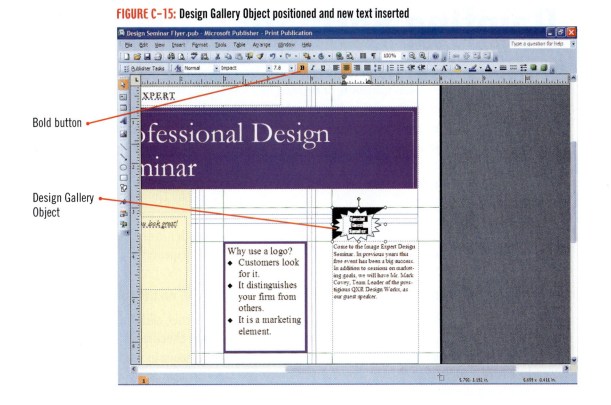

FIGURE C-16: Design Gallery Object replaced and resized

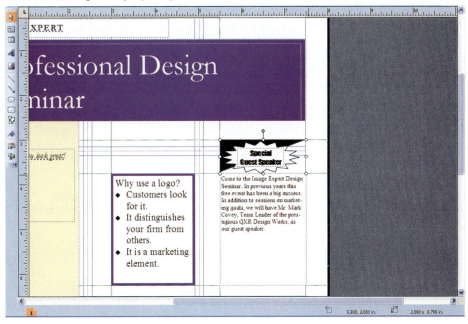

Nudging an object

You can use the keyboard arrow keys to move a selected object, a technique called **nudging**. This is helpful for moving an object a relatively small distance because the object only moves in the direction of the key you are pressing. Each time you press an arrow key, the object moves a fraction of an inch (0.13") in the direction of the key you pressed. You can change the distance an object is nudged by clicking Tools on the menu bar, clicking Options, and then clicking the Edit tab. Select the Arrow keys nudge objects by text box to edit the default nudging distance, then click OK.

Painting Formats

As you have learned, toolbar buttons can be used to apply object formatting or text attributes such as bold, italic, and underlining, as well as to increase or decrease font size. If you are applying the same formatting combinations to text in different locations in your publication, this process can get repetitive. To help you apply formats with consistency and without difficulty, you can use the Format Painter button on the Standard toolbar. Once you have applied formatting attributes, you use this feature to apply the formatting to other text. You want to spruce up the text about using a logo so that it stands out. Once you find a formatting combination you like, you want to paint the formatting to selected text.

STEPS

1. **Use the scroll bars to center the text box with the violet border in the work area**

   To draw attention to certain words in each sentence, you want to apply specific formats. One method of formatting is to use buttons on the Formatting toolbar.

TROUBLE

If you don't want the text to wrap, you can enlarge the text box slightly by dragging the middle right sizing handle slightly right.

2. **Select the text Why use a logo?, then click the Bold button B on the Formatting toolbar**

3. **Click Format on the menu bar, click Font, click the Color list arrow, click the Accent 1 (Violet) color box, (second from left) then click the Small caps check box**

   Compare the Font dialog box to Figure C-17. You can add as many attributes as you want by clicking the check boxes in this dialog box, but some are mutually exclusive. For example, Small caps and All caps cannot be selected at the same time.

4. **Click the Shadow check box, then click OK**

5. **Click the Format Painter button on the Standard toolbar, position in the text box, then click and drag over Customers**

   You can double-click to apply the same formatting to more than one location. To turn off the feature, press [Esc].

6. **Double-click , drag over firm, drag over marketing, then press [Esc]**

   You think the new color of the newly formatted bulleted text and small caps are too distracting.

TROUBLE

Once you save your work, you cannot undo the steps you performed.

7. **Click the Undo button three times, then press [Esc] twice**

   Your formatting of the text box is now complete. Compare your work to Figure C-18.

8. **Make sure your name displays in the email address in the lower-left corner of the newsletter**

9. **Press [F9], then click the Save button on the Standard toolbar**

FIGURE C-17: Font dialog box

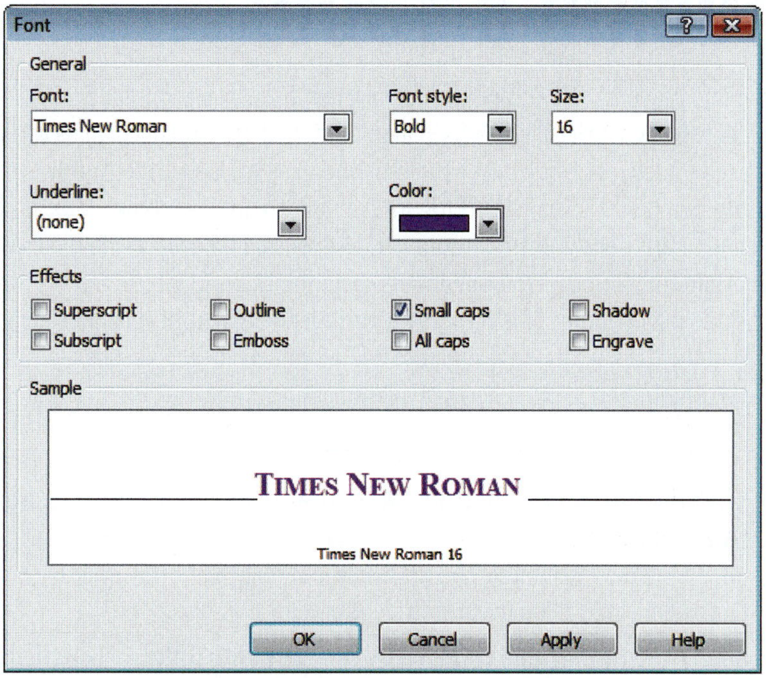

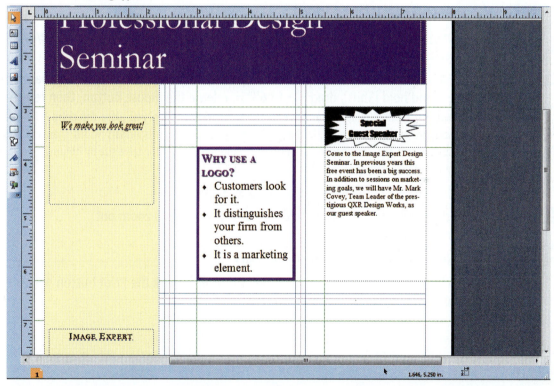

FIGURE C-18: Formatting applied

Design Matters

Creative deletion

Identifying poor design is an important skill, but mere recognition is not enough. Once a design flaw is identified, you have to either fix it or delete it. Not only is there nothing wrong with deleting flawed design elements, creative deletion is actually one of the most important skills a designer can learn. It is particularly important to be able to edit your own work. Look for elements that either detract from or fail to support the publication's message. If the element detracts or is unnecessary, it should be changed or deleted in favor of a constructive design element or more white space.

Adding a Table

Some information is more easily communicated in a table because its organization allows for quick reference. A **table** is a collection of information formatted in a grid of columns and rows. To create a table, you first need to determine how many columns and rows you need. You can always change the size of the table and the number of columns and rows if necessary. Publisher comes with 23 different table formats from which you can choose. To enter text in a table, you can type directly in the cells of the table, pressing [Tab] to move from cell to cell. You can also navigate the cells in a table using the arrow keys. 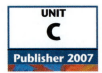 You need to include information in the flyer about the agenda for the seminar, including the title, description, and speaker for each. You decide to organize this information in a table. The table needs to contain six rows and three columns to hold all the necessary information.

STEPS

1. **Click the Insert Table button 🏢 on the Objects toolbar, then drag ╋ from 3" H / 7" V to 7½" H / 8¾" V**

   The Create Table dialog box opens, as shown in Figure C-19. The available table formats contain combinations of formatting attributes, borders, and shading.

   QUICK TIP

   You can move a selected table using the ⁺🔏 pointer. You can resize a table by clicking and dragging when the pointer is positioned over any of the handles.

2. **Scroll down the Table format list, click List with Title 2, click the Number of rows down arrow until 6 appears in the text box if necessary, click the Number of columns down arrow until 3 appears in the text box, then click OK**

   The table appears in the table frame.

3. **Press [F9], type Session Title, press [Tab], type Description, press [Tab], then type Speaker**

   QUICK TIP

   Use ➕ to change row height.

4. **Place ⌶ between the Description and Speaker columns until the pointer changes to ⁺‖⁺, press and hold [Shift], drag ⁺‖⁺ to 6½" H, release the mouse button, then release [Shift]**

   When first created, table columns are all the same width. When you place the pointer between column boundaries of a selected table, it changes to ⁺‖⁺. Changing the boundary width changes the size of the table; however, you can change the width of a column but retain the table size by holding [Shift] while dragging to the new width.

5. **Enter the table data using Figure C-20 as a guide**

   QUICK TIP

   Press [Tab] at the end of the last cell in a table to insert a new row in the table. Press [Enter] in any cell to insert lines within the row.

6. **Click outside the table to deselect it, then press [F9] to zoom out**

   You are pleased with the progress of the flyer.

7. **Delete the logo placeholder, if necessary**

8. **Click the Save button 💾 on the Standard toolbar, click the Print button 🖨 on the Standard toolbar, then exit Publisher**

Modifying the layout of a table

You can modify the layout of a Publisher table by right-clicking the table, then clicking Format Table. Using the Cell Properties tab, you can change the margins and vertical alignment within selected cells, as well as rotate text by 90 degrees. Use the Colors and Lines tab to change the fill or line color of selected cells. You can create a split cell effect for selected cells in a table by clicking Table on the menu bar, then clicking Cell Diagonals. The Cell Diagonals dialog box lets you divide a cell up or down, or remove a division entirely. You can also merge selected adjacent cells by clicking Table on the menu bar, then clicking Merge Cells. Merged cells can be split up by clicking Table on the menu bar, then clicking Split Cells. The contents of cells can be duplicated into adjacent selected cells by clicking Table on the menu bar, then clicking either Fill Down or Fill Right.

FIGURE C-19: Create Table dialog box

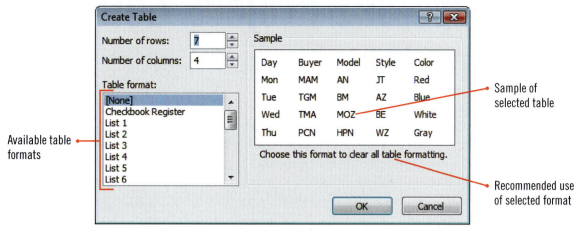

Available table formats

Sample of selected table

Recommended use of selected format

FIGURE C-20: Completed table

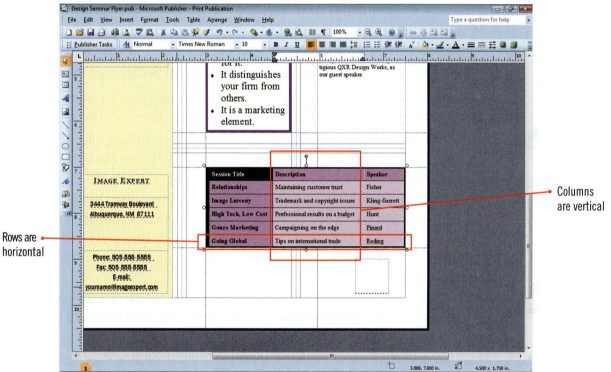

Columns are vertical

Rows are horizontal

Using AutoFormat

An existing table's design can be changed using the AutoFormat feature. The **Table AutoFormat** feature looks similar to the Create Table dialog box, except that it contains only table formats. Open the Auto Format dialog box by clicking Table on the menu bar, then clicking Table AutoFormat. Choose a new Table format, then click OK, and the new table format will replace the old. Figure C-21 shows the Numbers 3 format in the Auto Format dialog box. In order to use AutoFormat, you must select a table.

FIGURE C-21: Auto Format dialog box

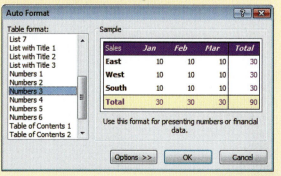

Capstone Project: College Brochure

You have learned how to change layout and margin guides and how to use ruler guides. You have also learned to format a text box, and add and modify bullets, numbering, and Design Gallery Objects. Additionally, you now know how to paint formats, add a table, and check spelling. You have been asked to create a flyer promoting the Camelback Community College Library Book Sale. The sale will feature the library's Great Books collection, so you want to call attention to this information in the flyer. The flyer needs to emphasize information about the great books available at the sale.

STEPS

1. **Start Publisher, click Flyers in the Publication Types list, scroll down to the Sale section, click Book Sale, click Create, then save it as Book Sale Flyer to the drive and folder where you store your Data Files**
   The template you selected has the right tone for the flyer.

2. **Change the color scheme to Sienna**

3. **Click the Book Sale placeholder, then change it to read Library Book Sale**

4. **Click Arrange on the menu bar, click Layout Guides, change all the margin guides to 0.4", change the grid guides to 3 Columns and 3 Rows, then click OK**

QUICK TIP
Draw ruler guides to help you position the object.

5. **Click the Design Gallery Object button 🖼 on the Objects toolbar, click Attention Getters, click Flag, click Insert Object, drag the object to ½" H, ½" V, then close the Format Publication task pane**

6. **Press [F9], resize the selected object to 2¾" H × 1½" V by dragging the lower-right handle, click the Free Offer text, type Great Books, press [Ctrl][A], click Format on the menu bar, click Font, click the All caps check box, click OK, press [F9], then press [Esc] three times**
   Making the Attention Getter larger and changing the text will help the reader decide immediately if he or she is interested in reading further.

7. **Click the text box at 7" H / 5" V, click Format on the menu bar, click Bullets and Numbering, click the diamond bullet, increase the bullet point size to 15 pt, then click OK**

8. **Click the text box at 7" H / 8" V, replace the text with the name of your school, click the text box at 7" H / 9" V, delete the logo placeholder if necessary, then replace the text with your school's address, and the email address with your name**

9. **Save the publication, print the page, compare your work to Figure C-22, then exit Publisher**

FIGURE C–22: Completed publication

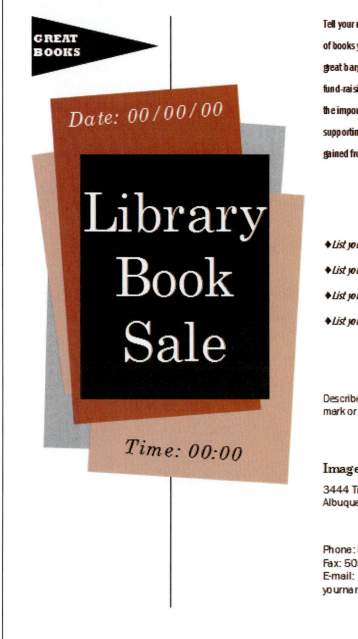

Tell your readers about the selection of books you have for sale and the great bargains they'll find. If this is a fund-raising event, be sure to convey the importance of the cause you are supporting and the benefits to be gained from the sale.

- List your most interesting items.
- List your most interesting items.
- List your most interesting items.
- List your most interesting items.

Describe your location by land-mark or area of town.

Image Expert

3444 Tramway Boulevard
Albuquerque, NM 87111

Phone: 505-555-5555
Fax: 505-555-5444
E-mail:
yourname@imageexpert.com

Practice

▼ CONCEPTS REVIEW

Label each of the elements of the Publisher window shown in Figure C-23.

FIGURE C-23

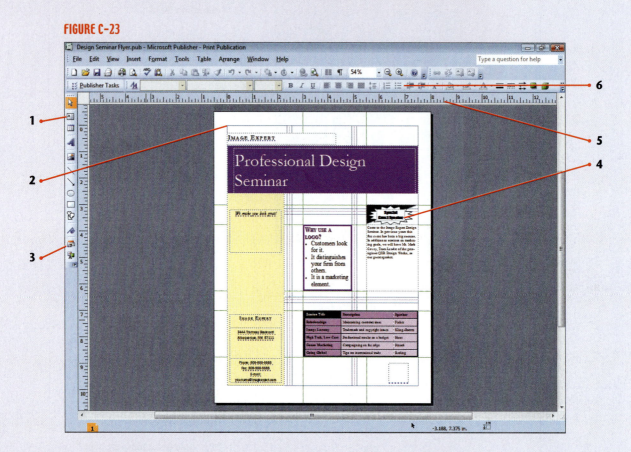

Match each of the buttons with the statement that describes its function.

7. ╋║╋
8. 🖌
9. ▢
10. ▦
11. 🖼
12. **B**

a. Paints formatting attributes
b. Changes a column's width
c. To move rulers
d. Inserts a table
e. Opens the Design Gallery
f. Makes text bold

Select the best answer from the list of choices.

13. The Spelling feature in Publisher:

a. Identifies misspelled words.
b. Finds all spelling and grammatical errors.

c. Gets rid of the blue wavy lines.
d. Cannot check words in a table.

14. Ruler guides are:

a. Blue.

b. Green.

c. Pink.

d. Red.

15. Which of the following is not a font attribute?

a. Bold

b. Snap

c. Italics

d. Shadow

16. To maintain a table's size, resize a column while holding the _____ key.

a. [Shift]

b. [Alt]

c. [Ctrl]

d. [Esc]

17. You can draw a table frame when the pointer turns to _____.

a. ⬉

b. ↔

c. +

d. I

18. In order to insert a new row in a table, position the pointer in the last cell, then press

a. [Enter]

b. [Tab]

c. [Shift][Enter]

d. [Page Down]

19. Each of the following buttons is used for formatting text, except _____.

a. *I*

b. ▣

c. 🖌

d. **B**

20. Each of the following is true about layout guides, except:

a. Objects can snap to them.

b. They are only visible onscreen.

c. They include margin guides and grid guides.

d. They appear in the foreground.

▼ SKILLS REVIEW

1. Use layout guides.

a. Start Publisher, click Flyers in the Publication Types list, then click the Company Picnic template in the Event category.

b. Use the Secondary Business Information Set and the Sapphire color scheme, create the file, close the task pane, then save the file as **Company Picnic Flyer** to the drive and folder where you store your Data Files.

c. Use the Arrange menu to open the Layout Guides dialog box.

d. Change the margin guides if necessary to 0.5 left, 0.5 right, 0.5 top, and 0.66 bottom.

e. Use the Layout Guides dialog box to create three columns and three rows of grid guides in this publication.

f. Save your work.

2. Use ruler guides.

a. Move the vertical ruler closer to the page.

b. Create horizontal ruler guides at ¼" V, 1" V, 7" V, and 9½" V. Create vertical ruler guides at ½" H, 4" H, 5¾" H, and 7" H.

c. Save your work.

3. Format a text box.

a. Move the vertical ruler back to the left side of the screen.

b. Click the text box at 2" H / 5" V, then zoom in to view the text box.

c. Create a 4 pt navy (Accent 1) border around the text box, zoom out so you can see the full page, then deselect the text box.

d. Save your work.

4. Add bullets and numbering.

   a. Select the text box at 5" H / 5" V, then zoom in to view the text box.

   b. Replace the text under the Highlights heading with the following information, pressing [Enter] after each activity except the last one, to create a bulleted list: **Volleyball, Live music, Sack race, Softball, Pie-eating contest**.

   c. Change the bullet style to a 12 pt open right-pointing arrow, zoom out, then save the publication.

5. Check spelling.

   a. Select and zoom in to the text box at 2" H / 5" V, then replace the existing text in the box with the file PUB C-2.docx from the drive and folder where you store your Data Files.

   b. Correct the spelling of the selected text, then AutoFit this text using the Best Fit command. (*Hint*: You should find four spelling errors.) Do not check the spelling in the rest of the publication.

   c. Zoom out so that you can see the entire publication, deselect the highlighted text if necessary, then save the publication.

6. Modify a Design Gallery Object.

   a. Click the Design Gallery Object button on the Objects toolbar, click the Attention Getters category, then insert the Double Slant Attention Getter.

   b. Move the object so that the upper-left edge snaps into place at the ruler guides at 5 ¾" H / ¼" V, then zoom in to the object.

   c. Change the default text to **Too Much Fun!**

   d. Zoom out, then save the publication.

7. Paint formats.

   a. Select the bulleted list and zoom in.

   b. Select the text Volleyball and format it using the Engrave effect and light blue (Accent 2) color.

   c. Use the Format Painter to paint Live music with the same formatting.

   d. Double-click the Format Painter button on the Standard toolbar.

   e. Paint the formatting to the following text: Sack race, Softball, and Pie-eating contest.

   f. Zoom out so that you can see the entire page, then save your work.

8. Add a table.

   a. Resize the three text boxes above the Time text box so that their right edges end at 4" H.

   b. Create a table from 4" H / 7⅞" V to 7¾" H / 9½" V, using the List 3 format.

   c. Create six rows and three columns.

   d. Zoom in, then enter the following text for the three column headings: **Activity**, **Contact**, and **Extension**.

   e. Enter the information in Table C-1, then resize the columns so the left edge of the Extension column begins at 6¾" H.

   f. Zoom out so that you can see the full page.

   g. Deselect the table, then delete the logo placeholder, if necessary.

   h. Replace the phone number for the Contact Person with your name, then save your work.

   i. Print the publication, then exit Publisher.

TABLE C-1

Activity	Contact	Extension
Volleyball	Lucy McMannus	4828
Live music	Frank Etherton	4689
Sack race	Roger Hubbard	5220
Softball	Gail Farnsworth	1096
Pie-eating contest	Greta Tolkmann	3117

▼ INDEPENDENT CHALLENGE 1

The firm of Top-Drawer Law Associates has hired you to design a postcard that invites people to a promotion party.

a. Start Publisher if necessary, use the Publication Types list to select the Blends Informational Postcard in the Classic Designs section, use the color scheme of your choice, save it as **Promotion Announcement** to the drive and folder where you store your Data Files, then close the task pane.

b. Change all four margin guides to .25".

c. Delete the text box containing placeholder text for a business tag line that is just under the upper margin.

d. Move the zero points to the top-left margin, then add a vertical ruler guide at 1" and a horizontal ruler guide at ⅛".

e. Move the Product/Service Information text box so that the upper-left corner is at 1" H / ⅛" V, create a 2 pt Accent 1 border around it, then type **TOP-DRAWER LAW ASSOCIATES ANNOUNCE**.

f. Align all of the text boxes so their left edges snap to the vertical ruler guide.

g. Select the text box that starts **Place text here** and insert the text found in PUB C-3.docx.

h. Use the Spelling Checker to correct any errors in the text. Do not check the rest of the publication.

i. Type the firm's name in the text box found at 1" H / 2 ⅜" V, then modify text and formatting to create a meaningful invitation.

j. Create text that has bold and embossed formatting, then use the Format Painter to copy formats for the text.

k. Add a text box that includes your name, delete the logo placeholder if necessary, save and print the publication, then exit Publisher.

▼ INDEPENDENT CHALLENGE 2

The seminar you are teaching in London on International Business Leadership is about to end. At the conclusion, you would like to present each attendee with a certificate of completion.

a. Start Publisher, if necessary, use the Publication Types list to select Award Certificates, choose the Celtic Knotwork Certificate, and the color scheme of your choice.

b. Save the publication as **International Leadership Certificate** to the drive and folder where you store your Data Files, then close the task pane.

c. Move the zero points to the top-left margin.

d. Replace the Name of Recipient with your name, then change the words "Certificate of Appreciation" to **CERTIFICATE OF COMPLETION**.

e. Format the Certificate of Completion text box border so it is a 5 pt, solid line.

Advanced Challenge Exercise

■ Change the solid line to a dash line. Compare your publication to Figure C-24.

f. Format the **Your Name** text using the formatting of your choice.

g. Change the "Business" name to **The International School of Business**.

h. Modify any other existing text to create a meaningful certificate of completion, then delete the logo placeholder if necessary.

i. Save and print the publication, then exit Publisher.

FIGURE C-24

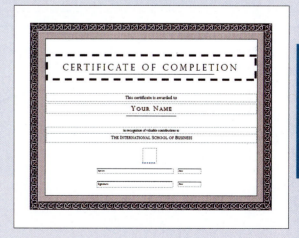

The local music appreciation society asks you to design a program for its upcoming festival.

a. Start Publisher if necessary, then use the Publication Types list to create a music program. Save the publication as **Music Program** to the drive and folder where you store your Data Files, then close the task pane.

b. On page 2, delete the existing table (for The Singers) and replace it with a 3-column, 8-row table with the format of your choice.

c. Make up the names of the singers, the songs they will sing, and the type of music (for example, opera, folk, or jazz).

d. Replace the **Conductor's Name** text with your name.

e. Replace any existing text on all pages with information that creates a meaningful music program.

f. Format text using at least two attributes, then use the Format Painter to copy the formatting to other text.

g. Use the Spelling Checker to correct any errors in the text.

h. Save and print pages two and three of the publication, compare your publication to Figure C-25, then exit Publisher.

FIGURE C-25

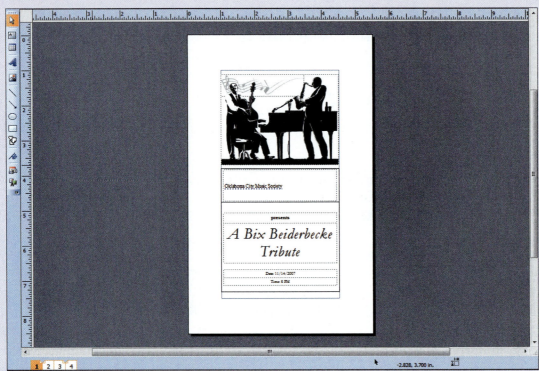

▼ REAL LIFE INDEPENDENT CHALLENGE

Your keen mind, artistic tastes, and desire to make money are leading you to pursue business opportunities that involve designing publications. To become more credible, you decide to learn more about different fonts.

a. Connect to the Internet, then using your favorite search engine or Web site (such as google.com or about.com), search for information on choosing fonts and typefaces.

b. Use the Publication Types list to create any style of flyer, then save it as **Different Font Flyer** to the drive and folder where you store your Data Files.

c. Create a heading that uses and names your favorite font.

d. Add a text box that contains a bulleted list that uses and names five other fonts that you find easy to read.

e. Add a text box that discusses the differences between serif and sans serif fonts.

f. Format the text to illustrate both sans serif and serif fonts.

g. Add a prominently placed text box with your name in a clearly readable font and point size.

h. Use your judgment to delete any objects that do not contribute to the design of your publication.

i. Add a colorful border to the text boxes.

Advanced Challenge Exercise

- Change the appearance of the bullets in the list.

j. Use the Spelling Checker to correct any errors in the text, then save and print the publication.

k. Compare your publication to Figure C-26, then exit Publisher.

FIGURE C-26

▼ VISUAL WORKSHOP

Use the Publication Types list to create an Estate Sale Flyer. Save this publication as **Estate Sale Flyer** to the drive and folder where you store your Data Files. Use Figure C-27 as a guide. Use the Tidepool color scheme and replace all text as shown in the figure. Include your name on the flyer. Save and print the flyer.

FIGURE C-27

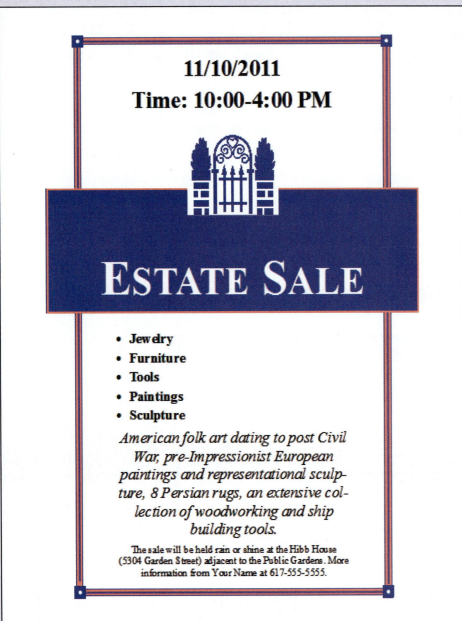

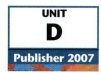

UNIT D
Publisher 2007

Working with Graphic Objects

Files You Will Need:

PUB D-1.pub
PUB D-2.tif
PUB D-3.pub
PUB D-4.pub
PUB D-5.pub

Artwork is much more than decoration. At its best, it expresses ideas and feelings that words cannot. In practical terms, artwork can be used to grab a reader's attention and clarify themes and messages in a publication. Proper positioning of graphic objects can relieve the monotony of text, add emphasis to the written word, and separate subjects. You have been asked to take over work on a flyer for a veterinary hospital fundraiser. The client wants the flyer to be inviting and friendly, with lots of graphics. Your first task is to choose appropriate artwork; the text will be added later.

OBJECTIVES

Insert and resize clip art

Copy and move an object

Crop an image

Align and group images

Layer objects

Rotate an image

Use drawing tools

Fill shapes with colors and gradients

Capstone Project: Flower Show
    Web Page

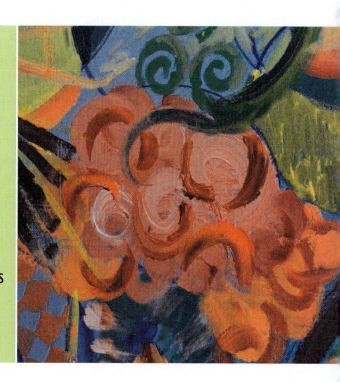

Inserting and Resizing Clip Art

The Clip Art task pane makes it easy to dress up any publication with images. There is so much clip art available, online and from commercial sources, that you can almost always find an image to represent a topic or round out a theme. With the Clip Art task pane, you can use the search feature to locate specific artwork by keyword or topic. Both the Microsoft Clip Organizer and the Clip Art task pane contain pictures, motion clips, and sounds, and are not limited to the artwork that comes with Publisher. You can customize the Clip Organizer by adding any electronic image you wish. The Clip Organizer also saves artwork from previous searches for future use. You are ready to search for artwork for the fundraiser flyer. You want to find art representative of a veterinary hospital setting, and then resize it to fit your design for the flyer.

STEPS

1. Start Publisher, open **PUB D-1.pub** from the drive and folder where you store your Data Files, click **File** on the menu bar, click **Save As**, then save the file as **Fundraiser Flyer**

2. Click the **Picture Frame button** 🖻 on the Objects toolbar, then click **Clip Art**

   The Clip Art task pane opens. It contains options that allow you to limit your search to specific collections, and search for different types of media, such as clip art, photographs, movies, and sounds, arranged by content.

3. Click the **Search for text box**, delete any existing text if necessary, type **animal**, click the **Results should be list arrow**, then remove the check marks next to Photographs, Movies and Sounds, if necessary so that **Clip Art** is the only checkbox that contains a check mark

4. Click the **Search in list arrow**, remove the check mark next to Web Collections, if necessary, so that **My Collections** and **Office Collections** are the only checkboxes that contain check marks, then click **Go**

   The results of the search appear, as shown in Figure D-1.

5. Position 🔓 over the **second image in the first row**, click the **down arrow** on the right side of the image, click **Preview/Properties**, verify that **j0216724.wmf** is the filename, then click **Close**

6. Right-click the selected **image**, click **Insert**, then click the **Close button** on the Clip Art task pane.

7. Press **[F9]**, position 🔓 over the **clip art** until the pointer changes to ⁺ᵏ, drag ⁺ᵏ so that the object's upper-left corner is at 2¾" H / 3¾" V, as shown in Figure D-2, then release the mouse button

8. Place 🔓 over the **lower-right corner frame handle** until the pointer changes to ↖↘, press and hold **[Shift]**, drag ↖↘ to the guides intersection at 5¼" H / 6⅞" V, then release **[Shift]**

9. Click the **Save button** 💾 on the Standard toolbar

FIGURE D-1: Clip Art task pane with search results

Image
j0216724.wmf

Pictures found in
the search

Connects to the Web
for additional clips

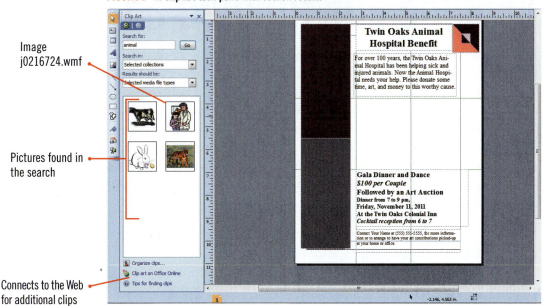

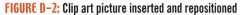

FIGURE D-2: Clip art picture inserted and repositioned

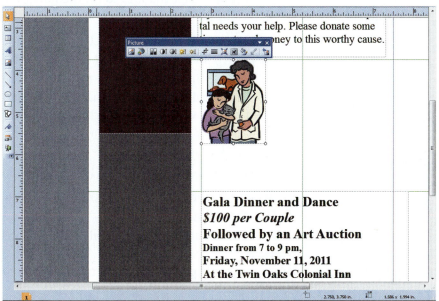

Resizing an object

As you work with objects, whether they originate from your own photos or from clip art, chances are good that you'll want to resize them to fit your publication. You can resize a selected object by dragging any of its displayed handles, but often this results in altered proportions that look, well, weird. You can resize a selected object in the following ways:

- resize an object and keep the object's center stationary by pressing and holding [Ctrl] while you drag a handle,
- maintain the object's proportions while resizing it by pressing and holding [Shift] while dragging a handle,

- keep the object's center stationary while maintaining its proportions by pressing and holding [Ctrl] while dragging a handle
- make the object a specific height and width by right-clicking it, clicking the Format command, clicking the Size tab, then entering measurements under Size and rotate
- specify proportions by right-clicking the object, clicking the Format command, clicking the Size tab, then entering the percentage of the original height or width you want

Copying and Moving an Object

You can move and copy images in a publication quickly and easily. By copying artwork, you can create interesting effects with duplicated images. You can also use copied images for experimentation in manipulating their colors, contours, cropping, dimensions, and orientations, without changing the design of your original publication. For example, you can manipulate an image to create a mirror image. A mirror image shows two identical images with one flipped, so that it appears as though you are viewing the object in a mirror. When you copy an image, the copy is held temporarily in the Windows **Clipboard**, a temporary storage area for copied or cut items. 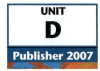 You want to create a mirror image using the image you just inserted. You are also considering using the image in another location in the publication. You decide to accomplish these tasks by using the Clipboard to copy and move the image.

STEPS

1. **Right-click the selected object, then click Copy**

   Although it looks as though nothing happened, the clip art object was copied to the Clipboard. Once an image is on the Clipboard, you can paste it repeatedly, using any pasting method.

2. **Right-click again, then click Paste**

   A copy of the object appears overlapping the original object, as shown in Figure D-4. The newly copied image is selected and is on top of the original image. This copy appears slightly offset from the original image's location.

3. **Position ⬚ over the selected copy until it changes to ⬚, then drag the selected object so the upper-left corner is at 5¼" H / 3¾" V**

4. **Press [F9], position the pointer over the selected object until it changes to ⬚, press and hold [Ctrl], press and hold [Shift], then drag ⬚ so that the upper-left corner is on the scratch area at 9" H / 3¾" V, release the mouse button, release [Shift], then release [Ctrl]**

   The second copy of the clip art is placed to the right of the original object, but off the page. You now have three images, two below the upper text box, and one on the scratch area. The **scratch area** is a convenient place to store design elements while working on the overall design of a publication.

5. **Right-click the selected object, then click Cut**

   The second copy is no longer visible, and because no image is selected, the Picture toolbar closes.

6. **Click the image whose upper-left corner is at 5¼" H / 3¾" V, click Arrange on the menu bar, point to Rotate or Flip, then click Flip Horizontal**

   The copy is flipped, as shown in Figure D-5, and you can see the original image next to the flipped copy. You decide you do not like its appearance.

7. **Right-click the flipped copy, then click Delete Object**

   The mirror image is no longer visible. Deleted items are not sent to the Office Clipboard.

8. **Click the Save button 💾 on the Standard toolbar**

Using the Format Painter on Clip Art

The Format Painter that you can use to copy multiple formats from one selection of text to another can also be used on objects, such as lines and shapes or even clip art. Suppose, for example, that you have several pieces of clip art that you want to enhance with a colorful line border and shadow. Apply all the formatting enhancements you want, click the Format Painter button, then click another clip art object. The formatting attributes will be applied to the clip art.

FIGURE D-4: Pasted object overlapping original object

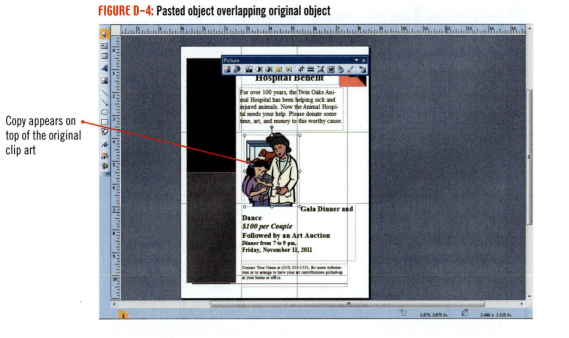

Copy appears on top of the original clip art

FIGURE D-5: Flipped image

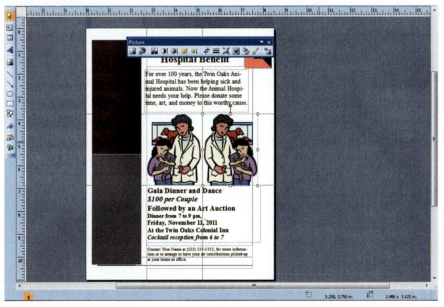

Using the Office Clipboard

The Office Clipboard is a Publisher task pane that lets you copy and paste multiple items, such as text, images, or tables, within or between Microsoft Office applications. The Office Clipboard can hold up to 24 items copied or cut from any Office program. You choose whether to delete the first item from the Clipboard when you copy the 25th item. The collected items remain in the Office Clipboard and are available to you until you close all open Office programs. You can scroll through the Clipboard task pane, shown in Figure D-6, to choose an item to paste; clicking the item inserts it at the current location of the cursor. You can specify when and where to show the Clipboard task pane by clicking the Options button at the bottom of the Clipboard task pane.

FIGURE D-6: Clipboard task pane

Cropping an Image

Even when you find the perfect image for a publication, you may find that it needs some modification to fit perfectly on the page. Perhaps a part of a picture's contents interferes with the publication's message or contains too much white space. When this happens, you can trim, or **crop**, portions of the artwork to modify it to fit your needs. A graphic image can be cropped vertically, horizontally, or both. Even though they are not visible, the cropped portions of an image are still there—they are just concealed, so you can make them visible again if you change your mind.  You want to add a photographic image to the flyer, and crop it so that it better suits your design.

STEPS

1. Click **Insert** on the menu bar, point to **Picture**, click **From File**, locate the drive and folder where you store your Data Files, click the file **PUB D-2.tif**, click **Insert**, then move the image so that the upper-left corner is at **9" H / 1" V** on the scratch area

   A photograph of kittens is placed on the scratch area, as shown in Figure D-7.

2. Scroll if necessary so you can see the entire image, click the **Crop button** ⌗ on the Picture toolbar, position ⬚ over the upper-left corner handle, when the pointer changes to ⌐ click the **upper-left handle**, then drag ⌐ to approximately **3" V**

   The Crop button stays selected until you turn it off, so you can continue cropping until you are finished. The surplus white space on the left edge will be concealed later.

> **QUICK TIP**
> To crop both edges simultaneously and equally, click the Crop button, press and hold [Ctrl], then drag ⌐.

3. Click the **lower-right handle**, drag ⌐ to approximately **15" H**, then press **[Esc]** to deselect the image

   The cropped image is much smaller, but it still needs to be resized so that it will fit next to the existing artwork on the page.

4. Click the **photo image** to select it, position ⬚ over the **lower-right corner handle**, when it changes to ⬂ press **[Shift]**, then drag ⬂ until the right border of the image is at **11½"** on the horizontal ruler

   The resized image now has a width of 2½" and can be placed on the page.

5. Click the **cropped and resized image**, then drag it using ⬚ so that the upper-left corner is at **2¾" H x 4½" V**

   The cropped image is directly on top of the clip art for now, but you will move it later. Compare your image to Figure D-8.

6. Click the **Save button** 💾 on the Standard toolbar

Design Matters

Browsing Office Online Clip Art and Media

If you have access to the Internet, you can add to the Microsoft Clip Organizer from Microsoft Office Online Clip Art and Media. You can access this site by clicking the Clip art on Office Online link at the bottom on the Clip Art task pane, or by going to office.microsoft.com/en-us/clipart/default.aspx. This site offers a constantly changing selection of artwork. Figure D-3 shows some of the choices offered at this Web site, although it will look different when you view it, as it changes constantly. This site lets you constantly update your clip art so you always have new, exciting types of artwork to include in your publications. You can download clip art, photographs, sounds, and video clips from this Web site.

FIGURE D-3: Microsoft Office Online Web site

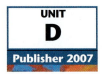

FIGURE D-7: Image before cropping

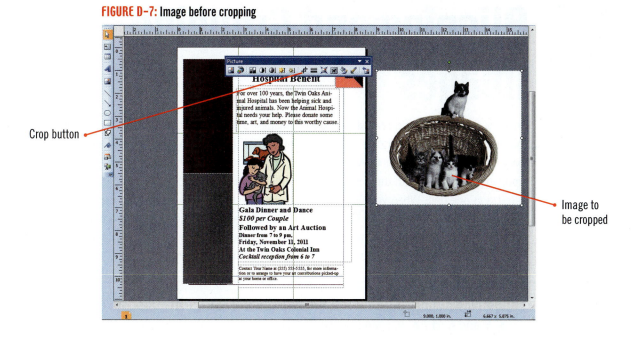

Crop button

Image to be cropped

FIGURE D-8: Image cropped, resized, and placed on page

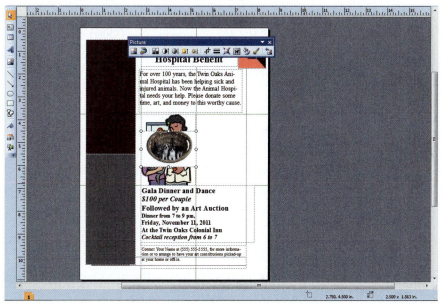

Design Matters

Cropping creatively

Cropping is used to remove portions of an image that do not support the publication's design. How do you decide what images should be cropped and how they should be cropped? Look for elements that either interfere with or fail to carry the publication's message. Just as with text or other objects, if a part of the image is distracting or unnecessary, it should be changed or deleted in favor of a beneficial design element. Often, it is white space in a photo or in clip art that should be cropped. If white space is needed, it can be added with a margin around the art.

Aligning and Grouping Images

Once you insert clip art, you can align multiple images so that the layout of the publication looks clean and balanced. Alignment helps guide the reader's eye across the page by avoiding isolated patches of white space that might be distracting. Artwork can be aligned from left to right or from top to bottom. You can group images to work with them more easily. A **group** is a selection of multiple images that you can move or resize as one unit. When you finish working with objects as a group, you can **ungroup** them to work with them individually again. You want to align the main text boxes and the two images in the flyer so that the overall appearance is neater. You also want to experiment with grouping the images to flip them as a single object on the page to see if this would improve your design.

STEPS

1. **With the cropped image still selected, press and hold [Shift], click the text boxes at 6" H / 3" V and 6" H / 8" V, then release [Shift]**

   Two text boxes and the image should be selected, as shown in Figure D-9.

2. **Click Arrange on the menu bar, point to Align or Distribute, then click Align Right**

   The text boxes and the photo image are lined up on the right edge, as shown in Figure D-10.

3. **Press [Esc] to deselect the objects**

4. **Press [Shift], click the cropped photo image, use ⬉ to drag the photo image until its bottom-left corner is at 5" H / 6⅞" V, then release [Shift]**

   Holding [Shift] while you move an object moves it in a straight line, either vertically or horizontally. The images are aligned along their bottom edges, and the text boxes are perfectly aligned with the photo image along their right edges.

5. **With the photo image still selected, press and hold [Shift], click the clip art image to select it, release [Shift], then click the Group Objects button 🖽 below the two selected objects**

   The two selected objects can now be manipulated as a single selected object.

6. **Click Arrange on the menu bar, point to Rotate or Flip, then click Flip Horizontal**

   Compare your work with Figure D-11. You don't like this change. The space above the kittens' heads is unusable white space, and the publication seems unbalanced with the objects reversed.

7. **Click the Undo button 🔄 on the Standard toolbar**

8. **Click the Ungroup Objects button 🖽 below the grouped object, then press [Esc]**

   The objects are deselected and the Picture toolbar is no longer visible.

9. **Click the Save button 💾 on the Standard toolbar**

Scanning artwork

If you have a favorite photo or piece of artwork that does not exist in electronic form, you can convert it to a digital computer file with a scanner. A variety of scanners are available in either handheld, sheetfed, or flatbed format. You can scan text, line art, or full-color images with amazing accuracy, enabling you to use virtually any image in publications. Every scanner comes with its own imaging software. With the camera or scanner in place and the software installed, Publisher lets you scan directly into a publication by clicking Insert on the menu bar, pointing to Picture, then clicking From Scanner or Camera.

FIGURE D-9: Three objects selected

Object 1

Object 2

Object 3

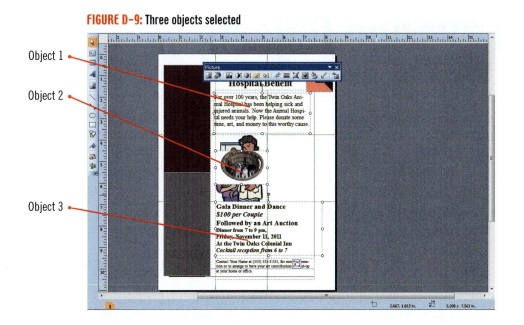

FIGURE D-10: Objects aligned right

Selected objects
right-aligned

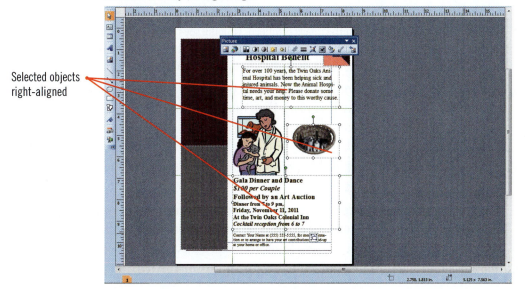

FIGURE D-11: Grouped objects flipped horizontally

Objects flip
horizontally
along the
vertical axis

Overlap from
the photo
image covers
part of the
clip art

Ungroup button

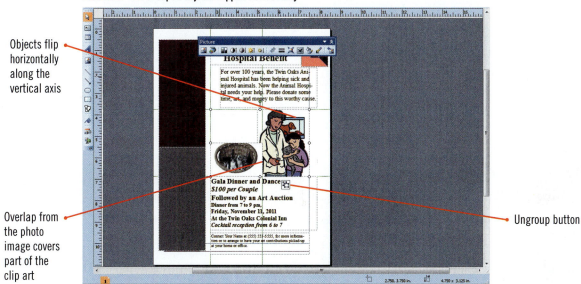

Layering Objects

When positioning objects, you might want some images to overlap, or appear as if they were in front of others. This layering effect can be used with any type of object. Sometimes you will want text to display on top of a shape, or one object to overlap another object to partially conceal it. You might want to superimpose a text box in front of one object or a collection of objects. There are four options for layering objects in Publisher. Table D-1 outlines the four Order commands on the Arrange menu. You can send an image to the back so that it appears to be underneath an object, or bring it to the front so it appears to be on top of an object. You want to experiment with layering and manipulating objects to improve the look of the flyer.

STEPS

1. **Click the clip art image at 4" H / 5" V, press [F9], then click the Bring to Front button** 🔳 ▾ **on the Standard toolbar**

   The clip art image of the animal hospital now overlaps the photograph, as shown in Figure D-12. You think the images look better with this amount of overlap because it reduces the white space separating the two images. You think the design might be improved by reversing the clip art image.

2. **Click Arrange on the menu bar, point to Rotate or Flip, then click Flip Horizontal**

   The overlap is maintained when the image is flipped. Flipping the clip art image lines up the subjects of the image in a strong diagonal that guides the eye from the upper-left to the lower-right. It also changes the apparent view of the veterinarian from one animal to all the animals and the little girl.

   > **TROUBLE**
   > You may have to use the vertical scroll bar to see 3½" V.

3. **Click the AutoShapes button** 🔯 **on the Objects toolbar, point to Callouts, click the Cloud Callout (fourth shape in the first row), then drag** ✛ **from 5¼" H / 3½" V to 8" H / 5" V**

   The image of the kittens now has a cartoon balloon to which you can add a caption. One of the effects of inserting a callout can be movement of some text in the upper text box to accommodate the object.

4. **Type They even love dogs!, press [Ctrl][A], click Format on the menu bar, point to AutoFit Text, then click Best Fit**

5. **Click the AutoShape to select it, position the pointer over the yellow handle, then drag** ▷ **to just above the head of the left-most kitten, at approximately 5⅞" H / 5¾" V**

   The callout is positioned so that it appears to originate from the kitten's mouth, as shown in Figure D-13.

6. **Click the Save button** 🔲 **on the Standard toolbar**

TABLE D-1: The Order commands

command	description
Send Forward	Moves the selected object or objects forward one level in the stack of layered objects
Send Backward	Moves the selected object or objects backward one level in the stack of layered objects
Bring to Front	Moves the selected object or objects to the topmost level in the stack of layered objects
Send to Back	Moves the selected object or objects to the backmost level in the stack of layered objects

FIGURE D-12: Image after it is brought to front

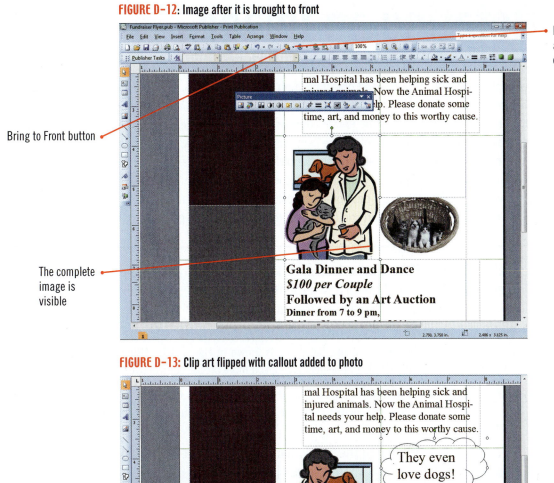

List arrow displays additional layering options

Bring to Front button

The complete image is visible

FIGURE D-13: Clip art flipped with callout added to photo

They even love dogs!

Gala Dinner and Dance
$100 per Couple
Followed by an Art Auction
Dinner from 7 to 9 pm,

Cloud callout

Using the Order commands

By creatively using the Order commands with text boxes and autoshapes you can superimpose text boxes on all kinds of objects and shapes to make them more dramatic. You can position objects in a specific stacking order to create a complex illustration. Figure D-14 shows layered text and graphics. Each object is on its own layer. This effect is achieved using the Bring Forward and Send Backward commands on the Arrange menu. Unlike Bring to Front and Send to Back, these commands move an image forward or backward only one layer at a time.

FIGURE D-14: Layered objects

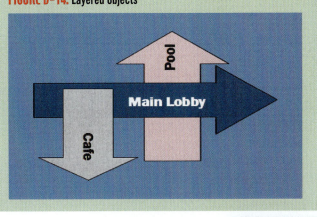

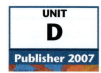

Rotating an Image

The **rotation** of an image—measured in degrees from a vertical plane—can be changed by dragging the green rotation handle on a selected object or using menu commands. Rotating images and other objects can change and guide the reader's focus and create visual interest. You can rotate a selected object in 90-degree increments by using the Rotate commands on the Arrange menu, or in specific degree increments by choosing the Format *item* (where item stands for AutoShape, Text box, Table, etc.) command on the shortcut menu and making selections in the dialog box that opens. You can rotate an object around a point on its base by pressing [Ctrl] while dragging the green rotation handle. You want to rotate the cartoon balloon, then change the position of the callout so it looks like a different kitten is speaking. This will help to catch the reader's attention and further lighten the tone of the publication, to create a sense of fun.

STEPS

QUICK TIP

You can also use the Measurement toolbar to adjust the rotation of the callout in addition to the spacing of the text.

QUICK TIP

Press [Ctrl][Alt] and an arrow key and you can rotate a selected object in 5-degree ° increments.

1. **Make sure the callout is still selected, click the green rotation handle • on the callout, then drag ↻ to the right until it is at 6¾" H / 3¼" V**
   The AutoShape is rotated to the right, as shown in Figure D-15.

2. **Right-click the callout, click Format AutoShape, then click the Size tab**
   The Size tab in the Format AutoShape dialog box is shown in Figure D-16. Using this dialog box lets you rotate an image a specific number of degrees giving you more precise control over the rotation.

3. **Select the contents of the Rotation text box, type 2, then click OK**
   The AutoShape is rotated two degrees clockwise. The object coordinates and object dimensions remain unchanged for a rotated object.

4. **Click the callout, then drag the yellow handle over the second kitten from the left (at approximately 6⅛" H / 5¾" V), then press [Esc]**
   Compare your image with Figure D-17.

5. **Press [F9], then click the Save button 🖫 on the Standard toolbar**

Design Matters

Using the Measurement toolbar

The Measurement toolbar lets you precisely move and resize graphic images or text boxes, and fine-tune text. To display the Measurement toolbar, click View on the menu bar, point to Toolbars, then click Measurement. You can adjust text point size, distance between characters, and line spacing using this toolbar, as well as an object's height, width, length, and rotation. This toolbar is context-sensitive, so the available options vary based on the type of object that is selected.

FIGURE D-15: Object rotated with handle

Rotation handle

FIGURE D-16: Size tab of Format AutoShape dialog box

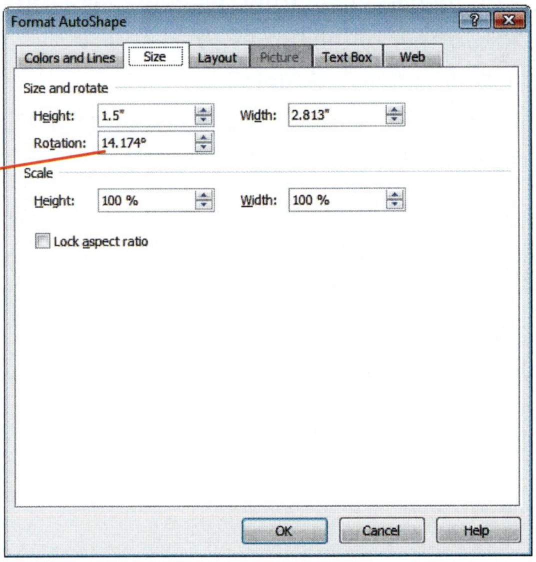

Precise degree
of rotation

FIGURE D-17: Precisely rotated object

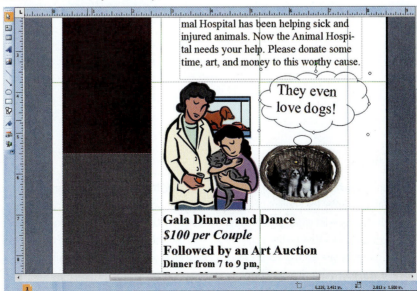

Publisher 2007

Using Drawing Tools

Publisher has a variety of drawing tools that you can use to create your own geometric designs. The Objects toolbar contains five drawing tools that let you draw lines, arrows, ovals, rectangles, and AutoShapes. Any shape drawn on a page can be moved, resized, or formatted to meet your design specifications. Like objects, shapes created with drawing tools can be flipped as well as rotated. Creating a shape is easy. You click the button for the tool you want to use, click where you want to start the shape, and drag to create the size you need. You want to add a geometric design to the gray rectangle at the lower-left corner of the page. You begin by drawing a border to frame the design and make it stand out.

STEPS

1. **Click the Rectangle button ▢ on the Objects toolbar**

2. **Drag ＋ from ½" H / 8¼" V to 2¼" H / 10" V, then press [F9]**
   The box is layered on the gray rectangle and has the dimensions 1¾" × 1¾".

3. **Click the AutoShapes button 🖫 on the Objects toolbar, then point to Basic Shapes**
   The Basic Shapes menu opens, as shown in Figure D-18.

4. **Click the heart, then drag ＋ from the upper left corner of the box at ½" H / 8¼" V to the lower right corner of the box at 2¼" H / 10" V**
   The heart is inside the box you just created.

   > **QUICK TIP**
   > If you want to repeat a designed shape with the identical dimensions, create one with all the formatting attributes you want, then copy and paste it.

5. **Click 🖫, point to Basic Shapes, click the heart, then drag ＋ to create a slightly smaller heart shape from ¾" H / 8½" V to 2" H / 9¾" V**

6. **Right-click the selected heart, click Format AutoShape, click the Line Color list arrow, click Accent 2 (RGB (255, 124, 128)) color box (third from the left), then click OK**
   The smaller heart shape is now outlined with a rose-colored border.

7. **Click the rectangle, then press [Delete]**
   You like the heart shape without the framing rectangle. Compare your work to Figure D-19.

8. **Press the Save button 🖫 on the Standard toolbar**

Using the Content Library

Any objects, text or graphics, can be organized and stored for future use using the Content Library. You can display the Content Library from any task pane by clicking the task pane list arrow, then clicking Content Library. (If no task pane is open, click View on the menu bar, then click Task Pane.) The Content Library lets you assign categories to its contents so you'll be able to retrieve them easily, and comes with three categories (Business, Personal, and Favorites) although you can add your own categories by clicking the Edit Category List button in the Add Item to Content Library dialog box. You can also add an object to the Content Library by right-clicking it, then clicking Add to Content Library.

FIGURE D-18: Basic Shapes menu

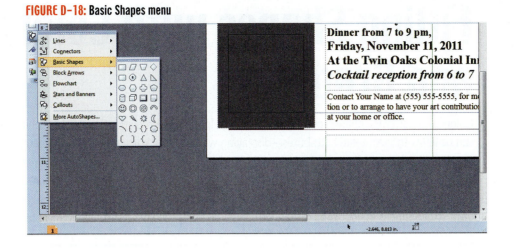

FIGURE D-19: Design created with drawing tools

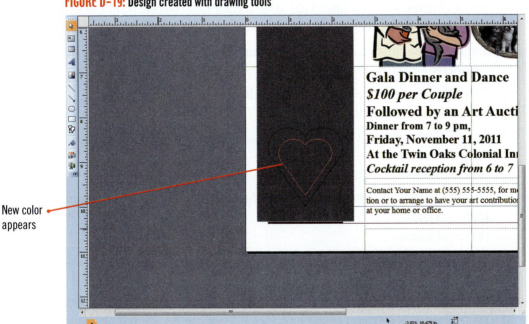

New color
appears

Design Matters

Drawing perfect shapes and lines

Sometimes you want to draw an exact shape or line. To draw a square, click the Rectangle button ▢ then press and hold [Shift] as you drag ┼. Press and hold [Shift] to create a circle using the Oval button ◯. Press and hold [Shift] to create a horizontal, vertical, or 45-degree angle straight line using the Line button ◥ (this method draws a line at 15 degree increments). To center an object at a specific location, click the tool to create the object, place the pointer where you want the center of the object to be, then hold [Ctrl] as you drag the mouse. Remember to always release the mouse button before you release [Ctrl] or [Shift].

Filling Shapes with Colors and Gradients

Colors and patterns enhance overall design and help you create elegant original graphics. Drawn shapes can be left with their default attributes—displaying whatever background exists—or you can fill them using a variety of colors, gradients and patterns. When choosing background colors, it's often effective to use the color scheme applied to the current publication. This includes a Main color, two or more Accent colors, and colors for hyperlinks that might be included in the publication. You want to add color and patterns to the shapes in your publication. You begin by adding color to the callout and one of the hearts.

STEPS

QUICK TIP

As you drag the mouse over each color displayed by the Fill Color list arrow, its name appears in a ScreenTip. The ScreenTip you see may display numeric color values rather than a generic color name.

1. Select the **smaller heart shape**, press **[F9]**, press **[Shift]**, click the **callout shape at 7" H / 4" V**, release **[Shift]**, click the **Fill Color list arrow** ▲ ▾ on the Formatting toolbar, then click the **Accent 2 (RGB (255, 124, 128)) color box**

   The rose color is added to the small heart shape and the callout, making them stand out.

2. Press **[Esc]**, right-click the **large heart**, click **Format AutoShape**, click the **Fill Color list arrow**, click the **Accent 1 (RGB (102, 0, 51)) color box** (second from the left), then click **OK**

   You want to experiment with changing the appearance of the smaller heart.

3. Right-click the **small heart**, click **Format AutoShape**, click the **Line Color list arrow**, then click **Accent 4 (RGB (204, 204, 204))**

4. Click **OK** to close the Format AutoShape dialog box

   A gray outline surrounds the small heart.

5. Press **[F9]**, click the **Line Color list arrow** ▲ ▾ on the Formatting toolbar, then click **Patterned Lines**

   The Patterned Lines dialog box opens with the Tint tab active.

QUICK TIP

You can also add pattern fills to objects by clicking the Pattern tab in the Patterned Lines dialog box and choosing a sample.

6. Click the **60% Shade box** (first box from the left in the third row) as shown in Figure D-20, then click **OK**

   The outline is darker.

7. Right-click the **rose heart shape**, click **Format AutoShape**, click the **Fill Color list arrow**, then click **Fill Effects**

8. Click the **Gradient tab** if necessary, click the **Diagonal up Shading styles option button**, click **OK** to close the Fill Effects dialog box, click **OK** to close the Format AutoShape dialog box, then press **[Esc]**

   Compare your work to Figure D-21.

9. Make sure your name displays in the **text box at 4" H / 10" V**, press **[F9]**, then deselect any objects

   Compare your work with the completed flyer in Figure D-22.

10. Click the **Save button** 🖫 on the Standard toolbar, click the **Print button** 🖨 on the Standard toolbar, then exit Publisher

FIGURE D-20: Tint tab of the Patterned Lines dialog box

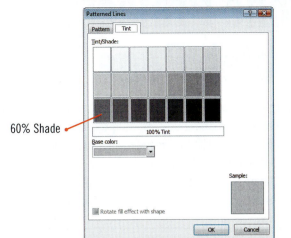

60% Shade

FIGURE D-21: Re-colored objects with gradient

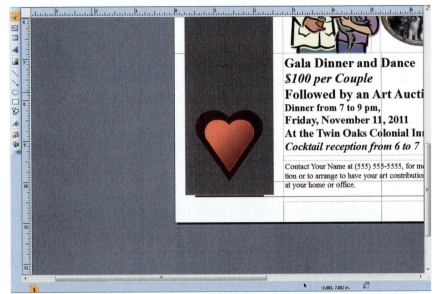

FIGURE D-22: Completed flyer

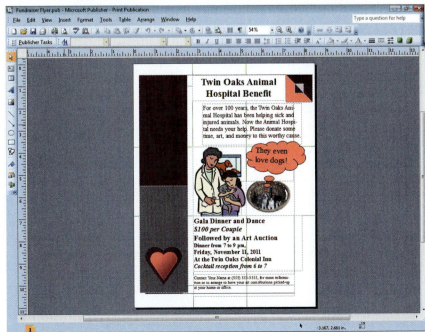

Capstone Project: Flower Show Web Page

You have learned the skills necessary to insert, resize, and rotate clip art. You can copy and move objects, and crop, align, and group objects. You have used drawing tools and added fill colors and gradients to drawn shapes. Now you will use your new skills to add and manipulate artwork on a Web site. 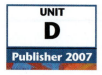 Image Expert was contracted to create a Web page for an annual flower show. Mike is heading up this project and has some preliminary work on a design, and has asked you to improve his work by adding images. Because the Web page is advertising a flower show, you decide to start by looking for photos and clip art related to flowers.

STEPS

QUICK TIP

Throughout this lesson, press [F9] to zoom in or out as necessary, to facilitate working with the publication.

1. Start Publisher, open PUB D-3.pub from the drive and folder where you store your Data Files, then save it as Flower Show Web Page

2. Click the Picture Frame button 🖼 on the Objects toolbar, then click Clip Art

3. Click the Search for text box, delete any existing text, type flowers, click the Search in list arrow, click My Collections and Office Collections if necessary to select them, click the Results should be list arrow, click Clip Art and Photographs to select them if necessary, click the list arrow again to close the list, then click Go

   Your search finds two objects, as shown in Figure D-23.

4. Insert the photograph of the daffodils (*Hint:* The filename is j0284916.wmf), then close the Clip Art task pane

5. Move the picture so that the upper-left corner is at 3½" H / 7½" V

6. Click Arrange on the menu bar, point to Rotate or Flip, then click Flip Horizontal

   Flipping the copy creates an attractive mirror image.

7. Create a text box at ¼" H / 3" V, type your name, modify the font and point size so that the text is readable, then preview the publication

   Compare your work to Figure D-24.

8. Click the Save button 💾 on the Standard toolbar, click File on the menu bar, click Print, select the Current page button, click Print, then exit Publisher

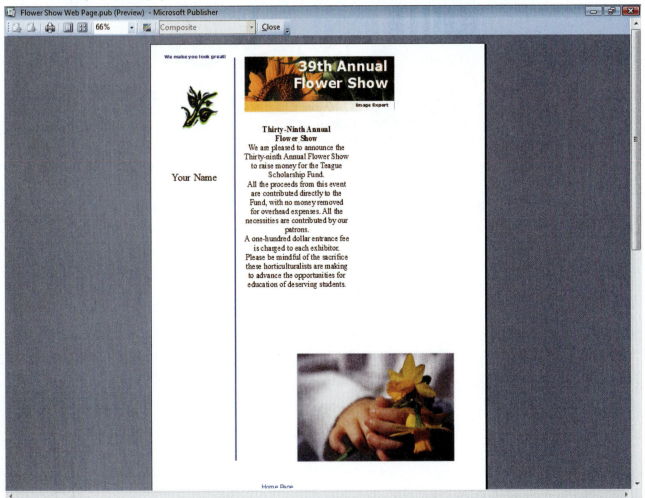

Publisher 2007

Practice

▼ CONCEPTS REVIEW

Label each of the elements of the Publisher window shown in Figure D-25.

FIGURE D-25

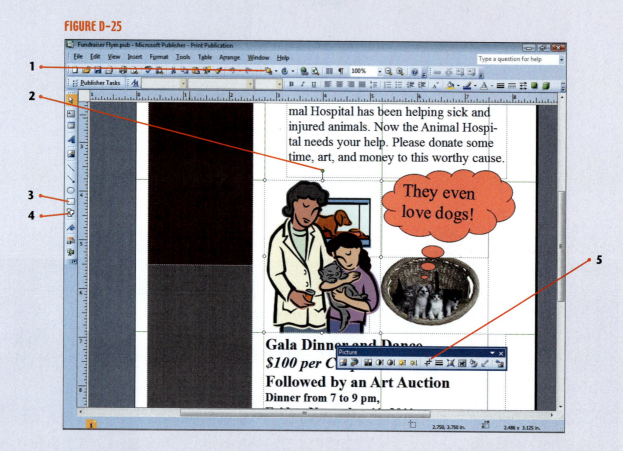

Match each of the buttons with the statement that describes its function.

6.
7.
8.
9.
10.
11.

a. Brings an object to the front
b. Colors a line or border
c. Contains clip art
d. Creates a custom shape
e. Conceals part of an image
f. Fills an object with color

Select the best answer from the list of choices.

12. To create a circle, click _____, then press and hold [Shift] while dragging the pointer.

   a. ⬭

   b. ▢

   c. ◺

   d. ◺

13. Which button is used to add colors and patterns to objects?

   a. 🪣

   b. 🖌

   c. ▦

   d. 🔲

14. You can do each of the following with clip art, except:

   a. Crop.

   b. Italicize.

   c. Flip.

   d. Rotate.

15. Which pointer is used to copy an object without placing a copy on the Clipboard?

   a. ▷

   b. I

   c. ▷⁺

   d. 🖌I

16. Create a square using the Rectangle button by holding _____ while dragging +.

   a. [Ctrl]

   b. [Alt]

   c. [Shift]

   d. [Esc]

17. To resize an object, maintaining its scale while dragging, press and hold _____.

   a. [Shift]

   b. [Alt][Shift]

   c. [Ctrl]

   d. [Alt]

18. Which button cannot be used with clip art?

   a. **B**

   b. ▦

   c. ⊹

   d. 🧹

19. Which pointer is used to insert an AutoShape?

   a. ⬚

   b. I

   c. +

   d. 🖑

20. Rotate an object clockwise in 90-degree increments by clicking:

   a. Flip Horizontal.

   b. Free Rotate.

   c. Rotate Left.

   d. Rotate Right.

▼ SKILLS REVIEW

Throughout this exercise, zoom in and out whenever necessary.

1. **Insert and resize clip art.**
   a. Start Publisher.
   b. Open PUB D-4.pub from the drive and folder where you store your Data Files, then close the task pane.
   c. Save the file as **Family Reunion Postcard**.
   d. Use the Microsoft Clip Organizer to search My Collections and Office Collections for clip art and photographs using the word **home**. Locate the black-and-white image of a house in the top row, second from the left in the Clip Art task pane (filename: j0185604.wmf).
   e. Insert the image in the lower left corner of the publication so that the upper-left corner is at ½" H / 3" V (the clip art's dimensions are approximately 1" H × 1" V), then close the task pane.
   f. Press and hold [Shift], then reduce the size of the image by positioning the pointer over the lower-right handle, then dragging until the lower-right corner is at 1¼" H / 3¾" V. The image should now be approximately ¾" H × ¾" V.
   g. Save the publication.

2. **Copy and move an object.**
   a. Copy the selected image, then paste the image anywhere on the publication.
   b. Move the newly pasted copy so that the upper-left corner is at 4¼" H / 3" V.
   c. Flip the copy horizontally, then deselect it. (*Hint*: The images' chimneys will be on opposite sides.)
   d. Save the publication.

3. **Crop an image.**
   a. Move the image of the flowers from the upper-right corner of the publication so that the upper-left corner of this image is at 2" H / 2" V.
   b. If the Picture toolbar is not visible, click View on the menu bar, point to Toolbars, then click Picture.
   c. Click the Crop button on the Picture toolbar. Crop the top edge of the image using the center cropping handle, hiding ⅛" of the image so that the top-left corner is now at 2" H / 2 ⅛" V, then press [Esc].
   d. Save the publication.

4. **Align and group images.**
   a. Press and hold [Shift], select the two clip art images of the house, then select the image of the flowers.
   b. Right-click, point to Align or Distribute, then click Align Bottom.
   c. Right-click, point to Align or Distribute, then click Distribute Horizontally.
   d. Save the publication.

5. **Layer objects.**
   a. Copy the object at 1" H / 3½" V, then paste and drag the copy so that its upper-left corner is at 1" H / 2¾" V.
   b. Send the copied object behind the original object.
   c. Copy the object at 4½" H / 3½" V, paste it, then drag the copy so that its upper-left corner is at 3¾" H / 2¾" V.
   d. Send the copied object behind the original object.
   e. Save the publication.

6. **Rotate an image.**
   a. Flip the image of the flowers horizontally.
   b. Right-click the image of the flowers, click Format Picture, use the dialog box to change the rotation to 300 degrees. (*Hint*: Use the Size tab in the Format Picture dialog box.)
   c. Deselect the image, then save the publication.

7. **Use drawing tools.**

   a. Click the AutoShapes button on the Objects toolbar, point to Basic Shapes, then click the heart (sixth row down on the left).

   b. Draw the heart so that its upper-left corner is at 4½" H / ¼" V and it has the dimensions ¾" H x ¾" V.

   c. Create a copy of this shape, paste the copy, then drag it so that the upper-left corner is at 4¼" H / ¼" V (the two hearts should overlap).

   d. Save the publication.

8. **Fill shapes with colors and gradients.**

   a. Add a red fill color to both heart shapes.

   b. Select the left heart, then change the fill transparency to 30%.

   c. Create a text box with the upper-left corner at ½" H / 2¼" V with the dimensions 2" H × ½" V, then insert your name, using AutoFit Text to adjust the point size as necessary.

   d. Save and print the publication, compare your screen to Figure D-26, then exit Publisher.

FIGURE D-26

▼ INDEPENDENT CHALLENGE 1

You have decided to market yourself more effectively in the business world. Your first priority is designing a new business card. You want to create a card that reflects your interests and personality.

a. Start Publisher, if necessary, use the Retro Business Card from the Publication Types list, with Landscape orientation, include a logo placeholder, then click Create.

b. Save the publication as **New Business Card Design** to the drive and folder where you store your Data Files.

c. Enter and use any appropriate information about yourself in the Primary Business Information Set, change the logo so it reads **Image Expert**, then change the color scheme to Solstice.

FIGURE D-27

d. Use at least three drawing tools to create an interesting series of shapes in the upper-right corner of the business card. Change the fill color and fill effects of at least two shapes.

Advanced Challenge Exercises

- Use [Shift] to create a perfectly round or square shape. (If you choose, you can delete any shapes created earlier.)
- Insert a piece of clip art downloaded from the Microsoft Office Online Clip Art and Media. Compare your publication to Figure D-27.

e. If desired, rotate and layer the artwork.

f. Save and print the publication, then exit Publisher.

▼ INDEPENDENT CHALLENGE 2

A local clothing store is planning a new sales promotion to increase their sale of gift certificates. The manager of the store asks you to use your design skills to create a gift certificate that is attractive and eye-catching.

a. Start Publisher, then use the Mobile Gift Certificate found in the Publication Types list.

b. Save the publication as **Gift Certificate** to the drive and folder where you store your Data Files.

c. Enter appropriate information in any Business Information Set, change the logo so it reads **Image Expert**, then change the color scheme to Meadow.

d. Use the Microsoft Clip Organizer to search My Collections and Office Collections for clip art and photographs using the word **maps**, then insert the globe (filename: j0335112.wmf) at approximately 0" H / 2" V.

e. Add an AutoShape of your own choosing.

f. Make at least two copies of the AutoShape, resize them, then place them according to your own sense of design.

g. Add different fill colors to the AutoShapes.

h. Type your name next to "Authorized by" in the Authorized by text box.

FIGURE D-28

i. Compare your publication to Figure D-28.

j. Save and print the publication, then exit Publisher.

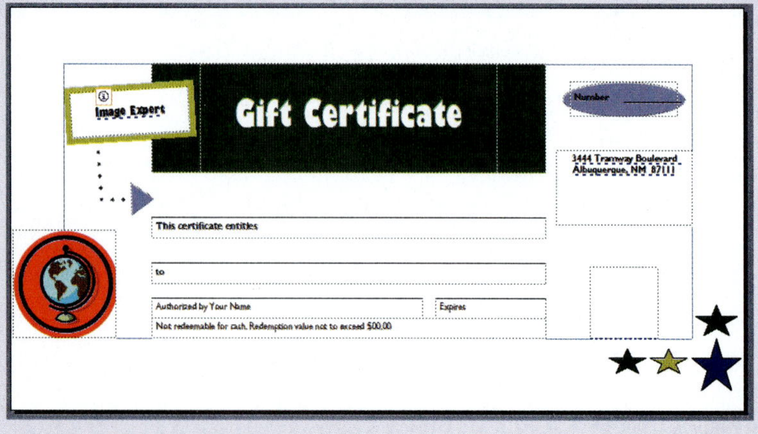

▼ INDEPENDENT CHALLENGE 3

You want to spruce up your work area. A customized calendar is just what you need to help organize and add visual interest to your surroundings.

    a. Start Publisher, if necessary, then use the Blocks template in the Full Page section of the Calendars category of the Publication Types list. Complete any necessary installations, if prompted.

    b. Create a one-month calendar using the next month from the current month. (Hint: Use the Set Calendar Dates button.)

    c. Save the publication as **Next Month's Calendar** to the drive and folder where you store your Data Files.

    d. Enter appropriate information about yourself in the Primary Business Information Set.

    e. Change the color scheme to one of your own choosing.

    f. Add clip art of your choosing to the calendar.

Advanced Challenge Exercises

    ■ Download and insert at least one piece of artwork from Microsoft Office Online Clip Art and Media.

    ■ Crop the new artwork.

    ■ Add objects created with drawing tools, and add color and patterns, if appropriate. If necessary, resize any drawn objects.

    g. Save and print the publication, then exit Publisher.

▼ REAL LIFE INDEPENDENT CHALLENGE

There are many sources on the Web for clip art. Some require payment to use an image, while other images are free to download. You need to find some free clip art that relates to your favorite hobby.

    a. Connect to the Internet, then use your browser and favorite search engine to find free clip art sites. Some possible free clip art sites are: www.free-clip-art.com, www.clipartconnection.com, and www.graphicsfree.com.

    b. Print out the home page from at least two of the sites you found. Take note of any restrictions regarding use of graphic images.

    c. Right-click any of the free clip art images that appeal to you, then download them by choosing the Save Picture As command in the shortcut menu. Save them to the drive and folder where you store your Data Files using the artwork's default name.

    d. Start Publisher, create any design you choose using the Quick Publications category in the Publication Types list, then save the publication to the drive and folder where you store your Data Files as **My Clip Art**.

    e. Replace a placeholder with a downloaded file, add appropriate text (if necessary) to describe the artwork, then add your name somewhere on the page.

    f. Format the artwork by cropping any undesirable elements, then copy or align images if necessary to enhance the publication.

    g. Save and print the publication, compare your screen to Figure D-29, then exit Publisher.

FIGURE D-29

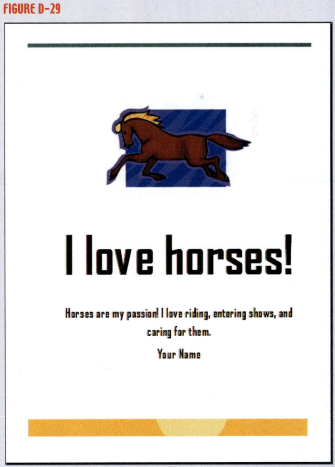

I love horses!

Horses are my passion! I love riding, entering shows, and
caring for them.

Your Name

Use the elements found in PUB D-5.pub to create the party invitation seen in Figure D-30. Save this publication as **Party Invitation** to the drive and folder where you store your Data Files. Make sure your name appears on the publication, then save and print it.

FIGURE D-30

Enhancing a Publication

Files You Will Need:

PUB E-1.pub
PUB E-2.docx
PUB E-3.pub
PUB E-4.docx
PUB E-5.docx
PUB E-6.pub
PUB E-7.pub

Text in a publication should be easy to read. Professionals advise using no more than two fonts per page because too many fonts make a page look busy and detract from the message. Instead, you can add visual interest by formatting fonts in different sizes, with bold, italic, or other effects. To further enhance readability, consider formatting story text in one or more columns, instead of running text in a single block between the page margins. If you are working on a story that is too long to fit on one page, you can use additional text boxes to continue it elsewhere in the publication. Publisher has tools to help map and link the text boxes to create a cohesive publication. Mike Mendoza has asked you to work on *Route 66 Traveler*, a quarterly newsletter for an Image Expert client. You begin by revising styles and formatting in the newsletter, so that it has a strong, consistent design, and is enjoyable to read.

OBJECTIVES

Define styles

Apply and modify a style

Change a format into a style

Create columns

Adjust text overflows

Add continued on/from notices

Add drop caps

Create reversed text

Capstone Project: Solar System Newsletter

Defining Styles

You can maintain consistent formatting, even in multi-page publications, by using styles. A **style** is a defined set of text and formatting attributes, such as font, font size, and paragraph alignment. As a reader moves from page to page, consistent styles make it easy to recognize what is an article headline, what is pull-quote text, and so on. The Styles task pane contains all of the styles specific to a particular publication, and displays each style exactly as it will look. You can create your own styles and modify those that already exist. These new styles apply only to the publication for which they are created, but they can also be imported into other publications. By naming a style, you can make it available for further use. It is important to assign a descriptive name to a style in order to distinguish it from other styles that exist. You want to define a new style for the body text in the newsletter. You want the body text to be easy to read and to complement other text in the publication.

STEPS

1. **Start Publisher, open PUB E-1.pub from the drive and folder where you store your Data Files, then save it as Route 66 Traveler**

QUICK TIP
You can also open the Styles task pane by clicking the list arrow on any open task pane, then clicking Styles.

2. **Click the Styles button on the Formatting toolbar**
   The Styles task pane opens, as shown in Figure E-1.

3. **Click New Style on the task pane**
   The New Style dialog box opens, as shown in Figure E-2. In this dialog box, you can change the font and font size, modify the alignment of indents and lists, change the line and character spacing, adjust the tabs, and even modify the appearance of the horizontal rules.

QUICK TIP
Choose font sizes and styles carefully. Text that is too large looks awkward; text that is too small or too ornamental is distracting and hard to read.

4. **Type 66 Body Text in the Enter new style name text box, then click the Font button**

5. **Click the Font list arrow, click Times New Roman, click the Size list arrow, click 14, then click OK to close the Font dialog box**
   The 66 Body Text style consists of the Times New Roman font, which is a very common type style for the body text of documents because it is easy to read, with a point size of 14.

6. **Click Paragraph, click the Alignment list arrow, click Right, then click OK to close the Paragraph dialog box**
   The sample in the New Style dialog box indicates how the new style will look, as shown in Figure E-3.

7. **Click OK**
   The New Style dialog box closes and the 66 Body Text style appears in the list of existing styles in the task pane.

8. **Click the Save button on the Standard toolbar**

FIGURE E-1: Styles task pane

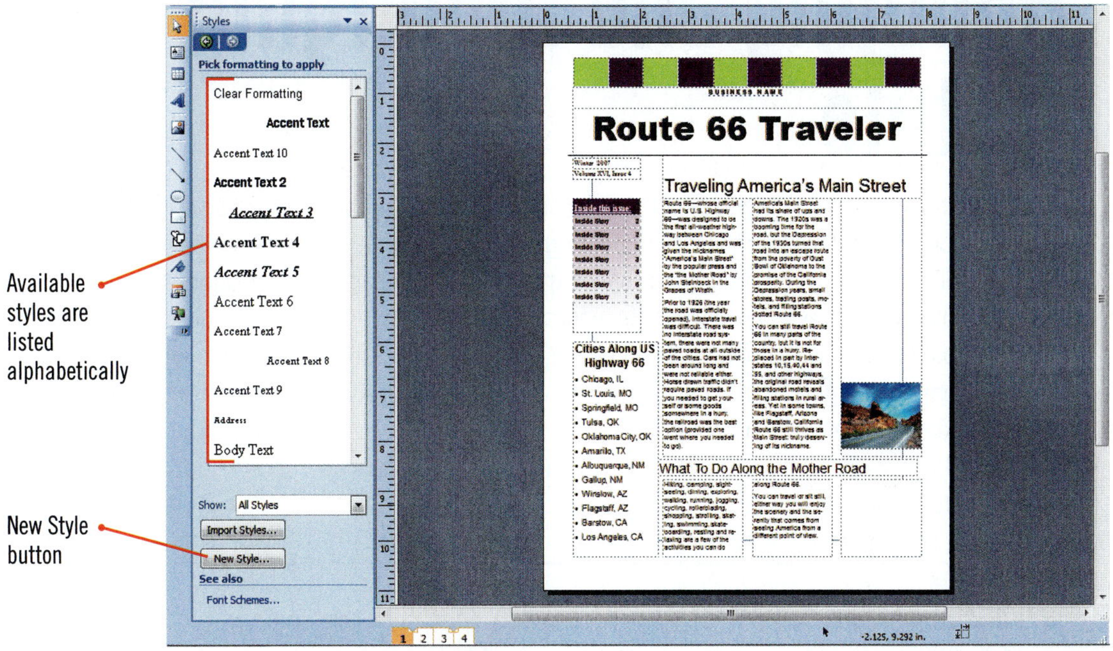

Available styles are listed alphabetically

New Style button

FIGURE E-2: New Style dialog box

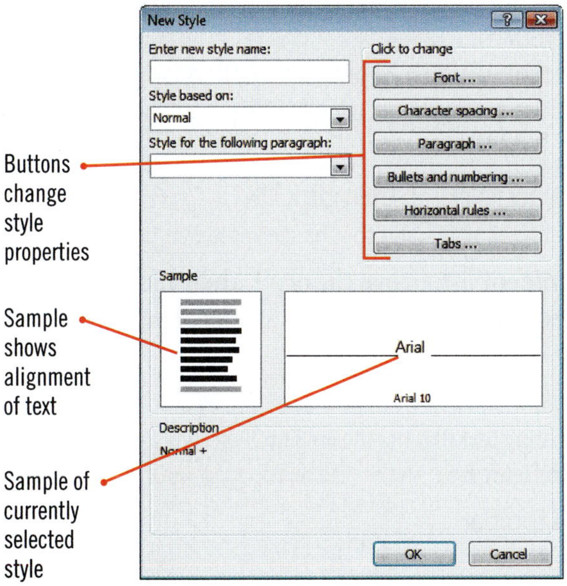

Buttons change style properties

Sample shows alignment of text

Sample of currently selected style

FIGURE E-3: Style changes appear in New Style dialog box

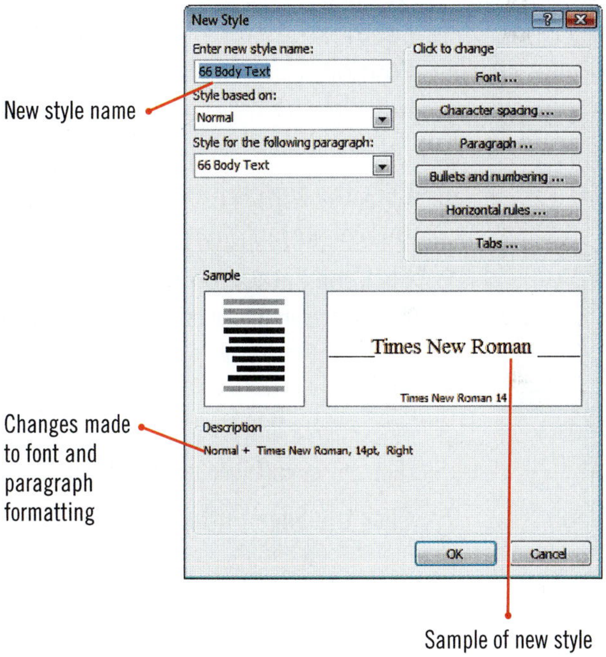

New style name

Changes made to font and paragraph formatting

Sample of new style

Publisher 2007

Design Matters

Choosing fonts

Font types generally fall into one of two categories: serif fonts and sans serif fonts. **Serifs** are small decorative strokes added to the end of a letter's main strokes. Serif, or Roman, types are useful for long passages of text because the serifs help distinguish individual letters and provide continuity for the reader's eye. Times New Roman and Courier are two popular serif fonts. **Sans serif** fonts are typefaces that do not have serifs. Examples include Arial or Helvetica. Sans serif faces lend a clean, simple appearance to headlines and titles but are avoided for long passages of unbroken text because they are more difficult to read than serif fonts.

Applying and Modifying a Style

Applying a style is easy. You simply select the text you want to format, then click the style in either the Style list on the Formatting toolbar or the Pick formatting to apply list in the Styles task pane. Because any style can be modified, you have the freedom to change the appearance of all the text assigned to a specific style within a publication. Once you define a style, you can apply it to text so that your publication develops a consistent look with similar attributes, or you can change the style, and the newly modified style will be applied automatically. You decide that the font size for the style you created is too large, so you want to modify it. Then you will be ready to apply the modified style to a story. Mike has provided you with a Word document containing a story for the publication, so you can insert the document instead of typing the story from scratch.

STEPS

1. **Click the text box at 3" H / 5" V, press [Ctrl][A], then click the Zoom In button 🔍 until 75% appears in the Zoom box on the Standard toolbar**
   You can see the task pane and the top and bottom of the text box.

2. **Click 66 Body Text in the Pick formatting to apply list in the task pane, then press [Esc] twice**
   The selected text was converted to the 66 Body Text style.

3. **Position ⬚ over 66 Body Text in the Pick formatting to apply area of the task pane (do not click the style), click the 66 Body Text list arrow, then click Modify**
   The Modify Style dialog box opens.

4. **Click the Font button, click the Size list arrow, click 12, then click OK**
   The font size for 66 Traveler changes from 14 point to 12 point, and the change appears in the sample.

5. **Click the Paragraph button, click the Alignment list arrow, click Left, then click OK**
   The Paragraph dialog box closes. The modified text size and alignment appears in the Modify Style dialog box, as shown in Figure E-4.

QUICK TIP
You can determine the attributes of any style in the Pick formatting to apply list by placing the pointer over the style name.

6. **Click OK**
   The Modify Style dialog box closes. Any new or existing text that has the 66 Body Text style applied to it will show the modified 66 Body Text style, as shown in Figure E-5.

7. **Click the Save button 💾 on the Standard toolbar**

FIGURE E-4: Modify Style dialog box

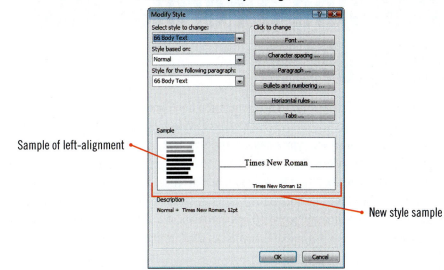

Sample of left-alignment

New style sample

FIGURE E-5: New style applied

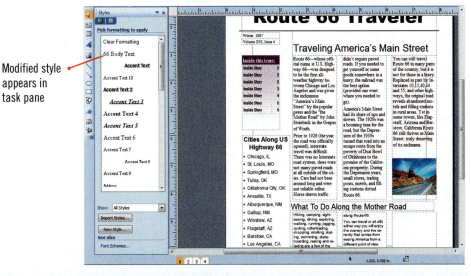

Modified style appears in task pane

Design Matters

Adjusting spaces between characters

Sometimes words on the page don't look quite right: they may seem packed too close together or spread too far apart. This is particularly true of typefaces at 14 points and larger. Adjusting the spacing between specific character pairs, or **kerning**, can make large text look better and be easier to read. Publisher automatically kerns characters with point sizes of 14 and larger, but you can kern any characters you choose by selecting the character pair(s) to be adjusted, clicking Format on the menu bar, then clicking Character Spacing. Using the Character Spacing dialog box, you can change scaling, the width of the text characters, and tracking, the distance between text characters, in addition to kerning, and the point size where automatic kerning begins, as shown in Figure E-6.

FIGURE E-6: Character Spacing dialog box

Changing a Format into a Style

You can create a style from formatted text even if you don't know all the attributes that make up the appearance of the text. To do so, you create what is called a **style by example**. First, you select the text whose format you want to use, then you type a name in the Style text box on the Formatting toolbar. Creating a style by example makes the style available for use over and over again in the publication. This may sound similar to using the Format Painter, but there is an important difference. The Format Painter reformats selected characters according to the formatting attributes of currently selected characters, but does not store or name the set of attributes, or update similarly formatted text automatically.  You like the style of the story title and want to create a style from this format that you can use throughout the publication.

STEPS

1. **Click anywhere in the headline Traveling America's Main Street in the text box at 3" H / 2¾" V**

   The text box containing the headline is selected. The current style displays in the Styles task pane, as well as in the Style box on the Formatting toolbar.

2. **Click Heading 2 in the Style box on the Formatting toolbar**

   The current style is selected.

3. **Type 66 Heading, then press [Enter]**

   The Create Style By Example dialog box opens, as shown in Figure E-7. You entered a new name in the Style box to create a style based on the formatting of the selected text in the lead story headline. The Sample box shows you the current style's font and size, as well as its alignment setting and new style name.

4. **Click OK**

   The Create Style By Example dialog box closes. Do you see that the new name, 66 Heading, appears in the Style box on the Formatting toolbar and in the Styles list in the task pane?

5. **Click anywhere in the text Route 66 Traveler in the text box at 5" H / 1½" V, click Title 2 in the Style box on the Formatting toolbar, type 66 Masthead, press [Enter], then click OK in the Create Style By Example dialog box**

   The new style is listed in the Pick formatting to apply list, and you can apply it to any text in the publication. Compare your publication to Figure E-8.

6. **Click the Save button [icon] on the Standard toolbar**

Using Styles in other publications

Suppose you've created styles in one publication that you want to use in other publications. Do you have to re-create them in the new publication? No, you only need to import them. You can import styles from any Publisher or Word document into the current, open publication. To do this, display the Styles task pane, then click Import Styles. Select the publication (or Word document) that contains the styles you want to import, then click OK. All the styles from the selected publication or document will be imported.

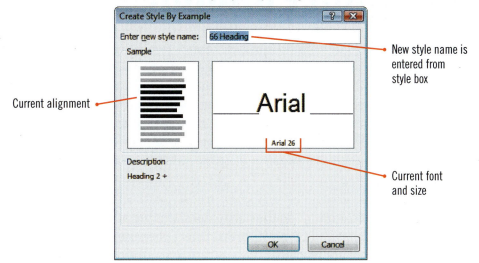

New style name is entered from style box

Current alignment

Current font and size

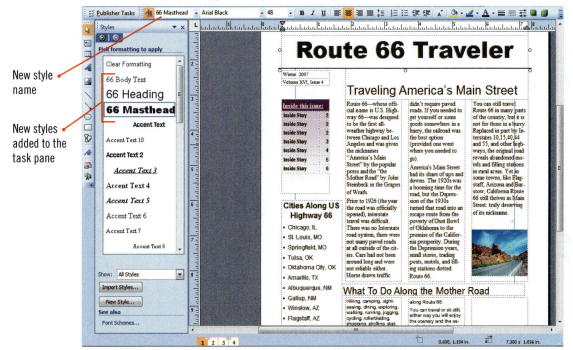

New style name

New styles added to the task pane

Design Matters

Horizontal text alignment

Text can be horizontally aligned in four ways: left-aligned so that text lines up at the left margin; right-aligned so that text lines up at the right margin; centered so that each line is equally spaced between the margins; and justified so that lines of text are balanced evenly between the right and left margins. Justified and left-aligned text are the most common settings for ordinary text. In most publications, text is left-aligned because the ragged right edge adds an element of white space, making it easier for the reader to move between lines. Some people are attracted to the neatness of text that lines up perfectly on the left and right when justified. While justified text may lend an air of formality to a publication, it requires extra attention to hyphenation and careful proofing to avoid awkward-looking gaps of white space. It does offer the advantage of letting you pack more text in the same amount of space than left-aligned.

Creating Columns

Most newsletter stories are formatted in multiple columns to make them easier to scan and to improve their appearance. Two or more narrow columns on a page tend to be easier to scan than a single wide column of text that spans the whole page. When you create a publication, a page may have a three-column layout, but you can use the Page Options task pane to change the layout to fewer columns, or a mixed number of columns, on the same page. These simple design techniques can add visual interest and help differentiate among stories.  You want to see different ways the columns can be arranged on page three to evaluate how the arrangement of the columns affects the overall design of the publication.

STEPS

1. Click the Page 2 icon ⎡2⎤ on the horizontal status bar at the bottom of the screen, click the Zoom box 51% ▾, type 45, press [Enter], then use the scroll bars if necessary so that both pages are visible

2. If necessary, click the Styles task pane list arrow, then click Page Options

3. Click the Select a page to modify list arrow, then click Right inside page

   Compare your screen to Figure E-9. The Page Options task pane lets you select the number of columns for specific pages.

4. Click the Mixed button under Columns on right page

5. Position ▷ over the 2 button under Columns on right page, click the 2 list arrow, then click Apply to the Page

   The layout of page three, the right inside page, changes to two columns. This provides some visual interest, but is less attractive than the mixed columns, and is not consistent with the rest of the publication.

6. Position ▷ over the 3 button under Columns on right page, click the 3 list arrow, then click Apply to the Page

   The layout changes to three columns, as shown in Figure E-10. The design is consistent with the rest of the publication and seems balanced.

7. Close the task pane, then click the Save button 🖫 on the Standard toolbar

Using Baseline guides to align columns

If you are working on a multi-column publication and want to align multiple columns of text so they are evenly spaced, you can use baseline guides. **Baseline guides** belong to the set of layout guides along with margin guides, column guides, and row guides. Text that is aligned to the baseline automatically adds equal line spacing so the text appears balanced along columns. You can adjust the baseline guides by clicking Arrange on the menu bar, then clicking Layout Guides. In the Layout Guides dialog box, click the Baseline Guides tab, adjust the settings, then click OK.

FIGURE E-9: Page Options task pane

Select a page to modify list arrow

One column on right page box

Content options for right page

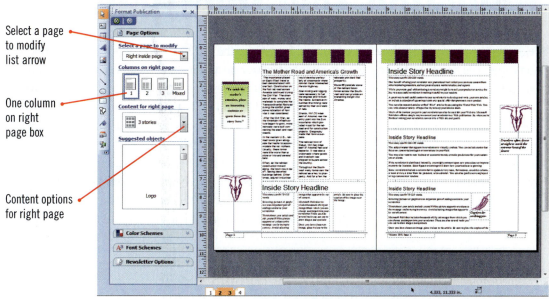

FIGURE E-10: Layout of pages with 3 columns

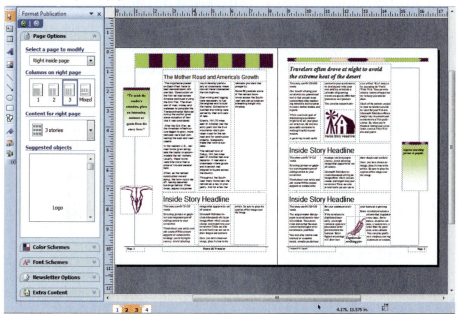

Manually creating multiple columns

Using the Text Box button  creates a text box with a single column. You can add multiple columns to a text box by clicking the Columns Dialog button on the Formatting toolbar and selecting the number of columns you want. The text box is then divided into multiple columns of equal width with equal space between them. The number of columns and the spacing between them can be changed using the Columns dialog box. To access the Columns dialog box, first right-click a text box, click Format Text Box, select the Text Box tab, then click the Columns button. The Columns dialog box appears, as shown in Figure E-11.

FIGURE E-11: Columns dialog box

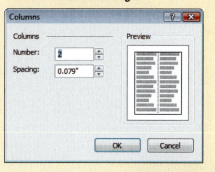

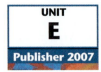

Adjusting Text Overflows

Text does not always fit neatly within a text box. Sometimes the text box is not large enough to contain it. Sometimes you don't want a story to fit in just one text box on a page, but instead you want it to continue on another page, or on several additional pages. Publisher makes it easy to take the overflow from one text box and flow it into another text box using the Connect button at the bottom of the text box. Text boxes that contain text flowed from another text box are linked to the previous text box, so it's easy to make editing and formatting changes to the entire story. You can use the **Autoflow** feature if you want text to flow automatically to another text box when necessary, or you can flow the text manually. Working manually gives you greater control over where the text is placed. You have a long story about Route 66 to insert in the newsletter. You want it to start on page two and continue on page three. First you need to import the text file into a text box on page two, then you can flow it into a text box on page three.

STEPS

1. Click the Zoom list arrow `51%    ▾`, click Whole Page, click the text box on page 3 at 10" H / 3" V, right-click, then click Delete Text

TROUBLE
If you get a warning saying that you need to install a converter, contact your instructor or technical support person.

2. Right-click the text box on page 2 at 5" H / 9" V, point to Change Text, click Text File, select PUB E-2.docx from the drive and folder where you store your Data Files, click OK, then click No when asked if you want to use autoflow

   The Text in Overflow button 🅰 ··· at the bottom of the text box indicates that there is overflow text. Text that does not fit in this text box can be continued in other text boxes, using the 🄰 and 🔗 pointers.

TROUBLE
If you do not see 🔗, click View on the menu bar, point to Toolbars, then click Connect Text Boxes.

3. Click the Create Text Box Link button 🔗 on the Connect Text Boxes toolbar

   The pointer changes to 🄰 when placed on objects on the page. When you place this pitcher over an empty text box, it changes to 🔗, as shown in Figure E-12.

4. Position 🔗 at 10" H / 3" V, then click

   The remaining text fills the text boxes. If there had been additional overflow (indicated by the appearance of 🅰 ···), you would repeat this process until no overflow text remained.

5. Click the text at 3" H / 9"V

6. Click View on the menu bar, click Task Pane, click the Format Publication task pane list arrow, then click Styles

   The list of available styles is displayed.

7. Press [Ctrl][A] to select the entire story, then click the 66 Body Text Style

   The text in the entire story is changed to 12 pt Times New Roman. Compare your pages to Figure E-13.

QUICK TIP
To break a link between connected frames, click 🔗.

8. Click the Save button 💾 on the Standard toolbar

FIGURE E-12: Preparing to pour overflow text

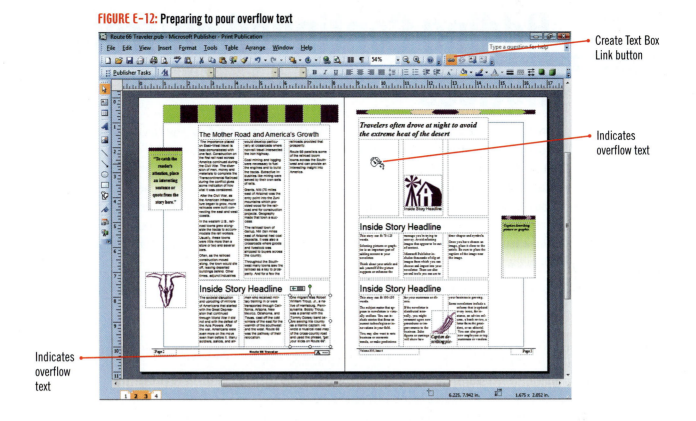

Create Text Box Link button

Indicates overflow text

Indicates overflow text

FIGURE E-13: Overflow text poured into text box

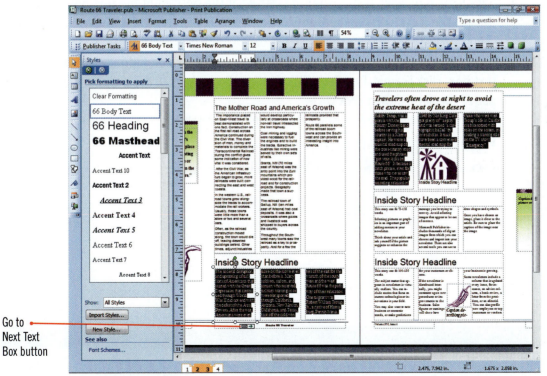

Go to Next Text Box button

Adding Continued on/from Notices

UNIT E — Publisher 2007

To make it as easy as possible to find and read all segments of a story, you can create continued on and continued from notices. A **continued on** notice tells the reader where to find the next segment of the story. A **continued from** notice tells the reader where the story's previous segment can be found. These notices automatically insert text with the correct page reference, and they update automatically if you move the text box. Sometimes publications are specifically designed with stories spanning several pages to encourage readers to see all the pages in the publication. Be aware that continued on/from notices may add a few lines of length to a story. You insert continued on and continued from notices in the story that spans two pages.

STEPS

1. **Click the text box at 7" H / 9" V, then press [F9]**
   You want the first continued on notice to appear at the bottom of this text box because the text continues on page three. You create a continued on notice by modifying the text box's properties.

2. **Click Format on the menu bar, click Text Box, then click the Text Box tab**
   The Text Box options appear, as shown in Figure E-14.

3. **Click the Include "Continued on page" check box, then click OK**
   Compare your page to Figure E-15. You want to insert a continued from notice in the text box on page three. If a single text box is connected to both continued from and continued to text boxes, you can insert the continued on and continued from notices at the same time.

   > **TROUBLE**
   > Continued on/from notices appear only if they refer to text on pages other than the current page.

4. **Click the Go to Next Text Box button ▭→ at the bottom of the text box on page two**
   The insertion point is on page three at the continuation of the story. The story needs a continued from notice on page three.

5. **Press [F9] twice to center the selected text box on the screen, right-click the selected text box, click Format Text Box, click the Text Box tab, click the Include "Continued from page" check box, then click OK**
   The continued from notice appears at the beginning of the text box, as shown in Figure E-16.

   > **QUICK TIP**
   > Continued on/from notices can be turned on or off for each text box. This can help you adjust the quantity of text in a text box to enhance its appearance.

6. **Press [Esc] twice, then press [F9]**

7. **Click the Save button 🖫 on the Standard toolbar**

Design Matters

Changing the style of continued notices

If the appearance of a continued on or continued from notice does not appeal to you, you can change it. Each type of continued notice has a defined style—you can see the style name of a selected continued notice in the Style box on the Formatting toolbar.

Change the style of a continued notice by selecting the notice you want to change, making formatting modifications, clicking the Style box, changing the name of the style, pressing [Enter], then clicking OK in the Create Style By Example dialog box.

FIGURE E-14: Format Text Box dialog box

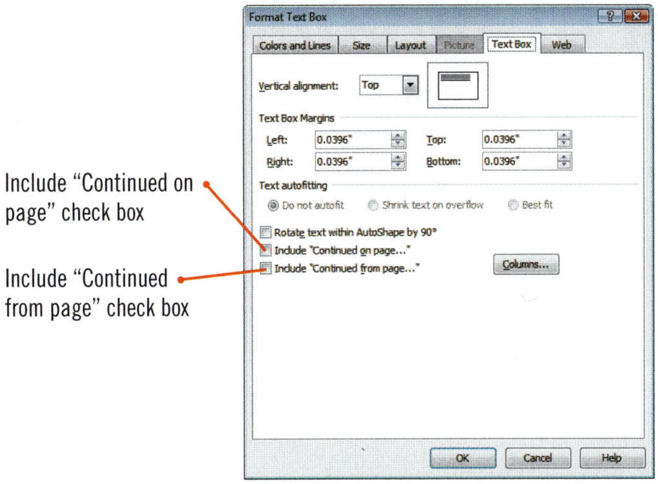

Include "Continued on page" check box

Include "Continued from page" check box

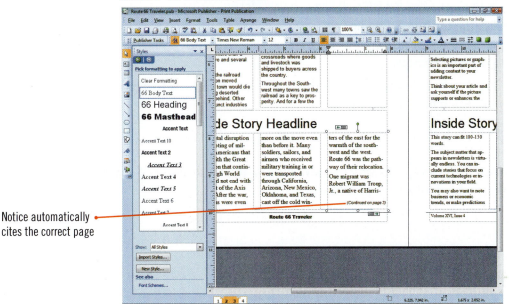

FIGURE E-15: Continued on notice

Notice automatically cites the correct page

FIGURE E-16: Continued notices

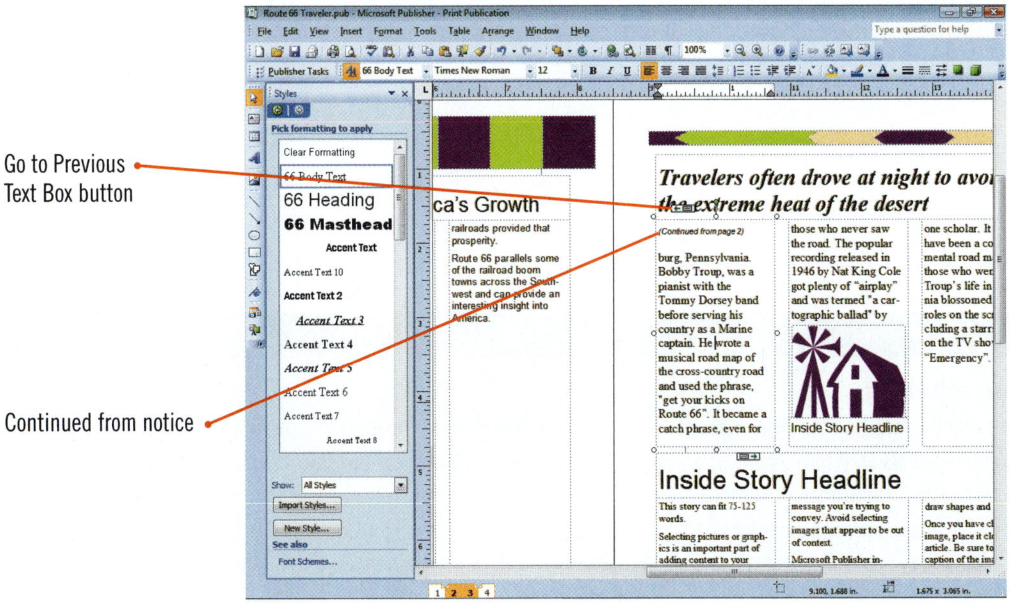

Go to Previous Text Box button

Continued from notice

Adding Drop Caps

To draw attention to the beginning of a story, you can add a **drop cap**, a formatting attribute that enlarges the first character in a story or paragraph. Depending on your design goals, you can add just one drop cap to a publication, or you can add a drop cap to every story or even every paragraph in a publication. You can even apply drop cap formatting to the entire first word instead of just the first character, if you prefer. In Publisher, you can choose from predefined character types that use different fonts and line heights, or you can create your own custom drop cap. Because the addition of a drop cap adds to the length of a story, this addition may cause a story to overflow.  You want to dress up several stories using drop caps. You start by applying a drop cap to the story you have been working on.

STEPS

1. **Click the text box on page two at 3" H / 9" V**

2. **Click Format on the menu bar, then click Drop Cap**

   The Drop Cap dialog box opens, as shown in Figure E-17.

3. **Click the Custom Drop Cap tab**

   You can use this tab to change the default drop cap height, precisely position the drop cap, and adjust other aspects of the drop cap.

4. **Click Dropped if necessary, click the Size of letters down arrow twice, then compare your dialog box to Figure E-18**

5. **Click OK, then press [F9]**

   Compare your work to Figure E-19.

6. **Press [Esc] twice, then click the Save button 🖫 on the Standard toolbar**

   Your work is saved with the modifications.

Design Matters

Working with Font schemes

Using a font scheme ensures that the fonts in a publication work together to create a well-coordinated result. A font scheme is a defined set of two or more fonts associated with a publication. For example, a font scheme might be made up of one font for headings, one for body text, and another for captions. Font schemes facilitate changing all the fonts in a publication to give it a new look. Within each font scheme, both a major font and a minor font are specified. Generally, a major font is used for titles and headings, and a minor font is used for body text. To use a font scheme, click Format on the menu bar, then click Font Schemes.

FIGURE E-17: Drop Cap dialog box

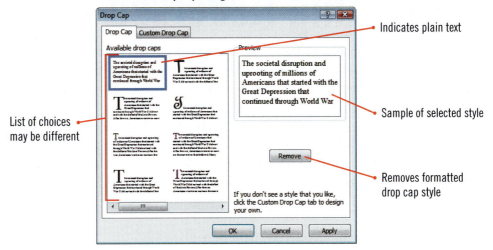

Indicates plain text

List of choices may be different

Sample of selected style

Removes formatted drop cap style

FIGURE E-18: Custom Drop Cap tab in Drop Cap dialog box

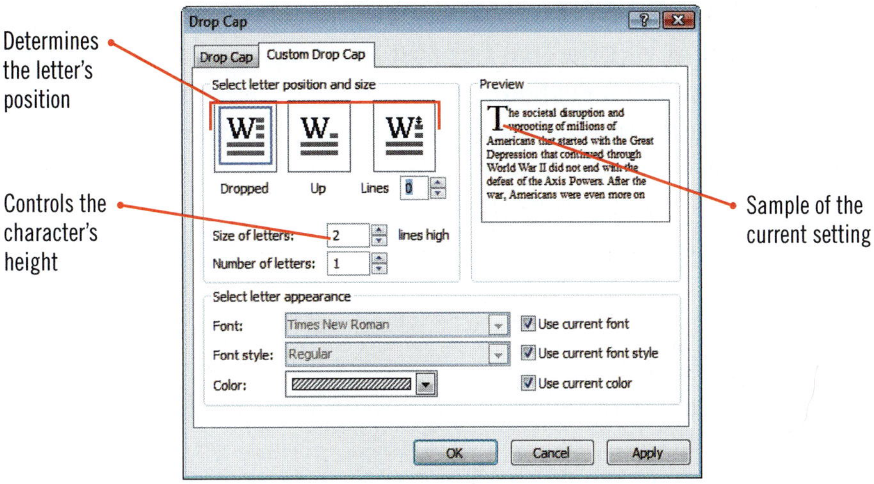

Determines the letter's position

Controls the character's height

Sample of the current setting

FIGURE E-19: Drop cap added

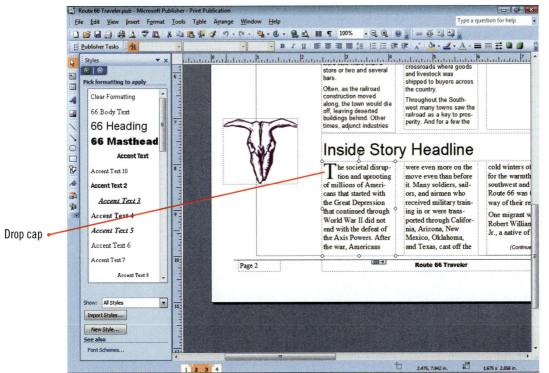

Drop cap

Enhancing a Publication

Creating Reversed Text

A great way to emphasize selected text on a page is to create reversed text. **Reversed text** is a formatting effect that changes text from the standard look of dark characters on a light background to the more dramatic look of light characters on a dark background. Although any color combination can be used, it is best to use contrasting colors to ensure readability. In print publications, reversed text is often used in titles and headings because it is eye catching and readable in larger text sizes. In smaller text sizes, reversed text can be more difficult to read, unless you are printing at high resolutions on good quality paper. To create this effect, you change the font color and the fill for the text you want to reverse. You want to format the inside story headline at the bottom of page two as reversed text.

STEPS

1. Click the Inside Story Headline text at 3" H / 7½" V

2. Type The Musical Map of Route 66
   The headline text is replaced.

3. Press [Ctrl][A], click the Font Color list arrow ![A] on the Formatting toolbar, then click the Accent 5 (White) option
   The text in the text box seems to disappear. When creating reverse text, the order in which you change the font color or fill color doesn't matter. Regardless of the order, when you create black and white reverse text, at some point, they will both be the same color.

4. Click the Fill Color list arrow ![fill] on the Formatting toolbar, then click the Main (Black) option
   The background changes to black and the text reappears.

5. Press [Esc] twice
   You can see the reversed text effect. Compare your work to Figure E-20.

6. Press [F9], click the pull quote placeholder at 1" H / 3" V, press [F9], then replace the existing text with the sample shown in Figure E-21, making sure Your Name displays
   You've made good progress on the newsletter, applying many enhancements to the text.

7. Click the Save button ![save] on the Standard toolbar, click File on the menu bar, click Print, then print page two of the newsletter

8. Click File on the menu bar, then click Exit

FIGURE E-20: Reversed text

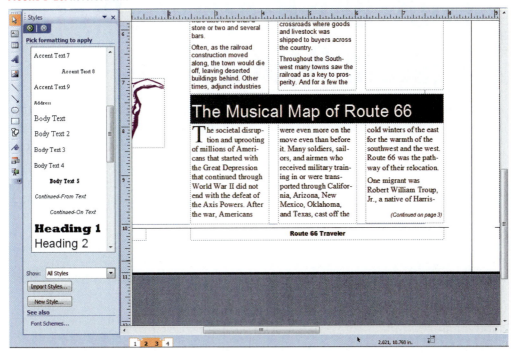

FIGURE E-21: Pull quote text

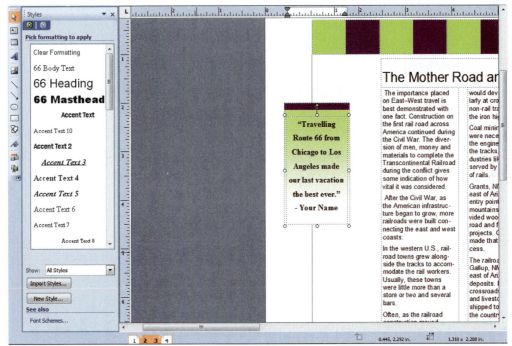

Design Matters

Attracting a reader's attention

Experts recommend that you never use more than three different fonts on a page, and usually suggest that two are enough. So, how do you make your publications attract a reader's attention? Instead of using more fonts, make full use of a limited palette. Use bold and italic versions of your fonts for prominence, and reverse text for a stylized headline. Never underline type, and don't use full capitalization in ordinary text. (In the past, this was done on typewriters for emphasis when there were no alternatives, but is considered outdated and poor form). With a desktop publishing program, you have the ability to attract readers with a wide variety of tools.

Publisher 2007

Enhancing a Publication

Publisher 117

Capstone Project: Solar System Newsletter

You have learned the skills necessary to enhance a publication. You can modify and apply text styles, change a format into a style, create columns, and adjust text overflows. You know how to add continued on/from notices, add drop caps, and create reversed text. Now you will use these skills to add and manipulate text in a newsletter. 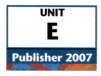 You have been asked to produce a sample copy of a newsletter for a group of astronomers. You want to keep the client's objectives in mind: clarity, color, and elegance. You decide to use styles, continued on/from notices, drop caps, and reversed text to enhance the publication and make it easier to read.

STEPS

1. Start Publisher, open PUB E-3.pub from the drive and folder where you store your Data Files, then save it as Solar System Newsletter

2. Create a style based on the headline at 3" H / 3½" V, name it Space Headline, apply it to the headline at 3" H / 8½" V, then press [Esc]

3. Click the text box at 3" H / 9" V, insert the text file PUB E-4.docx, click No when asked if you want to use autoflow, then adjust the text overflow to fill the two empty columns on page two

4. Add continued on and continued from text to the inserted story

5. Add custom drop caps to the first paragraphs of both stories on page one with two-line high letters

6. Reverse the text in the headline at 3" H / 2" V using Accent 5 (White) for the text and Accent 1 (RGB(102, 0, 51)) for the fill

   You like the way the newsletter looks. You made it easy to read, consistent, and emphasized key text.

7. Replace the pull quote at 1" H / 4½" V on page one with Your Name, save your work, print page one, then exit Publisher

   Compare your work to Figure E-22.

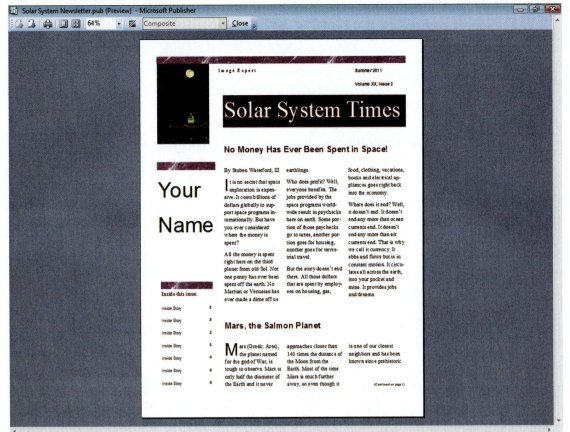

Practice

▼ CONCEPTS REVIEW

Label each of the elements in the Publisher window shown in Figure E-23.

FIGURE E-23

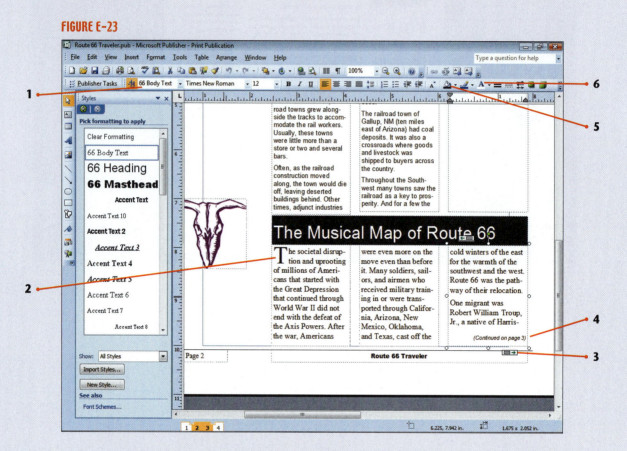

Match each of the buttons or pointers with the statement that describes its function.

7.
8.
9.
10.
11.
12.

a. Go to Previous Text Box button
b. Pouring pointer
c. Text in Overflow button
d. Create Text Box Link button
e. Go to Next Text Box button
f. Pitcher pointer

`Select the best answer from the list of choices.

13. Adjusting the spacing between a pair of characters is called:
- **a.** Spacing.
- **b.** Kerning.
- **c.** Fonting.
- **d.** Adjusting.

14. In which dialog box can you add, modify, or remove a drop cap?
- **a.** Drop Cap
- **b.** Format Text Box
- **c.** Fancy First Letter
- **d.** Spacing Between Characters

15. Which button indicates the existence of overflow text?
- **a.**
- **b.**
- **c.**
- **d.**

16. Changing a format into a style is called:
- **a.** Format stylization.
- **b.** Creating a style by example.
- **c.** Styling a format.
- **d.** Creating a format master.

17. Once you click the Connect Text Box button, the pointer looks like:
- **a.**
- **b.**
- **c.**
- **d.**

18. Which button takes you to the next text box?
- **a.**
- **b.**
- **c.**
- **d.**

19. Which dialog box is used to create continued on/from notices?
- **a.** Continued Notices
- **b.** Notices
- **c.** Frame Formatting
- **d.** Format Text Box

20. In which dialog box can you change the spacing of columns in a text box?
- **a.** Text Box Characteristics
- **b.** Columns in Text box
- **c.** Columns
- **d.** Text Box Formatting

21. Select the entire contents of a text box by pressing:
- **a.** [Shift][A]
- **b.** [Alt][A]
- **c.** [Ctrl][A]
- **d.** [Esc][A]

22. Which pointer do you use to flow overflow text into a different text box?
- **a.**
- **b.**
- **c.**
- **d.**

▼ SKILLS REVIEW

1. Define styles.
- **a.** Start Publisher.
- **b.** Use the Publication Types list to create a newsletter. Select the Southwest Newsletter (in Classic Designs) then use the Secondary Business Information set and the Orange color scheme.
- **c.** Save the file as **Guanajuato Newsletter** to the drive and folder where you store your Data Files.
- **d.** Create a new text style that is 18 point Franklin Gothic Demi, left-aligned.
- **e.** Name the new style **Southwest Headline**.
- **f.** Save your work.

2. **Apply and Modify a style.**

   a. Click the page 2 icon, then apply the Southwest Headline style to the inside story headline at 3" H / 7¾" V.

   b. Return to page one of the newsletter.

   c. Change the font size of the Southwest Headline style to 20 point.

   d. Change the effect of the Southwest Headline style to Shadow.

   e. Apply the Southwest Headline style to the Secondary Story Headline on page one.

   f. Save your work.

3. **Change a format into a style.**

   a. Click the Lead Story Headline on page one. Use the Style box to create a style called **Amigos Headline** that uses the same formatting.

   b. Apply the Amigos Headline style to the Inside Story Headline on page three at 10" H / 7¾" V.

   c. Save your work.

4. **Create columns.**

   a. Display the Page Options task pane.

   b. Change the number of columns on the left inside page to a mixed-column layout, then close the task pane.

   c. Create a new style called **Amigos body text**, that is left-aligned, 12 pt Times New Roman.

   d. Save the publication.

5. **Adjust text overflows.**

   a. Select the text box on page two at 3" H / 2" V, then delete the text.

   b. Above the empty text box, select the Inside Story Headline on page two and change it to **Guanajuato Rocks**.

   c. Select the text box on page three at 10" H / 6" V, then delete the text.

   d. Select the Inside Story Headline on page three at 10" H / 5" V, then change it to **Guanajuato Rocks**.

   e. Select the Lead Story Headline text on page one at 2½" H / 3" V, then change it to **Guanajuato Rocks**.

   f. Delete the text from the text box on page one at 3" H / 4" V and insert the text file PUB E-5.docx. Do not use autoflow.

   g. Select the entire new story, then apply the Amigos body text style.

   h. Click the Create Text Box Link button, then flow the text into the empty text box on page two.

   i. Click the Create Text Box Link button, then flow the remaining text into the empty text box on page three.

   j. Save the publication.

6. **Add Continued on/from notices.**

   a. Add a continued on notice in the third column text box in the **Guanajuato Rocks** story on page one.

   b. Click the Go to Next Text Box button, then add a continued from notice and a continued on notice in the single column of the Guanajuato Rocks story on page two.

   c. Click the Go to Next Text Box button, then add a continued from notice in the first column of the Guanajuato Rocks story on page three.

   d. Save the publication.

7. **Add drop caps.**

   a. Click anywhere in the first paragraph of the Guanajuato Rocks story on page one.

   b. Create a custom first letter drop cap three lines high, using the default font.

   c. Save your work.

8. **Create reversed text.**

   a. Select the contents of the Newsletter Title on page one at 1" H / 1½" V and replace it with the name **Guanajuato**.

   b. Change the font color to Accent 3 (Gold).

    c. Change the fill color to Main (Black).

    d. Replace the text "Special Points of Interest" on page one at 1" H / 6¾" V with your name.

    e. Print pages one through three of the publication.

    f. Save your work.

    g. Exit Publisher.

▼ INDEPENDENT CHALLENGE 1

A local investment company, Finance Wizardry, wants to hold monthly seminars to make people feel more comfortable with financial instruments. They have hired you to create a brochure that announces these free seminars. You decide to use the Publication Types list to create the brochure and start planning some of the brochure style elements.

    a. Start Publisher, if necessary, then create a new publication using the Slant Event Brochure from the Publication Types list. Use the Business Information set of your choosing to enter placeholder information.

    b. Change the color scheme to Prairie.

    c. Save the publication as **Finance Wizardry Brochure** to the drive and folder where you store your Data Files.

    d. Create a style called **Main Heading** that uses a 14 point Arial italic font and is center-aligned.

    e. Apply the Main Heading style to the Main Inside Heading at 1" H / ¾" V on page two.

    f. Select the story at 1" H / 4½" V and add a two-line custom drop cap.

    g. On page one, replace the text in the text box at 9" H / 4" V with the name **Finance Wizardry**.

    h. Create a reversed text effect in the text box at 9" H / 1¾" V. Change the text to the Accent 5 (White) color. Change the fill to the Main (Black) color.

    i. Substitute your name for the business name at 5" H / 6½" V.

    j. Save and print both pages of the publication.

    k. Exit Publisher.

▼ INDEPENDENT CHALLENGE 2

To attract new homebuyers and businesses, the Chamber of Commerce hires you to create an informational Web site about your community. This Web site will be available to anyone seeking information about your community.

    a. Start Publisher, if necessary, then open PUB E-6.pub from the drive and folder where you store your Data Files.

    b. Change the color scheme to Mountain.

    c. Save the publication as **Community Promotion Web Site** to the drive and folder where you store your Data Files.

    d. Create a style by example called **Homepage Headline** based on the Our Home Town Home Page Headline.

    e. Apply the new style to the "A Great Place To Live" headline.

    f. Use your word processor to write a four- to six-paragraph story about what you like about your community. Save this story as **A Great Place**.

    g. Delete the text in the text boxes at 2" H / 5½" V and 2" H / 2" V.

    h. Insert the "A Great Place" text file into the text box at 2" H / 2" V. Do not use autoflow.

    i. Pour the overflow text from the first text box into the second text box at 2" H / 5½" V.

    j. Add a two-line-high custom drop cap to the first paragraph of your story.

    k. Insert your name in the e-mail address at the bottom of the page.

    l. Replace the text in the text box at 2½" H / 1¼" V with your city and state.

    m. Save and print the publication.

    n. Exit Publisher.

▼ INDEPENDENT CHALLENGE 3

Your school wants to hold a fundraiser for the local homeless shelter. You volunteer to create this flyer and choose the type of fund-raising activity.

a. Start Publisher, if necessary, use the Mobile Flyer (in the Fundraiser section) from the Publisher Types list to create a new publication. Use the Personal Information set of your choice to enter your own placeholder information.

b. Choose your own color scheme.

c. Save the publication as **Homeless Shelter Flyer** to the drive and folder where you store your Data Files.

d. Decide on a title for your fundraiser, then enter it in the text box at 2" H / 2" V.

e. Make up your own text describing the event for the text box at 5" H / 8" V.

f. Create a new style called **Fundraiser Text** using 14 point Times New Roman, right-aligned.

g. Apply this style to the text box at 5" H / 8" V.

h. Insert your name in the e-mail address at 1" H / 8½" V.

i. Enter the time and date of the fundraiser in the text box at 1½" H / 7½" V.

Advanced Challenge Exercises

- Apply the Casual font scheme.
- Adjust the spacing between two letters in your flyer's title by 80%.
- Replace the placeholder artwork with appropriate clip art. (*Hint*: If you have Internet access, you can use clip art from Microsoft Office Online.) Compare your publication to Figure E-24.

j. Save and print the publication.

k. Exit Publisher.

FIGURE E-24

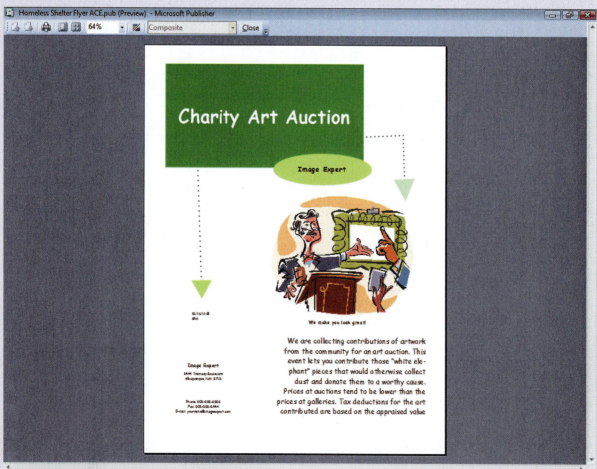

▼ REAL LIFE INDEPENDENT CHALLENGE

This Independent Challenge requires an Internet connection. BBB Road Club is organizing a bus trip to see the leaves change in New England during late September and October. They have asked you to design a promotional brochure for this event. Before you design this brochure, you want to use the Internet to find out more about the New England countryside and its foliage.

a. Connect to the Internet, then use your browser and favorite search engine to find information about the New England countryside and its foliage. Find out what towns and attractions might be of interest when the leaves are changing.

b. Start Publisher, if necessary, use the Profile Informational Brochure (in the Classic Designs section) from the Publisher Types list. Use the Business Information set of your choice.

c. Change to the color scheme of your choice.

d. Save the publication as **New England Foliage Brochure** to the drive and folder where you store your Data Files.

e. Use the information you obtained from the Internet to write a four- to six-paragraph document about what to see and do in New England using a word processor program. Save this document as **New England Attractions** to the drive and folder where you store your Data files.

f. Replace any default text with text about New England. (You do not have to replace the placeholder images or the caption placeholders.)

g. Choose two locations on different pages for the New England Attractions document. Create additional text boxes if necessary.

h. Delete any placeholder text from the text boxes, then flow the story into the text boxes.

i. Add drop caps to the beginning of each paragraph, and add continued on/from notices where appropriate.

j. Insert your name in the e-mail address on page two of the publication.

Advanced Challenge Exercises

- Remove the drop caps from all but the initial paragraph on page 2.
- Change the style of the continued on/from notices using the style by example method. (Use a Bold Arial 7-point font. Name the new style "New Continued-On Text". You can also create a new continued from style called "New Continued-From Text".) Compare your publication to Figure E-25.

k. Print the publication.

l. Save the publication.

m. Exit Publisher.

FIGURE E-25

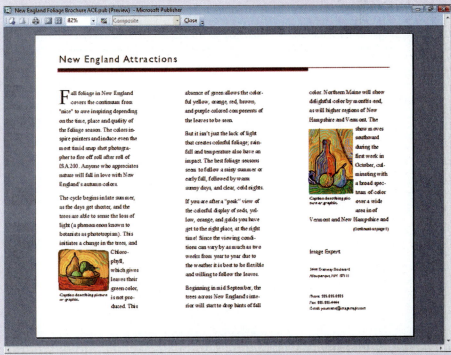

Open PUB E-7.pub from the drive and folder where you store your Data Files. Save this publication as **SW Brochure**. Using Figure E-26 as a guide, modify the styles and add additional formatting as necessary so your publication matches the one shown. Save the publication, then print it.

FIGURE E-26

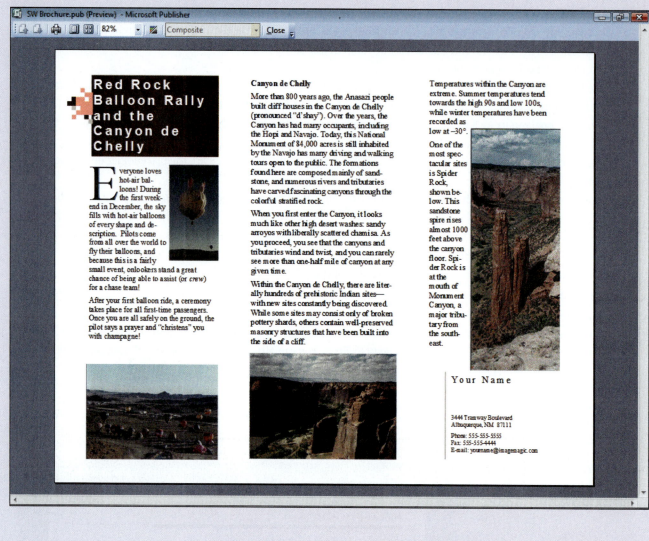

UNIT F
Publisher 2007

Improving a Design

Files You Will Need:

PUB F-1.pub

PUB F-2.pub

PUB F-3.pub

PUB F-4.pub

PUB F-5.pub

PUB F-6.pub

You can be proficient at using features and tools in Publisher, but in order to create an attractive, professional publication you also need to focus on its design. **Design** involves the selection, formatting, and placement of elements on a page, as well as coordinating the elements throughout all pages within a publication. You can resize and reposition elements to make them more effective and better convey the message of your publication. The non-profit organization, Global Parenting, is an Image Expert client. You have been assigned the task of reviewing their in-house monthly newsletter and improving its design.

OBJECTIVES

Critique a publication

Strengthen publication text

Rearrange elements

Modify objects

Refine a page

Experiment with design elements

Capstone Project: Flower Shop Flyer

Critiquing a Publication

Casting a critical eye toward someone's work can be challenging for both the reviewer and the designer. Some of us feel uncomfortable criticizing someone else's work, and even more uncomfortable when that criticism is directed at our own work. But when done constructively, critiquing can be a positive learning experience for everyone involved. Many of us learn best by having our mistakes pointed out, and then making corrections. While design is a highly subjective process, there are some fundamental principles that can be applied to any critiquing process. Examining the strengths and weaknesses of another person's work can be a helpful method of refining a publication so that it looks professional and achieves its goals. It can also help you develop a more constructive eye toward your own designs. As you learn to critique designs, you may find that the most effective designs are the simplest. You are ready to review the client's in-house monthly newsletter, *Creative Parent*. You open the publication shown in Figure F-1 and think about the critiquing process:

DETAILS

• Take in all the elements

To get started, ask yourself a series of questions that determines the purpose of a particular page, and the arrangement of elements that helps you achieve that goal. These questions include: To what elements are your eyes drawn? Where is the text? Is the text legible? Are any/all of the elements on the page necessary? Are any elements distracting? In Figure F-1, your eyes may be drawn to the central graphic and the blue text box because they are colorful, and because of their size and position. Unfortunately, the text in the blue box is illegible, and the caption above and below the central graphic is broken up, which makes it difficult to read and comprehend the safety message. Also, the elongated table of contents distracts the eye from the image of the children and the crossing guard.

• Decide what is important

Every publication has a goal, and each page should support that overall goal. While the goal of this issue of *Creative Parent* is children and safety, the goal of a particular page may be getting readers to read the executive director's article on the topic. During the critiquing process, you should continually ask yourself whether the design achieves the goal—and if not, why not. What's getting in the way? What needs to be changed, removed, or strengthened to reach your audience and guide them toward important information?

• Share the message with the reader

As the designer, your focus is on assembling various visual elements—graphic images, text, or tables—that share the message with the reader. Figure F-2 shows a preliminary rearrangement of the cover elements. In this design, the central element is the children and the crossing guard. This graphic has been cropped to eliminate unnecessary imagery. By rearranging the elements on the page, the message of children and safety is featured more prominently. The use of white space and elimination or refining of distracting elements, such as the blue text box and the table of contents, force the reader's eye to focus on the central image.

• Keep it simple

Microsoft Publisher offers so many exciting and interesting design elements that it's often tempting to use as many objects from the Design Gallery as possible. Such overindulgence can lead to a cluttered, ineffective design that will not help readers see the whole message, and they may miss the point entirely. It's usually best to choose a few key elements that convey the message, then feature those items prominently. In the redesigned cover, there is only one central design object. The reader is free to read the text beneath the image, but it is not necessary to understanding the safety message.

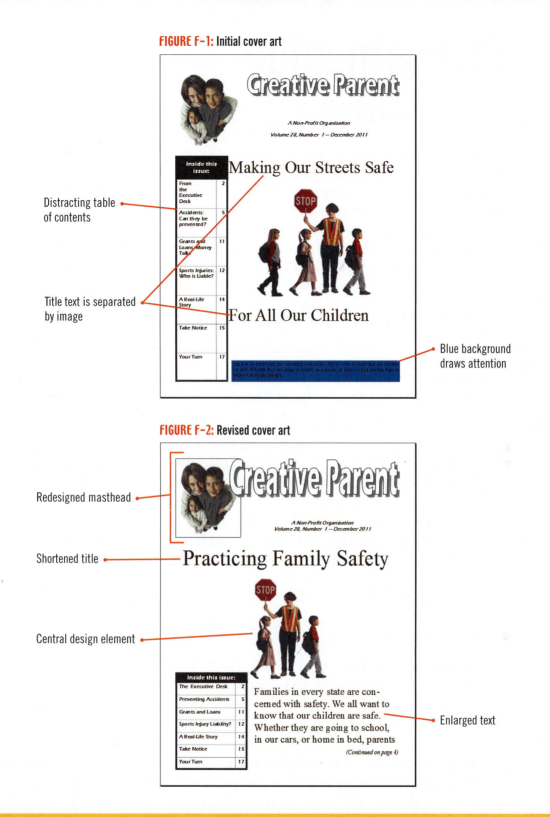

FIGURE F-1: Initial cover art

Distracting table of contents

Title text is separated by image

Blue background draws attention

FIGURE F-2: Revised cover art

Redesigned masthead

Shortened title

Central design element

Enlarged text

Using diplomacy

How do you tell people that their work could use some improvement? People's designs are a reflection of their own opinions about what makes an effective and attractive publication. Therefore, it isn't easy to tell people why and how their publications could be improved, and you must be sensitive to their feelings when delivering feedback. You may be able to minimize hurting someone's feelings by involving the person whose work you're critiquing in the solution phase. If you make the changes yourself, or instruct someone else to, not only will you create friction in the workplace, but the original author may be offended, and will have learned nothing in the process. By working with people to help them revise their work, they will benefit from maintaining control over it, and will learn some important design concepts in the process.

Strengthening Publication Text

Most newsletters feature a **masthead**, an arrangement of text and graphic elements that provide important information about the publication. A masthead contains important information that rarely changes, such as the newsletter's title. The only changing information in a masthead is the issue information, such as the publication month, or the number and volume. The masthead is generally featured prominently, and provides a first impression of the publication. When fine-tuning a design, you may find you need to use a mask. A **mask** is an object designed to hide a specific area so that the final result looks seamless. You've found several elements to improve in the newsletter. First, you want to modify the masthead so the graphic and text create a stronger, more unified impression. To achieve this, you want the title to be more prominent, and to overlap slightly with the graphic. You want to call more attention to the graphic with a border, and realize you'll need to mask part of the border to combine all the elements smoothly.

STEPS

1. Start Publisher, open **PUB F-1.pub** from the drive and folder where you store your Data Files, then save it as **Creative Parent Newsletter**

2. Click the **text box** at 4" H / 2½" V, press **[F9]**, then close the task pane if necessary

3. Position ▷ over the **top-center handle**, click and drag ↕ down to 2½" V, click the **blank line** above the first line of text, if necessary, press **[Delete]**, click the **blank line beneath the text A Non-Profit Organization**, press **[Delete]**, then press **[Esc]** twice

   The text box containing the issue information has been resized and is now in better proportion to the elements around it, as shown in Figure F-3.

4. Click the **WordArt object** at 4" H / 1" V, position ▷ over the **bottom-center handle**, click and drag ↕ to 1¾" V, position over the **left-center handle**, then click and drag ◁▷ to 2¼" H

   The title is larger and partially obscured by the graphic image, as shown in Figure F-4.

5. Click the **Bring to Front button** 🔳 on the Standard toolbar

   The newsletter title appears to overlap part of the image.

6. Right-click the **image** at 2" H / 2" V, click **Format Picture**, click the **Colors and Lines tab**, click the **Line Color list arrow**, click **Main (Black) (the first box)**, then click **OK**

   The masthead image is surrounded by a black outline. The black outline visible between the "C" and the "r" in the title can be hidden using a mask.

7. Click the **Rectangle button** 🔳 on the Objects toolbar, drag + over the vertical portion of the black line at the letter C from the **top of the black line** to the **bottom of the black line** to create a skinny rectangle that surrounds the segment of the line

8. Right-click the **rectangle**, click **Format AutoShape**, click the **Line Color list arrow**, click **No Line**, click the **Fill Color list arrow**, click **Accent 5 (White) (the eighth box)**, click **OK**, click the **Bring to Front list arrow** 🔳, then click **Send Backward**

   The rectangle was formatted to blend into the background, and is positioned between the text and the graphic image.

9. Press **[Esc]** to deselect the rectangle, then click the **Save button** 💾 on the Standard toolbar

   Compare your masthead to Figure F-5.

Smaller text box reflects decreased importance

Masthead text partially hidden

Design Matters

Examine the components

As it can be overwhelming to critique an entire publication, you may find it helpful to examine its individual components. In the case of a newsletter cover, the components include the masthead, the artwork and text, and the table of contents. Within the masthead, you can consider the size, appearance, and placement of the newsletter title, and artwork, and the size and placement of other text boxes. On inside pages, the elements can include the number of stories, related artwork, and the surrounding white space. When viewed in their entirety, it can be difficult to spot specific strengths and weaknesses. Looking at them individually, however, can make it easier to locate and refine problem areas, so that the end result is a cohesive, powerful publication.

Rearranging Elements

The appearance of elements on a page is important, but of equal importance is the way in which the elements are arranged. The components of any page should form a cohesive unit so that the reader is unaware of all the different parts, yet influenced by the way they work together to emphasize a message or reveal information. For example, if a large image is used, it should be easy for the reader to connect the image with any descriptive text. There should be an easily understood connection between the text and the artwork, and the reader should be able to seamlessly connect them. You want to rearrange the elements so that the table of contents is smaller and the title for the story on page 1 is more concise and eye-catching.

STEPS

1. **Press [F9], click the table at 1" H / 3½" V, then drag the top-center sizing handle ↕ down to 7⅞" V**

   The table is reduced in size, which opens up the left side of the page.

2. **Right-click the text box that reads "For All Our Children" at 4" H / 8½" V, then click Delete Object**

   Compare your screen to Figure F-6.

3. **Click the text box that reads "Making Our Streets Safe" at 3" H / 3½" V, then use ⟺ to drag the left-center handle left to ½" H**

4. **Click anywhere in the text box, press [Ctrl][A], click the Font Size list arrow** `40 ▾` **on the Formatting toolbar, then click 48**

   The text is selected and enlarged. The location of this text is now at the optical center of the page. The **optical center** occurs approximately three-eighths from the top of the page and is the point around which objects on the page are balanced.

5. **Type Practicing Family Safety, click Center button ▤ on the Formatting toolbar, then press [Esc] twice**

   The title is centered and better expresses the message of the cover. Compare your work to Figure F-7.

6. **Click the Save button 🖫 on the Standard toolbar**

Design Matters

Overcoming the fear of white space

What is the most important difference between the file open now and the one opened at the beginning of this unit? White space. The best example of the use of white space is margins surrounding a page. This white space acts as a visual barrier—a resting place for the eyes. Without white space, the words on a page would crowd into each other, and the effect would be a cluttered, ugly page. This technique makes it possible for you to guide the reader's eye from one location on the page to another. One of the first design hurdles that must be overcome is the irresistible urge to put too much *stuff* on a page. When you are new to design, you may want to fill each page completely. Remember, less is more. Think of white space as a beautiful frame setting off an equally beautiful image.

FIGURE F-6: Text box deleted

Text box removed from beneath image

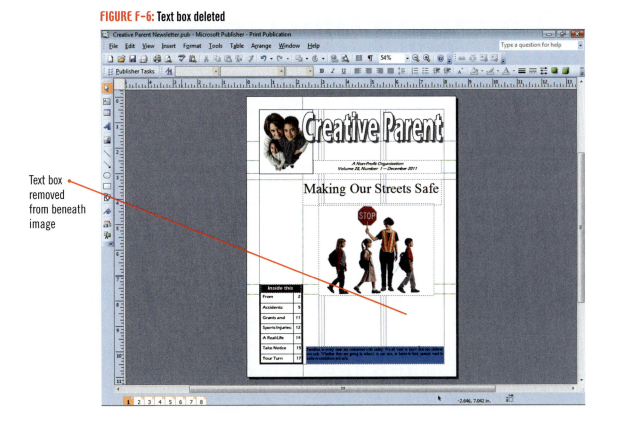

FIGURE F-7: Title text completed

Optical center containing centered text

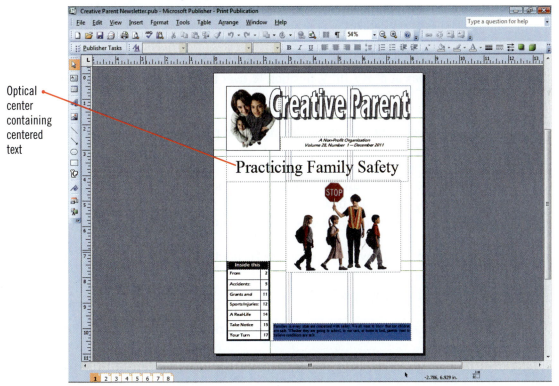

Modifying Objects

Once the optical center is located, objects can be positioned around it. A page can have a symmetrical or asymmetrical balance relative to an imaginary vertical line in the center of the page. In a **symmetrical balance**, objects are placed equally on either side of the vertical line. This type of layout tends toward a restful, formal design. In an asymmetrical balance, objects are placed unequally relative to the vertical line. **Asymmetrical balance** uses white space to balance the positioned objects, and is more dynamic and informal. A page with objects arranged asymmetrically tends to provide more visual interest because it is more surprising in appearance. 🎨 You want to balance the few objects on the page using an asymmetrical layout. You want to crop the image and rearrange a few elements to make better use of the white space. You begin by zooming into the image on the page.

STEPS

QUICK TIP

If the Picture toolbar does not appear, click View on the menu bar, point to Toolbars, then click Picture. You can click the Picture toolbar's title bar and drag it to a new location if it obscures your view.

1. Click the object at 5" H / 5" V, then click the Zoom In button 🔍 on the Formatting toolbar until the Zoom factor is 75%

   The image containing the crossing guard is selected, and the Picture toolbar appears.

2. Click the Crop button ⊞ on the Picture toolbar, position the pointer over the left-center handle, drag ⊣ to 4⅛" H as shown in Figure F-8, release the mouse button, then click ⊞

   The little girl on the left is no longer visible. The object handles reappear when the cropping tool is turned off.

TROUBLE

If the Picture toolbar is still visible, click the Close button on the toolbar.

3. Position ⬚ over the selected object, press and hold [Shift], drag the selected object so its left edge is at 3" H, release [Shift], click the Send Backward list arrow 🔲▾ on the Standard toolbar, click Send to Back, then press [Esc]

   The object is centered on the page, and the Picture toolbar is no longer visible. Holding [Shift] while you moved the object maintained the vertical measurement as you changed the horizontal position.

4. Click the Zoom Out button 🔍 on the Formatting toolbar until the Zoom factor is 66%, click the text box at 5" H / 10" V, position ⬚ over the upper-left handle, then drag ⬚ to 3⅛" H / 7¾" V

5. Press [Ctrl][A], click the Format on the menu bar, point to AutoFit Text, then click Best Fit

   The text is readable.

6. Click the Fill Color list arrow 🪣▾ on the Formatting toolbar, then click the Accent 4 (RGB(204, 204, 204)) color box

   The background is now a light gray, making the text box easy to read.

7. Click the Zoom list arrow 51% ▾ on the Formatting toolbar, click Whole Page, then click [Esc] twice

   Compare your publication to Figure F-9.

8. Click the table at 1" H / 9" V, use ⇐ to drag the right-center handle right to 3" H, then press [Esc]

   The table width is increased, making it easier to read. Your screen should look like Figure F-10.

9. Click the Save button 💾 on the Standard toolbar

FIGURE F-8: Image cropped

Cropped image outline

FIGURE F-9: Text box improved

Text enlarged and blue background changed to gray

FIGURE F-10: Objects moved and resized

Title reworded and centered

Image cropped and moved

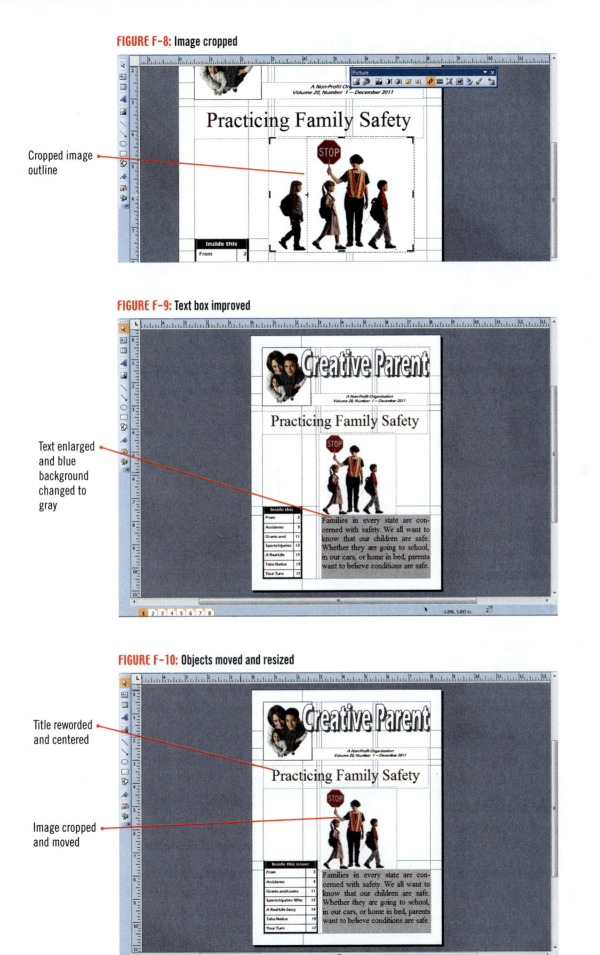

Refining a Page

The goal of page design is getting readers to read each story. Pages that contain nothing but text can overwhelm the reader, causing them to quit reading before the story is finished. To encourage readers to keep reading, you can break up the monotony of a large story with art and other elements. You can also split a story into multiple text boxes on two or more pages. The Executive Director of *Creative Parent* wrote an important article that will be featured in this issue. The current layout has this story occupying the entire page. You decide to refine this page by adding vertical lines between the columns, splitting the story onto multiple pages, and formatting the story with a drop cap.

STEPS

1. **Click the Page 2 icon, click the Line button** ◳ **on the Objects toolbar, press and hold [Shift], drag** + **from 3" H / 1½" V to 3" H / 10" V, then release [Shift]**

   Pressing [Shift] assures that the line is straight. The vertical line between the two columns provides a visual boundary that makes the column text easier to read.

   > **TROUBLE**
   > Before dragging a selected object, reposition the pointer until ⬚ appears, or the object will not be copied.

2. **Press and hold [Ctrl] [Shift], position** ⬚ **over the selected object, click the left mouse button, drag** ⬚ **to 5½" H / 1½" V, release the mouse button, then release [Ctrl] [Shift]**

   Compare your page to Figure F-11.

   > **QUICK TIP**
   > Distributing story text in columns and chunks across a page can open up the design and can provide visual relief from too much text.

3. **Click the text box at 7" H / 9" V, position** ⬚ **over the bottom-center handle, then drag** ↕ **to 3" V**

   The majority of column 3 is now available, as shown in Figure F-12. At a later date, you may want to include another story, an advertisement, or a graphic image in this space.

4. **Click the text box at 2" H / 2" V, click Format on the menu bar, then click Drop Cap**

   The Drop Cap dialog box opens.

5. **Click the first choice below the current selection, then click OK**

   The drop cap appears in the first paragraph of the story. The addition of this feature caused the text to be slightly rearranged, but because there are no other elements on this page, the effect on the current layout is not important.

6. **Press [Esc] twice to deselect the text box, then click the Save button** 💾 **on the Standard toolbar**

   Compare your publication to Figure F-13.

Design Matters

Working with advertisements

Publications often depend on advertising dollars to defray costs and increase profits. So it's in a publisher's interest to display ads in a manner that will gain the greatest exposure. That's one reason stories usually are not laid out in one continuous text box, with ads lumped together in another section. If a reader turns through several pages to finish reading a story, he or she is more likely to see the ads that are interspersed with editorial content. This means that advertising artwork can become an integral part of page layout.

Your advertisers and your readers want clever, attractive ads that potential clients will remember. In many cases, your advertisers will give you camera-ready artwork. This artwork is complete and only needs to be included in the layout. The good news is that you don't have to do the work of designing the ad. The bad news is that you often have no say in terms of the ad's appearance or design values. In most publications, the cost of running an advertisement is determined by size, color, and placement on the page.

FIGURE F-11: Vertical lines between columns

Lines provide visual boundary between columns

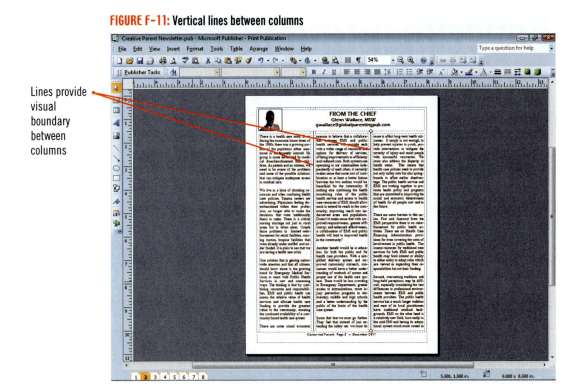

FIGURE F-12: Text box shortened

Additional elements can be placed here

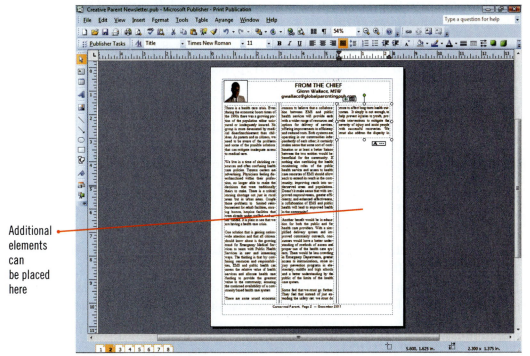

FIGURE F-13: Drop cap added

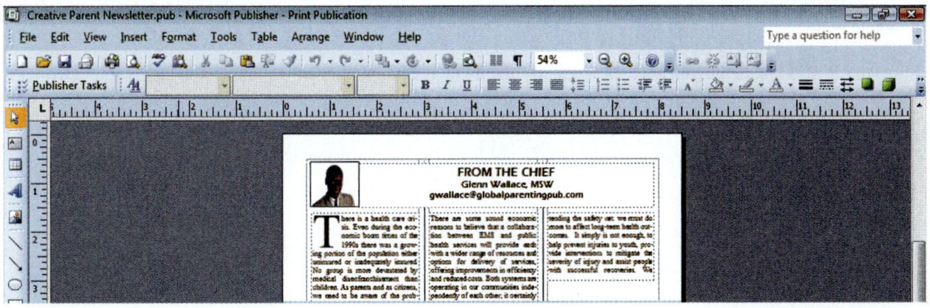

Experimenting with Design Elements

Solving layout problems often requires experimentation. Design elements should guide the reader from story to story, without providing unnecessary distractions. Some design elements, such as a relevant graphic image, or an interesting advertisement, can provide a nice mental break. Among the elements you can use to enhance the layout of a page are pictures, drop caps, and pull quotes. It's hard to say which element will best improve a particular page; sometimes you must experiment with a variety of elements and configurations until you find the layout that works. 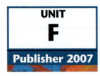 You want to experiment with several design elements to see which ones look most effective in the new space in the third column. In order to generate the reader's interest, you'd also like to extract a compelling sentence from the story, modify it slightly, then use it as a pull quote. Finally, this page seems to need some color so you decide to include a health-related graphic image. The previous designer placed a piece of clip art on page 5 that you think will complement this article.

1. Click the **Design Gallery Object button** 🖼 on the Objects toolbar, click **Pull Quotes** in the categories list, click **Bars**, then click **Insert Object**

   The pull quote is inserted on the page.

2. Using ⭦, move the selected **pull quote** until the upper-left corner of the object is at **2" H / 3" V**, then press **[F9]**

3. Click the **center of the pull quote**, type "**No group is more devastated by the lack of medical attention than children.**", press **[F9]**, then press **[Esc]**

   Compare your page to Figure F-14. The text box is still selected, but you're not sure you like the effect of this element on the page because the page still looks busy.

4. **Select the pull quote**, if necessary, then use ⭦ to drag the pull quote to **10" H / 3" V** on the scratch area

   The object can be used later, if necessary.

5. Click the **Page 5 icon**, click the image at **7" H / 9" V**, click the **Copy button** 📋 on the Standard toolbar, then click the **page 2 icon**

   The clip art is on the Clipboard, and can be placed on page two.

6. Click the **Paste button** 📋 on the Standard toolbar, then use ⭦ to drag the image so that its **upper-left corner is at 2" H / 4" V**

   You feel that the graphic image adds a splash of color to the page and looks more inviting than the pull quote, as shown in Figure F-15. This page is far from finished, but you are done working on it for now.

7. Click the text box at **4" H / 1" V**, press **[F9]**, replace Glenn Wallace with **Your Name**, press **[Esc]** twice, then press **[F9]**

8. Click the **Save button** 💾 on the Standard toolbar, print pages one and two, then exit Publisher

FIGURE F-14: Pull quote in story

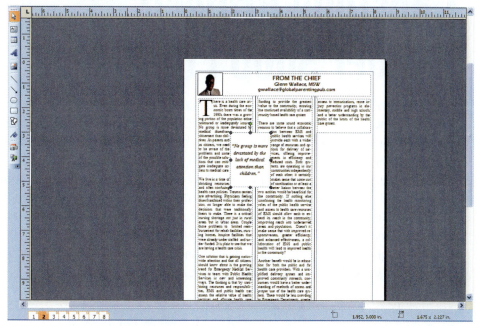

FIGURE F-15: Clip art in story

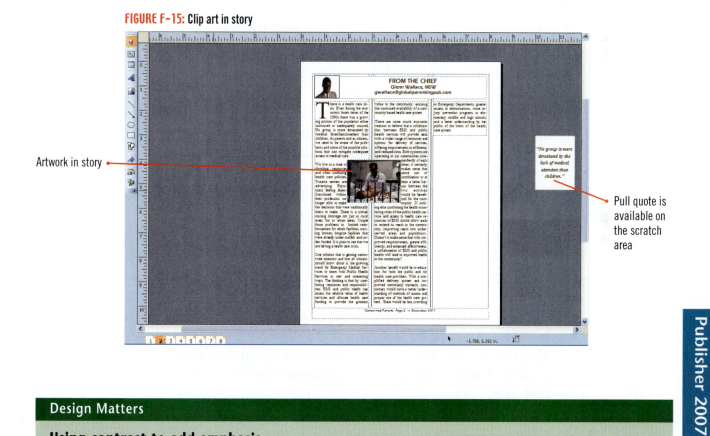

Artwork in story

Pull quote is available on the scratch area

Design Matters

Using contrast to add emphasis

Contrast is an important design principle that provides variety in the physical layout of a page and publication. Just as you can use a font attribute to make some text stand out from the rest, you can use contrasting elements to make certain graphic objects stand out. You can create contrast in many ways: by changing the sizes of objects; by varying object weights, such as making a line heavier surrounding an image; by altering the position of an object, such as changing the location on the page, or rotating the image so it is positioned on an angle; by drawing attention-getting shapes or a colorful box behind an object that makes it stand out (called a **matte**); or by adding carefully selected colors that emphasize an object.

Capstone Project: Flower Shop Flyer

You have learned how to critique a publication, strengthen publication text to grab your reader's attention, rearrange elements so they work together effectively, and work with objects and page layouts to create a professional publication.  You are asked by the owner of a flower shop to critique a problematic flyer. The flyer is for a newly opened flower shop, and the owner wants to offer a 50% discount on annuals during the grand opening celebration. The initial publication is colorful, but it is disorganized and fails to promote the discount. In critiquing the flyer, you find that the border of roses distracts from the text and central object in the flyer. Instead of having many images of flowers, you think it might be more dramatic to make one image the focal point of the flyer. You also think that the text at the top of the flyer is too long and poorly aligned. The name of the shop should stand out more, and you think using WordArt could help achieve this. You start improving this design by removing the border of roses.

STEPS

1. Start Publisher, open **PUB F-2.pub** from the drive and folder where you store your Data Files, then save it as **Flower Shop Flyer**

   Compare your screen to Figure F-16.

2. Click the **graphic object** at **7" H / 4" V**, then press **[Delete]**

3. Click the **tulips** at **5" H / 5" V**, press and hold **[Ctrl]**, then use ⤡ to drag the upper-left sizing handle up and to the left until the sizing handle snaps to the ruler guides at **1½" H / 2½" V**

4. Click the **text box** at **4" H / 7" V**, use ⌖ to drag the object so that its upper-left corner is at the guides at **1½" H / 8" V**, select the **date and time text**, click the **Bold button** **B** on the Formatting toolbar, change the font size of the selected text to **20**, then press **[Esc]**

   The repositioned text box and the contrasting text are more attractive.

5. Click the **text box** at **2" H / 2" V**, press **[Ctrl][A]** to select the text, type **Your Name's Flowers**, press **[Enter]**, then type **Grand Opening and Sale**

QUICK TIP
You can resize the text box or use a smaller point size if all the text doesn't fit.

6. Press **[Ctrl][A]**, click the **Center button** ▤ on the Formatting toolbar, select the text **Your Name's Flowers**, click the **Font Size list arrow** `40` on the Formatting toolbar, then click **48**

   The text now looks balanced, and the name of the shop is more prominent.

7. Click the **Rectangle button** ▭ on the Objects toolbar, create a shape from **1" H / 1" V** to **7½" H / 8" V**, click the **Dash Style button** ▤ on the Formatting toolbar, click **No Line**, click the **Fill Color list arrow** on the Formatting toolbar, click the **fourth color box from the left**, click the **Bring to Front list arrow**, click **Send to Back**, then press **[Esc]**

8. Click the **Design Gallery Object button** on the Objects toolbar, click **Coupons**, click **Open Background** if necessary, click **Insert Object**, modify the text to advertise **Featured Annuals** at **50% OFF**, with the flower shop name and address shown in the flyer, then delete the expiration date and modify the size and placement of the object as shown in Figure F-17

   Your design changes have resulted in a stronger flyer that is sure to capture the attention of potential customers.

9. Save your work, print the publication, then exit Publisher

Practice

▼ CONCEPTS REVIEW

Identify the design flaw in each element in Figure F-18.

FIGURE F-18

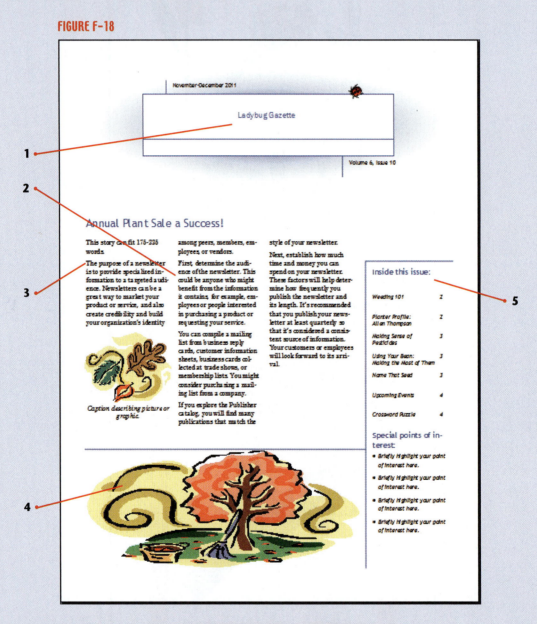

Match each of the design flaws noted below with a solution.

6. Stories that span several pages have no reference to where the next part of the story is located
7. Too many design elements on the page
8. Columns of text run together
9. The publication looks monotonous and boring

a. Add contrast, such as a matte, to the publication
b. Increase the amount of white space
c. Insert continued on/continued from notices
d. Add a visual boundary

Select the best answer from the list of choices.

10. Objects placed equally on either side of an imaginary vertical line in the center of the page is called:
    a. Asymmetrical objectivity.
    b. Asymmetrical balance.
    c. Symmetrical balance.
    d. Symmetrical positioning.

11. A consistent arrangement of text and graphic elements that appears at the top of each issue of a publication is called a:
    a. Mask.
    b. Matte.
    c. Masthead.
    d. Mark.

12. The optical center occurs where on the page?
    a. three-eighths from the top
    b. In the center of the publication
    c. three-eighths from the bottom
    d. Upper-right corner

13. Which of the following is *not* an example of white space?
    a. Margins
    b. Space between lines of text
    c. Space around a graphic
    d. Lines separating columns of text

14. In asymmetrical balance, the elements on a page are _____.
    a. Placed equally on either side of the vertical line
    b. Grouped near the center of the page
    c. Placed unequally on either side of the vertical line
    d. Placed in the white space

15. Which of the following is *not* true about working with advertisers?
    a. They may give you camera-ready artwork to place.
    b. They help support your publication financially.
    c. The cost of running an advertisement is determined by its size, amount of colors, and placement in the publication.
    d. Ads are most likely to be read when grouped together on a single page.

16. _____ is an important design principle that provides variety in a physical layout.
    a. Contrast
    b. Symmetrical balance
    c. White space
    d. Diplomacy

▼ SKILLS REVIEW

1. Critique a publication.

    a. Start Publisher, open PUB F-3.pub from the drive and folder where you store your Data Files, then save it as **Daily Specials Menu**. Throughout this exercise, zoom in and out as necessary.

    b. Take a look at each visual element on the page, and determine where the focal points are, and whether there are any unnecessary or distracting elements on the page. Find three things you would change to improve the publication.

    c. Create a text box on page 2 that includes your thoughts on what the goals of the publication are, and how well you think the publication meets the goals.

    d. Create a second text box on page 2, type **Critiquing the publication**, then write your three improvements and how you would implement them.

2. Strengthen publication text.

    a. Think about how you can use what you've learned about effective design to strengthen text in the menu.

    b. Move the text boxes for the name of the restaurant, the text **Daily Specials**, and the text box that includes the date (in this order) up near the top of the page. Leave a 2" margin between the top of the page and the restaurant name text box. Leave a 3½" margin between the left edge of the page and the three text boxes.

    c. Delete the graphic in the upper-right corner of page one, then increase the size of the graphic in the upper-left corner of the page to 2¾" H x 2¾" V.

    d. AutoFit the text containing the restaurant name, left-align the text in the text box, then change the font color from black to something more colorful. Adjust the size of the text box as necessary.

    e. Increase the font size of the **Daily Specials** menu item text to 9 point, if necessary, left-align the text in the text box, then make it the same font and font color as the restaurant name.

    f. Increase the font size of the date text to 12 point, and make it the same font but a different font color than the restaurant name. Adjust the size of the text box if necessary.

    g. Save your work.

3. Rearrange elements.

    a. Move the table so that its upper-left corner is 1" H / 4¼" V.

    b. Delete the graphics in the lower-left and right corners.

    c. Move the text box containing the payment information to the bottom of the page at ¾" H / 8¼" V.

    d. Move the text box containing the address, phone number, and Web site so that its upper-left corner is ¾" H / 9½" V.

    e. Save your work.

▼ SKILLS REVIEW (CONTINUED)

4. Modify objects.
  - **a.** Click the table.
  - **b.** Press [Ctrl][A] twice, then increase the font size by pressing [Ctrl] []] (right bracket) five times.
  - **c.** Resize the table so that its dimensions are 6½" H x 3½" V. Adjust any rows as necessary so that the text fits.
  - **d.** Use the fill color of your choice on the table to provide contrast between the background and the table. Make sure that the fill color complements the font colors you used in the masthead.
  - **e.** Save your work.

5. Refine a page.
  - **a.** Select all the cells in the table on page 1.
  - **b.** Format the table so that black lines surround each cell. (*Hint*: Use the Colors and Lines tab in the Format Table dialog box.)
  - **c.** Save your work.

6. Experiment with design elements.
  - **a.** Click the Design Gallery Object button on the Objects toolbar, click Coupons, click Top Oval, then click Insert Object.
  - **b.** Drag the coupon to the scratch area.
  - **c.** Click the **2 for 1** text box, then type **Dessert Special.**
  - **d.** Click the **Name of Item or Service** text box, then type **Free dessert with lunch entrée.**
  - **e.** Click the **Describe your location by landmark or area of town** text box, then type **12 Kimball Street.**
  - **f.** Enter an expiration date of September 1, 2011 in the remaining text box, and replace 'Carole' with Your Name.
  - **g.** Move the coupon to 4¼" H / 8¼" V, then compare your publication to Figure F-19.
  - **h.** Save the publication, print it, then exit Publisher.

FIGURE F-19

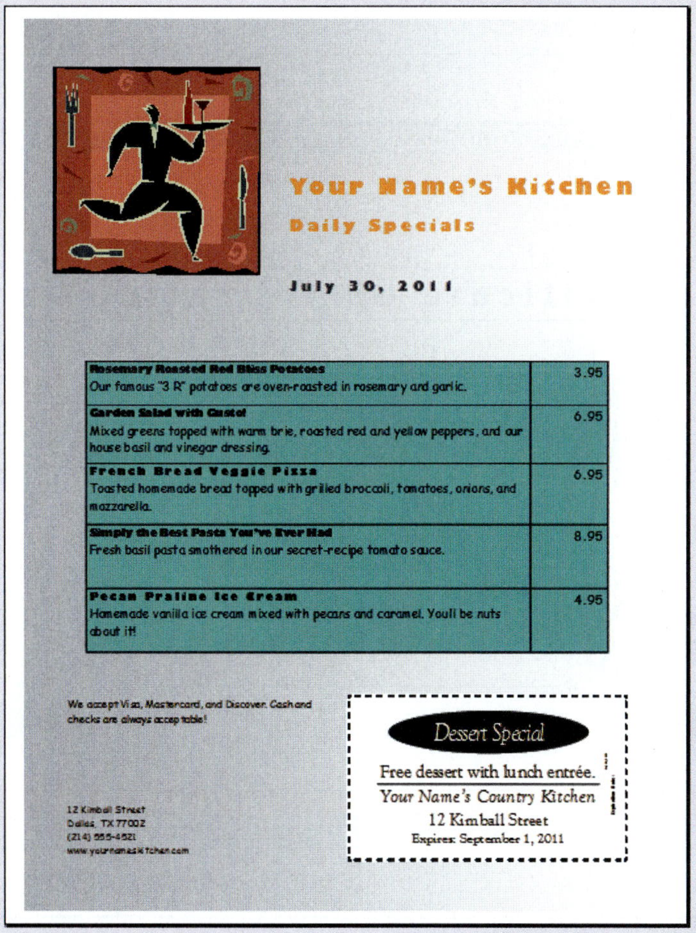

Publisher 2007

▼ INDEPENDENT CHALLENGE 1

Pastiche Martinez is an attorney who has hired you to redesign his business card. He is concerned that the layout of his current card makes it too hard to read and does not convey an elegant, organized image. Start Publisher, open PUB F-4.pub from the drive and folder where you store your Data Files, then save it as **Corporate Business Card**. Use your design knowledge to make corrections, then replace the existing name in the business card with your name. Save the changes, print the publication, then exit Publisher.

▼ INDEPENDENT CHALLENGE 2

Your design services consulting firm is really taking off. A local business has asked you to redesign a certificate they use to recognize excellence among their staff. The firm wants to convey a professional, cutting-edge image, although they are not averse to having fun.

a. Start Publisher, open PUB F-5.pub, then save it as **Certificate of Appreciation** to the drive and folder where you store your Data Files.

b. Change the name in the existing publication to Your Name.

c. Print the publication before any other changes are made, then mark at least five areas that need improvement.

d. Make the changes you noted in the previous step.

Advanced Challenge Exercises

- Change the color of the green line color in the AutoShape to blue, to add contrast.
- Find and insert appropriate clip art, then compare your publication to Figure F-20.

e. Save and print the publication.

f. Exit Publisher.

FIGURE F-20

▼ INDEPENDENT CHALLENGE 3

As the Design Coordinator at Super Design and Layout, you want to find convincing examples of good and bad design in print and on Web sites. Seeing both types of examples will be helpful to your students. You can use the Web to find examples of good and bad design.

a. Connect to the Internet, then open your browser and favorite search engine.

b. Find one site that offers design tips, then print the home page.

c. Find one example of a site you consider to have bad design, then print the home page. Mark on the printed page the elements you think exhibit bad design, and note how you would fix these elements.

d. Create a document describing your findings using your favorite word processor and save it as **Good and Bad Design Critique** in the folder where you store your Data Files. (Make sure your name appears somewhere on each printed page.) If you wish, you can illustrate the document with examples of the Web pages by navigating to the page in your browser, pressing the Print Screen button, then switching to the document and pressing [Ctrl][V].

▼ REAL LIFE INDEPENDENT CHALLENGE

You are asked to be the guest speaker at an upcoming class on Microsoft Publisher, and the topic is design techniques. As part of the class, you want to show a publication that has elements of poor design. During the class, you plan an active discussion to address the flaws in this problematic publication.

a. Start Publisher, create a newsletter using your choice of design, then save it as **Design Techniques** to the drive and folder where you store your Data Files.

b. Using the first page in the publication, incorporate improper techniques, such as a page that has too little white space, text that is too small, or a story that has no visual boundaries. Use as many incorrect elements as possible. (*Hint:* You can use any graphic elements and text stories available on your computer.)

c. Add your name to the masthead at the top of the first page.

Advanced Challenge Exercises

■ Save this publication as **Design Techniques-Good ACE** to the drive and folder where you store your Data Files.

■ Fix all the areas you consciously created using poor design techniques. See Figure 21 as an example.

d. Save the publication, then print the first page.

e. Exit Publisher.

FIGURE F-21

Open PUB F-6.pub and save it as **Tour Guide Flyer** to the drive and folder where you store your Data Files. Use your knowledge of design techniques and your Publisher skills to make the Data File look like the flyer in Figure F-22. Print the publication.

FIGURE F-22

Your Name's Vacation Nation Hospitality Enterprises – Invites YOU

Apply for Tour Guide Training. The hospitality industry is booming and you can capitalize on its growth. You can become a Certified Tour Guide.

- Retirement benefits
- 401 K plans
- Interesting people
- Exotic locales
- Unlimited growth
- Subsidized shelter
- Good pay
- Rapid promotions

Call 555 555-5555 today for an application packet and complete information

Working with Multiple Pages

Files You Will Need

PUB G-1.pub
PUB G-2.docx
PUB G-3.tif
PUB G-4.tif
PUB G-5.pub
PUB G-6.tif
PUB G-7.docx
PUB G-8.pub
PUB G-9.tif

Many publications, such as flyers, business cards, and signs, consist of a single page. However, other publications, such as catalogs and newsletters, require multiple pages. You can easily add, copy, and delete pages in Publisher; the bigger challenge is planning a multipage document that is easy to understand and reference. For a more professional and compelling design, you'll want to repeat informative text, such as the page number, the date, or a company tagline, at the top or bottom of each page. You can also add a table of contents so readers can find specific stories. You have been asked to design a catalog of Navajo rugs for a Native American trading company. The client wants a tasteful catalog that educates potential customers, but lets the colorful rug designs speak for themselves. When finished, this catalog will be approximately 65 pages long. For now, you'll focus on getting the major design elements in place.

OBJECTIVES

Add pages

Delete pages

Work with a master page

Create a header and footer

Add page numbers

Edit a story

Modify a table of contents

Create labels

Capstone Project: Jewelry Tools Catalog

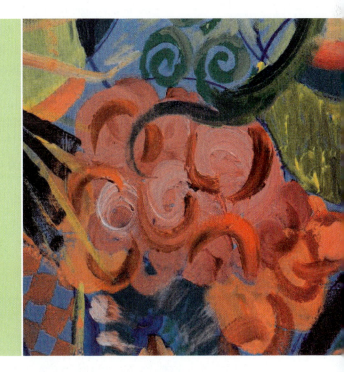

Adding Pages

You can add pages to a publication one at a time or in batches. Depending on the type of publication you are creating and how it is laid out for printing, you may want to add pages in multiples of two or four. A catalog, for example, prints pages in sets of four, so adding pages in multiples other than four can make printing difficult. You can add background items (such as layout guides) and objects (such as headers and footers) to new pages using the Master Page feature. A **master page** is the background of a publication page, where repeated information such as a pattern, header, or footer, can be viewed and edited. You also have the option to copy text or graphic objects from any page to a newly inserted page. You have created a new publication for the catalog, and are ready to add pages to it.

1. **Start Publisher, open PUB G-1.pub from the drive and folder where you store your Data Files, then save it as Rug Catalog**

   The catalog appears on the screen, and the Format Publication task pane opens. You can use this task pane to make changes in the design and layout of a catalog.

2. **Click the Close button on the Format Publication task pane**

   This catalog has eight pages. You can add pages either before or after the current page. To retain a consistent design, you can insert pages and place text boxes and picture frames in the same locations on each page.

3. **Click the Page 2 icon [2] on the status bar, click Insert on the menu bar, then click Page**

   The Insert Catalog Pages dialog box opens, where you can choose from 19 catalog-style layouts for the new page or pages.

4. **Click the Left-hand page list arrow, click 4 items, offset pictures, click the Right-hand page list arrow, then click 4 items, squared pictures**

   Compare your Insert Catalog Pages dialog box to Figure G-1.

QUICK TIP

To move a page, insert a new page, duplicate the objects from the page you want moved, then delete the original page.

5. **Click More**

   The Insert Page dialog box opens, as shown in Figure G-2. You can use this dialog box to control the number of new pages to add, as well as options, such as inserting blank pages and duplicating all of the objects on a specific page.

6. **Click Cancel in the Insert Page dialog box, click OK in the Insert Catalog Pages dialog box, then click Yes to automatically insert four pages**

   Compare your work to Figure G-3. The page 4-5 icon button is selected on the status bar, and the additional icon buttons indicate that the publication now has 12 pages. By clicking Cancel in the Insert Page dialog box, the page types in the Insert Catalog Pages dialog box were reset to the default, and the newly inserted pages (4–7) have the default layout (One column, all text) on both pairs of pages.

7. **Click the Save button [icon] on the Standard toolbar**

Using multiple master pages

A master page gives you the freedom to create a consistent background for pages. In Publisher, you can also create multiple master pages. This means, for example, that in a newsletter publication you can have a specific master page for Classified Ads, and another master page for daily news stories. You can view a master page by clicking View on the menu bar, then clicking Master Page. This automatically displays the Edit Master Pages task pane. When the Edit Master Pages task pane is visible, click the New Master Page button at the bottom of the task pane to create a new master page. You can also create a new master page by clicking the New Master Page button [icon] on the Edit Master Pages toolbar.

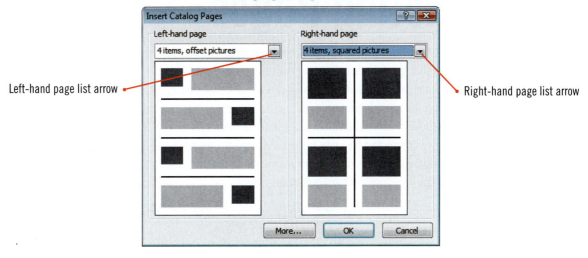

Left-hand page list arrow

Right-hand page list arrow

FIGURE G-2: Insert Page dialog box

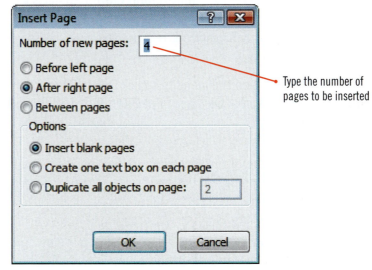

Type the number of pages to be inserted

FIGURE G-3: Publication with added pages

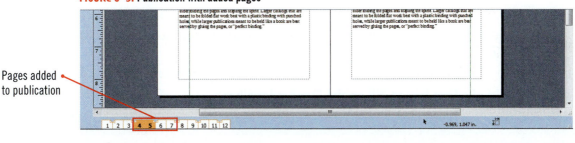

Pages added to publication

Publisher 2007

Design Matters

Printing multi-page documents

When you think of a page, you probably think of one 8½" × 11" sheet of paper; but from a printer's point of view, several pages may actually fit on one sheet of paper. A four-page brochure can be printed front and back on one sheet of paper and folded in half so that there are four pages. Commercial printers of publications larger than four pages print pages this way, then the folded pages are

bound together. This is why catalogs print in multiples of four, because they are printed on the front and back of a single piece of paper. When printing books or other large publications, paper is printed in multiples of eight, called **signatures**. Blank pages at the end of a book indicate there was not enough text to fill the last signature.

Deleting Pages

You should delete unnecessary pages to streamline your publication and keep file sizes down. Always view the pages that you are deleting to ensure that you are deleting the correct pages, and that there aren't any elements you want saved, such as clip art or a pull quote. You can store any elements that you want to retain on the scratch area or in the Content Library. When you delete a page, any objects on that page are deleted from the publication, continued on/continued from notices are automatically recalculated, and text in a connected text box is moved to the closest available text box on the next page. You need to eliminate some unnecessary pages in the catalog. You want to delete a total of eight pages: the four new pages as well as four additional pages.

STEPS

1. **Verify that pages 4–5 are selected, click Edit on the menu bar, then click Delete Page**
   The Delete Page dialog box opens, as shown in Figure G-4. The Both pages option button is selected, although you could just delete the left or right page.

2. **Click the Left page only option button, then click OK**
   The warning dialog box shown in Figure G-5 opens. This tells you that you can delete a single page, but your layout may be negatively affected, or you can cancel the single page deletion.

QUICK TIP
If you delete a page in error, immediately click the Undo button on the Standard toolbar.

3. **Click Cancel**

4. **Click Edit on the menu bar, click Delete Page, verify that the Both pages option button is selected, click OK, then click OK in the Multiple page spread warning box**
   The Multiple page spread warning box appeared because you were deleting only two pages, not a multiple of four. Your publication now has 10 pages.

5. **With pages 4–5 still active, click Edit on the menu bar, click Delete Page, verify that the Both pages option button is selected, then click OK**
   The Multiple page spread warning box does not appear because the total number of remaining pages is a multiple of four. There are now eight pages in the publication.

6. **With pages 4–5 still active, click Edit on the menu bar, click Delete Page, verify that the Both pages option button is selected, click OK, then click OK in the Multiple page spread warning box**
   The catalog now contains six pages.

7. **With pages 4–5 still active, click Edit on the menu bar, click Delete Page, verify that the Both pages option button is selected, click OK, then click the Page 2 icon 2 to select pages 2–3.**
   Compare your catalog to Figure G-6. There are now four pages in the publication.

8. **Click the Save button on the Standard toolbar**

Design Matters

Understanding mirrored layout guides

In a publication with both left and right pages (such as a bound book or magazine), you can use **mirrored guides** so that facing pages have opposite margins and layout guides. This can make your material easier to read and more consistent in appearance. When you click the Two-page master check box in the New Master Page dialog box, the names of the Left and Right margin guides become Inside and Outside margin guides. A bound publication should have larger inside margins to allow for the space taken up by the binding. You can switch the layout guides for the publication pages on the master page by dragging a layout guide. The pointer changes to a resize pointer. Drag the guide to any location, using the vertical and horizontal rulers for exact measurements. You can also return layout guides to their original locations by clicking the Undo button on the Standard toolbar before performing any other action. You can open the Layout Guides dialog box by clicking the Layout Guides button on the Edit Master Pages toolbar that displays when the master pages are in view.

FIGURE G-4: Delete Page dialog box

Delete Page
Delete
Both pages
Left page only
Right page only
OK
Cancel

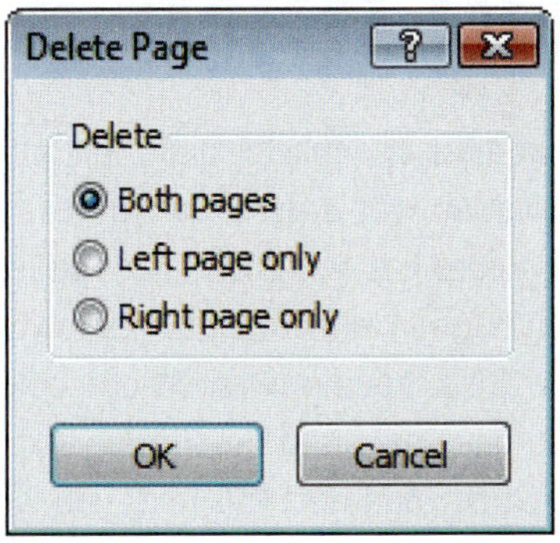

FIGURE G-5: Multiple pages warning dialog box

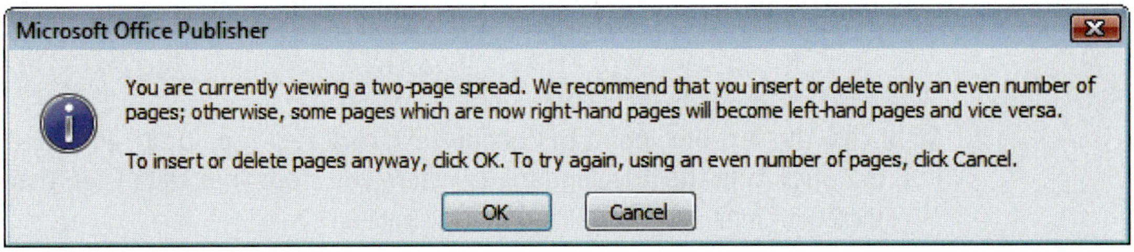

Microsoft Office Publisher
You are currently viewing a two-page spread. We recommend that you insert or delete only an even number of pages; otherwise, some pages which are now right-hand pages will become left-hand pages and vice versa.
To insert or delete pages anyway, click OK. To try again, using an even number of pages, click Cancel.
OK
Cancel

FIGURE G-6: Two-page spread

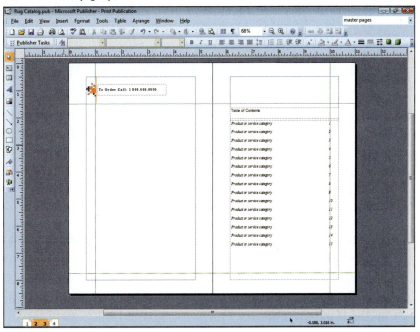

Rug Catalog.pub - Microsoft Publisher - Print Publication
File Edit View Insert Format Tools Table Arrange Window Help
master pages
Publisher Tasks
Table of Contents

Design Matters

Saving objects on a page

When a page is deleted, all the objects on that page are also deleted. But what if you want to save some of those objects for later use? Simply drag the object onto the scratch area. Objects in the scratch area are saved along with the publication, and can be viewed and accessed from all pages in the publication. When you decide where you want an object from the scratch area to be used, move it to its new location using any copying or pasting technique. Alternately, you can cut an object before deleting the page so it will automatically be stored on the Office Clipboard, where you can easily retrieve it until you close the publication. You can also store an object in the Content Library by clicking the object, then clicking Add selected items to Content Library on the Content Library task pane.

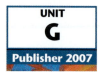

Working with a Master Page

Every publication has at least one master page that can be used to add text or objects that you want on every page. A publication with **mirrored guides** has both left and right master pages, a publication without mirrored guides has a single master page. You can use a master page to add an object, such as a logo, to each page. A **washout**, also known as a **watermark**, is another element you can add to the master page. It's a faded or washed-out looking image that appears behind text and objects on a page. You have prepared descriptive text about Navajo rugs which you want to insert in a text box on page 2. Once you insert this text, you will add a watermark of a rug image to the background page.

STEPS

1. Click the **Text Box button** 📄 on the Objects toolbar, then drag ✛ from 1" H / 1½" V to 4⅞" H / 7¾" V

   The text box appears on the page.

2. Right-click the **text box**, point to **Change Text**, click **Text File**, locate and select the file **PUB G-2.docx** from the drive and folder where you store your Data Files, then click **OK**

   All of the text fits within the text box, as shown in Figure G-7.

   QUICK TIP

   You can modify an existing master page by switching to the master page view and editing objects.

3. Click **View** on the menu bar, then click **Master Page**

   The master pages appear, with guides and placeholders for headers and footers. Because this is a mirrored page publication, the master pages are mirrored pages as well. You can easily tell that master pages are being displayed when you see the yellow background in the scratch area. Regular pages display against a gray background. The Edit Master Pages toolbar and Edit Master Pages task pane open for working with all elements of the master pages. Master pages can accommodate both text and graphics.

4. Click the **Rename Master Page button** 📄 on the Edit Master Pages toolbar, type **Intro Master** in the Description text box, then click **OK**

5. Click **Insert** on the menu bar, point to **Picture**, click **From File**, navigate to the drive and folder where you store your Data Files, click **PUB G-3.tif**, then click **Insert**

   The picture is placed across the two master pages.

6. Close the **Edit Master Pages task pane**, then position the picture so that its top-left corner is at 1" H / 1½" V

   The picture is positioned within the master page.

7. Right-click the **picture**, click **Format Picture**, click the **Picture tab** if necessary, click the **Color list arrow**, click **Washout**, then click **OK**

   Compare your screen to Figure G-8.

   QUICK TIP

   You can toggle between the regular and master page views by pressing [Ctrl][M].

8. Click **Close Master View** on the Edit Master Pages toolbar, then click the **Save button** 💾 on the Standard toolbar

   The washout image appears behind the text in the frame. Compare your publication to Figure G-9.

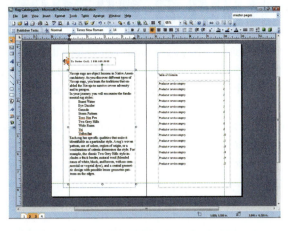

FIGURE G-8: "Washout" image added to master page

Image on left
master page

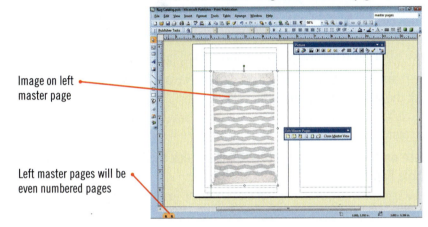

Left master pages will be
even numbered pages

FIGURE G-9: Text in foreground, image on master page background

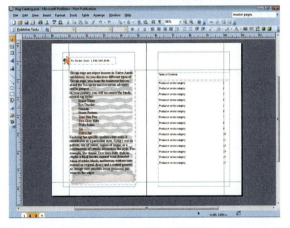

Using left and right master pages

If you have mirrored layout guides, you also have left and right master pages. Having both a left and right master page increases your design options. For example, you might want to have an image appear in the bottom-left corner on the left master page, and the bottom-right corner on the right master page. To change from double to single master pages, click Arrange on the menu bar, click Layout Guides, then deselect the Two-page master check box in the Layout Guides dialog box. When this check box is not selected, you have only one master page. What was previously the right master page is now used as the publication's background page and is applied to all the pages.

Publisher 2007

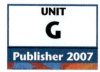
Creating a Header and Footer

Text you commonly see in a header or footer can include the document title, page number, or date. Text that appears on the top of each page is called a **header**, and text that appears on the bottom of each page is a **footer**. Special text boxes for the header or footer text are located on the right and left master pages. Images can also be included in headers and footers to enhance the publication. Usually, the headers and footers are not shown on the first page of a publication, although you can choose to display them. Table G-1 describes the buttons on the Header and Footer toolbar. You want to give the catalog a more professional look and feel, so you decide to add descriptive headers. In this case, the name of the trading company is Navajo Rugs: Cultural Expressions, and the theme for this catalog is Navajo Rugs: Strong Visual Statements.

STEPS

1. **Click View on the menu bar, then click Header and Footer**

   The view changes to the master page. The Header and Footer toolbar is open, and the background page Header text box at the top of the left page is selected.

2. **Type Navajo Rugs: An Expression of Culture in the Header text box on the left master page**

   Because you typed this in the Header text box, this text will appear in the publication on all left-hand pages.

3. **Click the Header text box at 6¼" H / ¼" V, type Navajo Rugs: Strong Visual Statements, then click the Align Text Right button**

   When you clicked the right-page text box, the display changed so that the left-page text box was no longer visible. Compare your page to Figure G-10.

4. **Click Close on the Header and Footer toolbar, click the Zoom list arrow 51%, then click Whole Page**

   The page background is gray, indicating that the publication pages, rather than the background pages, are visible. The headers appear on pages 2 and 3, as shown in Figure G-11.

5. **Click the Page 1 icon on the status bar**

   The header is visible on page 1. Catalogs, like other multi-page publications, typically don't display headers on the first page.

6. **Click View on the menu bar, then click Ignore Master Page**

   Because you chose to ignore the background on this first page, any objects on the right master page are not visible on this page.

7. **Click the Save button on the Standard toolbar**

TABLE G-1: Header and footer toolbar buttons

button	name	description
	Insert Page Number	Inserts a page number automatically into a header or footer
	Insert Date	Inserts current date into a header or footer
	Insert Time	Inserts current time into a header or footer
	Show Header/Footer	Used to toggle between the header and footer

FIGURE G-10: Header on right master page

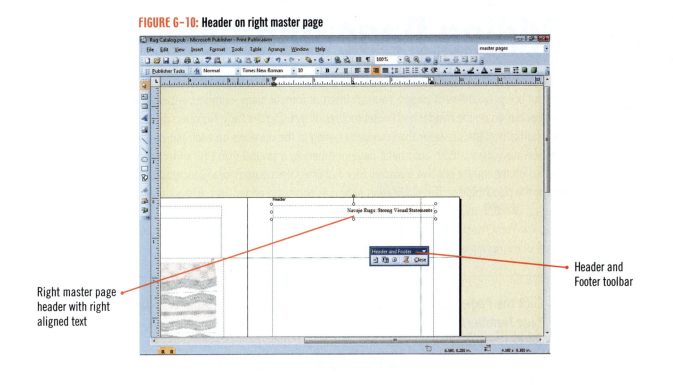

Right master page header with right aligned text

Header and Footer toolbar

FIGURE G-11: Headers visible on left and right pages

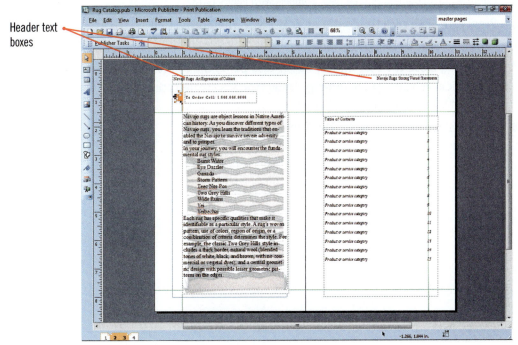

Header text boxes

Adding Page Numbers

Page numbers help readers find specific stories, and find the continued parts of stories that appear in multiple text boxes on different pages. You can insert automatic page numbers either by using the Insert Page Number button on the Header and Footer toolbar, or by using the Page Numbers dialog box. Using Publisher's page numbering tools is easier than manually typing in the numbers on each page yourself—and ensures the numbers stay correct. With automatic page numbering, a pound sign (#), rather than an actual number, is inserted on the master page as a placeholder. Publisher then automatically substitutes the correct page number for the placeholder in the publication pages. As pages are added and deleted, your page numbers remain accurate. 🎨 You want page numbers to appear in the footers at the bottom of each page, except the first page. You want the page numbers to appear in the bottom-left corner of the left pages and the bottom-right corner of the right pages.

1. **Click the Page 2 icon 2 on the status bar, click Insert on the menu bar, then click Page Numbers**

   The Page Numbers dialog box opens, as shown in Figure G-12.

2. **Click the Position list arrow, then click Bottom of page (Footer)**

3. **Click the Alignment list arrow, then click Outside**

4. **Deselect the Show page number on first page check box**

   The page numbering feature will count the first page, but the number will not appear. In most cases, it's not necessary to display the page number on the first page of a publication.

5. **Click OK**

   Compare the placement of your page numbers with Figure G-13.

> **QUICK TIP**
>
> Clicking Close Master View on the Edit Master Pages toolbar has the same effect as pressing [Ctrl][M].

6. **Press [Ctrl][M], click the footer at 7" H / 8" V, then press [F9]**

   The master page shows the page number feature as "#" inside the footer.

7. **Press [F9], close the Edit Master Pages task pane, then press [Ctrl][M]**

   The publication is displayed in Two-Page Spread view. You like the balanced look of the headers and footers aligned at the outer margins of both pages.

8. **Click the Save button 🖫 on the Standard toolbar**

FIGURE G-12: Page Numbers dialog box

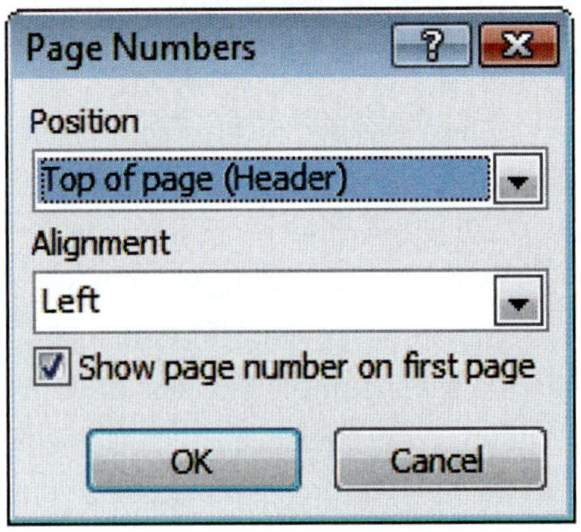

Page Numbers

Position

Top of page (Header)

Alignment

Left

☑ Show page number on first page

OK   Cancel

FIGURE G-13: Page numbers on both pages

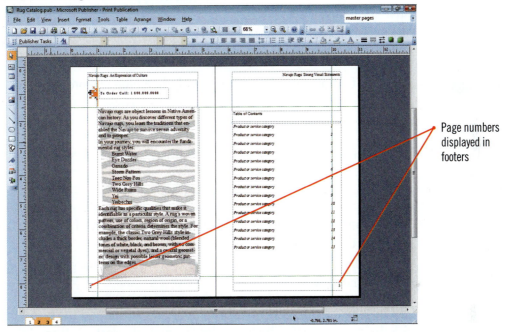

Page numbers displayed in footers

Publisher 2007

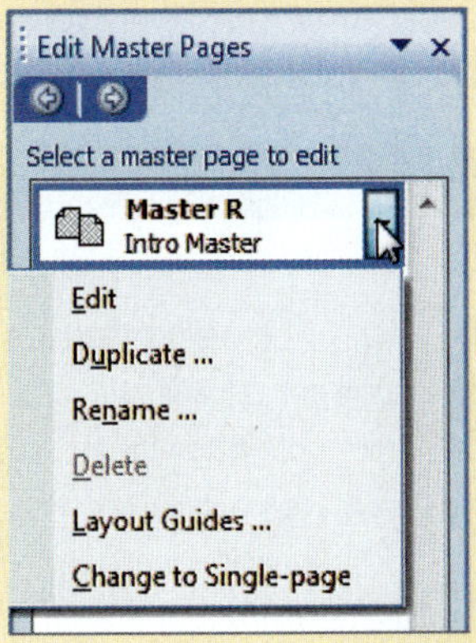

Editing a Story

As you have learned, you can type a story directly into a text box, or prepare it in another program and insert it as a text file. Once you have placed a story in a publication, you have a choice when editing it: You can do your normal editing in Publisher or you can use the Edit Story in Microsoft Word command to edit your text in Word from within Publisher. Any changes you make to the text are automatically updated in the publication when you save and close the Word document. To use this feature, you must have Microsoft Word 6.0 or later installed. If you are not dealing with a lot of text, you might find it easier to edit the story using Publisher's editing features. If you edit in Publisher, your changes are saved only to the publication, not to the original text file. After reading the publication, you realize you need to edit the descriptive text on page 2, to tighten up some of the wording.

STEPS

TROUBLE
If Word isn't installed on your computer or you receive a low memory error message, edit the story directly in Publisher.

1. **Right-click the text box at 3" H / 3" V, point to Change Text, click Edit Story in Microsoft Word, then click the Maximize button in the upper-right corner of the Document in Rug Catalog window if necessary**

   Microsoft Word opens, displaying the story's text, as shown in Figure G-15. Any edits you make to this text in Word will be applied to the selected story in the Publisher text box.

QUICK TIP
When working in Microsoft Word, you can save your changes to the Word document by clicking the **Save button** on the Standard toolbar (Word 2003) or the Quick Access Toolbar (Word 2007).

2. **Select the text discover different types of, then type explore**

   You changed the phrase "discover different types of" to "explore" in the first paragraph to make it more succinct.

3. **Click to the right of Yei (the eighth bullet text), press [Spacebar], type and, press [Spacebar], then press [Delete] twice**

   You combined the two related bulleted items into one bullet. Your edits are complete.

4. **Click File on the menu bar or on the Office Button menu (if you have Office 2007 installed), then click Close & Return to Rug Catalog**

   (If you are editing directly in Publisher, skip this step.) Word closes and you see your edits applied to the text in the Publisher story.

QUICK TIP
Some text formatting, such as drop caps, are lost when moving from Word to Publisher.

5. **Click anywhere within the first paragraph, click Format on the menu bar, click Drop Cap, click the drop cap style directly under the current selection, then click OK**

6. **Select the word Burnt, press and hold [Shift], click to the right of Yeibeichai, then release [Shift]**

7. **Click the Bullets button on the Formatting toolbar, then press [Esc] twice**

   The drop cap and bullets are added to make the story stand out. Compare your work to Figure G-16.

8. **Click the Save button on the Standard toolbar**

Design Matters

Copyfitting text

As you create a publication, you may find that you have either too much or too little text to fit comfortably in a column or page. **Copyfitting** is a term used to describe the process of making the text fit the available space within a publication. If you have too much text, you can narrow the margins, decrease the point size of the font, enlarge the text box, flow text into a text box on another page, or delete some text by editing. You can solve the problem of too little text by inserting a graphic image or pull quote, making margins wider, increasing the point size of the font, or adding some text. The AutoFit Text command found on the Format menu works by increasing or decreasing the point size of the fonts.

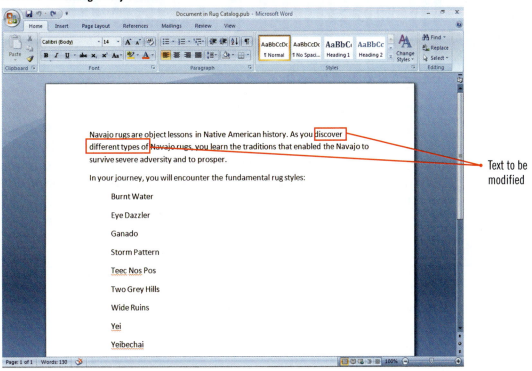

Text to be modified

Drop cap

Text combined

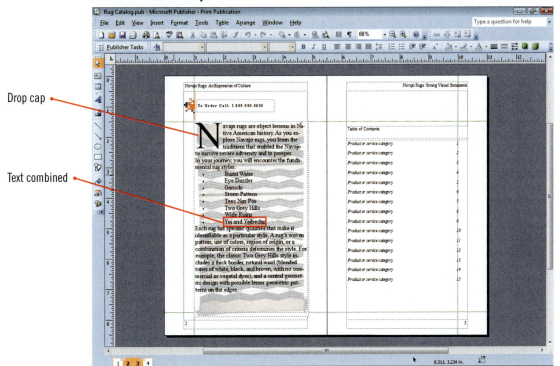

Modifying a Table of Contents

A **table of contents** helps readers locate specific information in a multi-page publication. A table of contents in Publisher uses tabs to align columns of information concerning content and the page numbers of the content. To create a table of contents, type text into a text box, then add tabs and leaders to connect the text and page numbers. A **tab**, or tab stop, is a defined location to which the insertion point advances when you press [Tab]. **Leaders** are a series of dots, dashes, or lines that lead up to a tab, and automatically adjust to fit the space between the columns. You want to modify the table of contents in the catalog by adding dot leaders to make reading easier. Although you still have several pages of content to add to this publication, you'll also make entries to approximate where information will be located.

STEPS

1. **Click the text box at 7" H / 2½" V, then press [F9]**
   The first item in the table of contents is for page 1. The reference to this page is not necessary, as the reader can easily see everything that's on page 1.

2. **Select the first line of text, then press [Delete]**
   The first line is deleted, and the second line begins with page 2.

3. **Press [Ctrl][A], right-click the text, point to Change Text, then click Tabs**
   The Tabs dialog box opens, as shown in Figure G-17.

4. **In the Leader section of the Tabs dialog box, click the Dot option button, click OK, then click outside of the text box to deselect the text**
   Each of the entries in the text box now has a dot leader preceding the page number.

5. **Select the text Product or service category in the first line, then type Introduction to Navajo Rugs**
   The first entry in the table of contents is complete.

6. **Delete the entry for page 3, then delete the entries for pages 13-15**

7. **Type the table of contents information as shown in Figure G-18 using the techniques described in Step 5, then substitute Your Name as a final entry to the table of contents**
   The table of contents looks good and is a tool that will help clients locate information about the rugs when the catalog is complete.

8. **Press [F9], click the Save button 🖫 on the Standard toolbar, then click the Print button 🖨 on the Standard toolbar**
   Review the four printed pages of the catalog.

9. **Click File on the menu bar, then click Close**
   The publication closes. Publisher remains open and available for additional work.

FIGURE G-17: Tabs dialog box

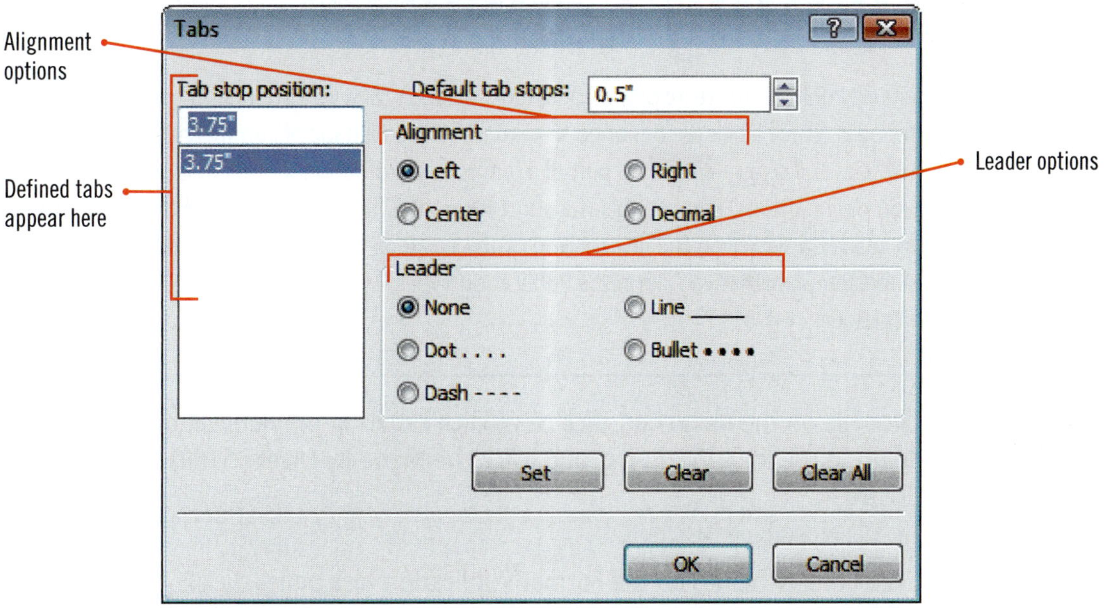

Alignment options

Defined tabs appear here

Leader options

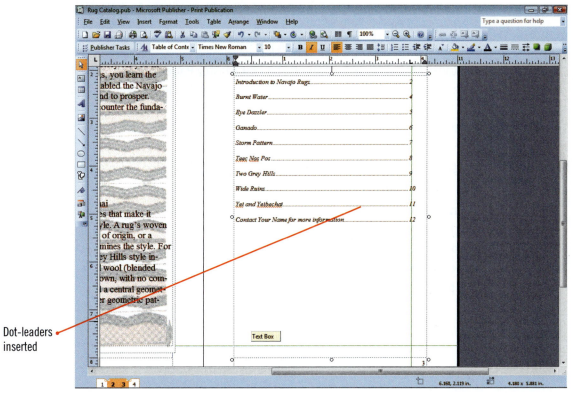

Dot-leaders inserted

FIGURE G-18: Completed table of contents

Publisher 2007

Creating Labels

You can use Publisher to create professional-looking labels for a variety of items, such as retail products, CDs, or notebooks. These labels are designed to print directly on a page of commercially available labels in a wide range of sizes and styles. As part of a temporary promotion, the client is planning to offer a 15% discount on online orders. Because this is a short-term offer, it won't be printed directly on the catalog. You plan to include a sticker on the first mailing of the catalogs that indicates the amount of the discount. You find a label template that you like in the Publication Types list to create a sheet of labels that can be attached to the catalogs.

STEPS

QUICK TIP

The label brand and model number required for printing varies based on the label design you use. You may need your Microsoft Publisher Installation CD to complete this step.

1. **Click File on the menu bar, click New, click Labels in the Publication Types list, scroll down to the Identification group, click the Made By (Avery 5160) template, then click Create**

   The label appears on the screen.

2. **Click Color Schemes on the Format Publication task pane, click Eggplant, then save the publication as Rug Label to the drive and folder where you store your Data Files**

3. **Click the Close button on the Format Publication task pane, press [Ctrl][M], click Insert on the menu bar, point to Picture, click From File, click PUB G-4.tif from the drive and folder where you store your Data Files then click Insert**

   Compare your label to Figure G-19.

4. **If necessary, use ✛ to drag the picture so that it is centered on the label, right-click the object, click Format Picture, drag the Brightness slider to 75%, drag the Contrast slider to 25%, then click OK**

   The image is now a much lighter shade than before.

5. **Click the Close Master View button on the Edit Master Pages toolbar, close the task pane, select the text Made especially for you by:, type Authentic Navajo Rug, then press [Ctrl][T]**

   Pressing [Ctrl][T] changed the text box fill from white to transparent. You can now see the image of the rug very clearly behind the text.

6. **Click the text box at 1" H / ¾" V, press [Ctrl][A], type 20% online discount, press [Ctrl][A], then click the Bold button B on the Formatting toolbar**

7. **Click Format on the menu bar, point to AutoFit Text, click Best Fit, press [Ctrl][T], then press [Esc] twice**

   Compare your label to Figure G-20.

8. **Click the Save button ⊟ on the Standard toolbar, click File on the menu bar, click Print, then exit Publisher**

FIGURE G-19: Label master page with image inserted

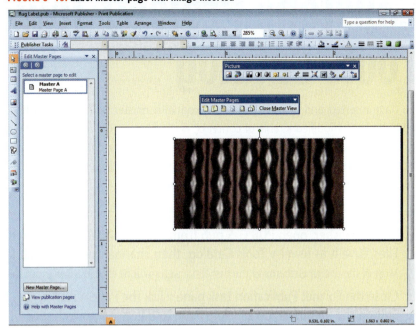

FIGURE G-20: Completed label with recolored image

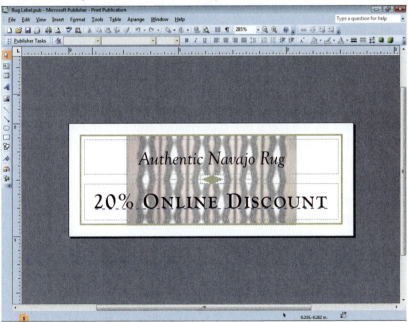

Creating CD/DVD labels

If you like creating CDs of your original music and photographs, or DVDs of converted VCR tapes, you may want to create jewel case labels for them. To do so, open the Publication Types list, then click the Labels category. When you scroll down to the CD/DVD Labels, you'll see a variety of case inserts and jewel case labels you can use.

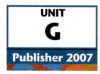

Capstone Project: Jewelry Tools Catalog

You have inserted and deleted pages, worked with master pages, created headers and footers, added page numbers, modified a table of contents, and edited a story in Word. You will use these skills to work on a new catalog. ▰▰▰ You are designing a metal workers' catalog. The target customers for this catalog are jewelers. You think they will appreciate a simple, uncluttered design that conveys the elegance of their craft. The client will add pictures and text later.

STEPS

1. Start Publisher, open PUB G-5.pub from the drive and folder where you store your Data Files, save it as Jewelry Tools Catalog, then change the color scheme to Tropics

   Most of the design elements in the first three pages will be carried throughout the catalog.

2. Close the Format Publication task pane, click the Page 4 icon ④ on the status bar, click Edit on the menu bar, click Delete Page to delete pages 4–5, click OK at each warning or dialog box, then repeat the process to delete the next two pages, which are now pages 4 and 5

   The publication now has four pages.

3. Click the Page 2 icon ② on the status bar, click View on the menu bar, click Master Page, click Insert on the menu bar, point to Picture, click From File, then double-click PUB G-6.tif from the drive and folder where you store your Data Files

4. Position the image so that its top-left corner is at 1¼" H / 3" V, resize it so the bottom-right corner is at 4½" H / 6" V, right-click the image, click Format Picture, click the Picture tab if necessary, click the Color list arrow, click Washout, then click OK

   The image is now centered and washed-out, and will look elegant with black text imposed over the gold color.

5. Click View on the menu bar, click Header and Footer, type Picasso Tools for the Jewelry Arts in the Header text box on the left master page, click the Show Header/Footer button 🔳 on the Header and Footer toolbar, type Page, press [Spacebar], click the Insert Page Number button 🔳, copy the entries in the left footer to the right footer, click the Align Text Right button 🔳 to right-align the right footer, then click Close Master View on the Edit Master Pages toolbar

   Page numbers will help customers navigate to specific items.

6. Press [F9], click the text box at 6½" H / 2" V, click Format on the menu bar, click Tabs, click the Line option button, then click OK

   There is still an entry for page 1 that must be deleted.

7. Right-click the text box, point to Change Text, click Edit Story in Microsoft Word, delete the entry for page 1, click File on the menu bar or the Office Button menu, then click Close & Return to Jewelry Tools Catalog

8. Click the text box at 2" H / ¾" V on page 2, substitute your name for the phone number, press [Esc] twice, then compare your work to Figure G-21

9. Click the Save button 🔳 on the Standard toolbar, print pages 2 and 3, then exit Publisher

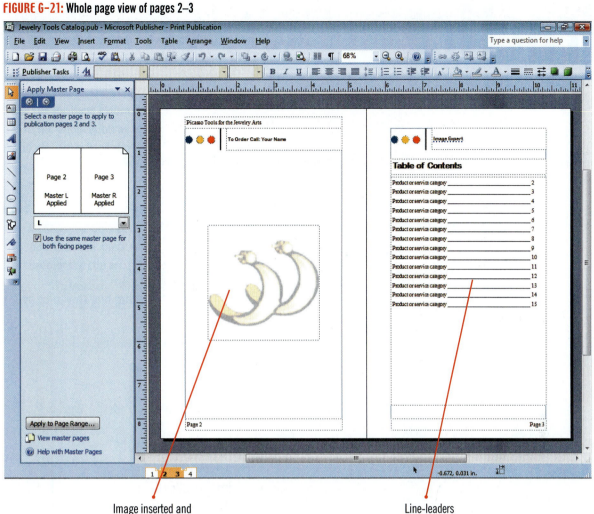

Image inserted and
formatted with
"Washout" color

Line-leaders
inserted

Publisher 2007

Practice

If you have a SAM user profile, you may have access to hands-on instruction, practice, and assessment of the skills covered in this unit. Log in to your SAM account (http://sam2007.course.com/) to launch any assigned training activities or exams that relate to the skills covered in this unit.

▼ CONCEPTS REVIEW

Label each of the elements in the Publisher window shown in Figure G-22.

FIGURE G-22

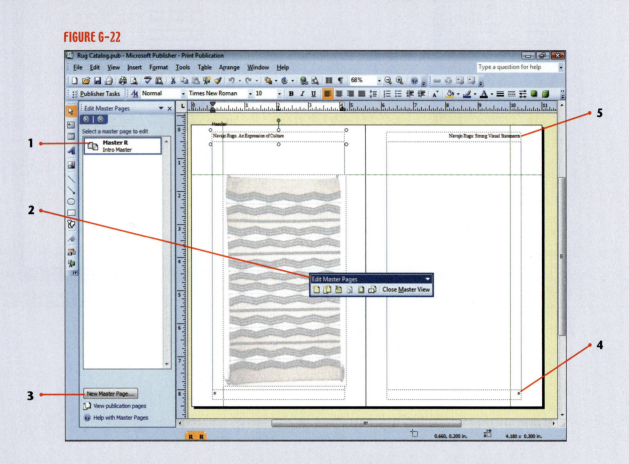

Match each of the features with the correct term, menu, dialog box, or command.

6. Footer

7. Format menu

8. Header

9. [Ctrl][M]

10. Tabs dialog box

11. Edit menu

a. Switches in and out of Master Page view

b. Text that repeats on the bottom of each page

c. Text that repeats at the top of each page

d. Contains the command that deletes a page

e. Contains the command that adds dot leaders

f. Contains the command that adds a drop cap

Select the best answer from the list of choices.

12. **Each of the following is true about adding a page, except:**
    a. Pages can be added before or after the current page.
    b. You can only add one page at a time.
    c. Existing layout guides are added to the new page(s).
    d. You can duplicate objects found on other pages in the publication.

13. **Which command is used to change the text box fill from white to transparent?**
    a. [Ctrl][M]   c. [Ctrl][N]
    b. [Ctrl][T]   d. [Ctrl][B]

14. **Where in a publication are headers and footers usually placed?**
    a. In AutoShapes   c. On the Clipboard
    b. In picture frames   d. On the master page(s)

15. **Which character symbolizes automatic page numbers?**
    a. @   c. !
    b. #   d. &

▼ SKILLS REVIEW

1. **Add pages.**
   a. Start Publisher, then choose the Marquee template in the Classic Designs section of the Catalogs category. Use the Secondary Business Information set, change the color scheme to Verve, then close the task pane.
   b. Save the file as **Video Store Catalog** to the drive and folder where you store your Data Files.
   c. Display pages 2–3.
   d. Insert four pages after page 3 (with the default settings). You now have 12 pages.
   e. Save your work.

2. **Delete pages.**
   a. Display pages 8 and 9, delete them, then display and delete the new pages 8 and 9.
   b. Display pages 6 and 7, delete them, then delete pages 4 and 5. You now have four pages.
   c. Display pages 2 and 3, then save your work.

3. **Work with a master page.**
   a. Change to Master Page view.
   b. Open the Insert Clip Art task pane, search My Collections and Office Collections using all media file types and the text **TVs**, select the image with the filename j0229385.wmf, then close the Clip Art task pane.
   c. Position the image so that its top-left corner is at ¾" H / 3" V.
   d. Press and hold [Shift], then drag the lower-right sizing handle until the image is approximately 4" wide and 2¾" high.
   e. Save your work.

4. **Create a header and footer.**
   a. Open the header on the left master page, type **Video Classics**, then make the text bold.
   b. Type **Video Classics** in the header on the right master page.
   c. Right-align the text in the right Header text box, make the text bold, then save the publication.

5. **Add page numbers.**
   a. View the footer on the right page, then add page numbers to the footers on both pages aligned at the outer margins.
   b. Close the Header and Footer toolbar, then close the master view.
   c. Delete the Page Number text boxes at the bottom of pages 2 and 3 (at 1" H / 7¾" V, and 9½" H / 7¾" V), then go to page 1.
   d. Prevent the page number from appearing on the first page, (*Hint*: use the Insert menu) then save the publication.

6. **Edit a story.**

   a. Use the page icon button on the status bar to return to page 2.

   b. Draw a text box at 1¼" H / 2½" V to 4¼" H / 6½" V.

   c. Insert the text file PUB G-7.docx into the text box, then open Word to edit the story.

   d. Add the following text in a matching font and text size as a new paragraph at the end of the story: **If we don't have what you're looking for, we can get it for you**. Close Word and return to the catalog, then verify that the text was added to the story.

   e. Add a three-line custom drop cap character to the first paragraph, then save the publication.

7. **Modify a table of contents.**

   a. Select the text box at 6½" H / 2" V on page 3 (the table of contents text), then open it in Word.

   b. Delete the entries for pages 1–3, then close Word and return to the catalog.

   c. Select the table of contents text, then change the tabs for the remaining entries to dot leaders.

   d. Change the remaining entries, using Table G-2 below. Delete any unnecessary text.

   e. Add a final entry to the Table of Contents that contains your name.

   f. Save your work, then print pages 2 and 3. Close the publication, but do not exit Publisher.

8. **Create a label.**

   a. Create a label using the Video Face (Avery 5199A) design and the Concourse color scheme.

   b. Save the label as **Video Store Label** to the drive and folder where you store your Data Files.

   c. Change the Video Title text to **All About Eve**.

   d. Change the date text to the current date.

   e. Change the company name text to your name.

   f. Save your work, print the publication, then exit Publisher.

TABLE G-2

page headings	page #
1930s	4
1940s	6
1950s	8
1960s	10
Award Winners	12
Independent Films	14

▼ INDEPENDENT CHALLENGE 1

You are a member of a small theater group. You are asked to create the program for the next production.

a. Start Publisher, then use the Publication Types list and the Theater template in the Programs category.

b. Use the Business Information set of your choice to enter appropriate information, then close the Format Publication task pane.

c. Save the publication as **Play Program** to the drive and folder where you store your Data Files.

d. Use the Master Page view to add a header displaying the name of the play. Choose any play with which you are familiar, such as Rent, A Chorus Line, or Man of La Mancha. Right-align the header on the right page.

e. Insert page numbers at the bottoms of the pages. If necessary, move any information so that your header and footer fit correctly and are visible.

f. Add any appropriate clip art to the master page, recoloring the clip art if necessary.

g. Return to the publication pages view, then make sure the page number, header, and footer do not appear on the first page.

h. Replace the text in the table containing the cast with the names of characters and cast members. Use the names of friends and family members or make up fictitious names.

i. Use Word to create and edit a paragraph describing the play in the existing text box on page 3.

j. Replace any placeholders so that all of the text in the program pertains to the play you chose.

k. Add your name as the director on page 1.

l. Rearrange and format any objects to create an attractive, effective design.

m. Check the spelling in the publication, save and print the publication, then exit Publisher.

▼ INDEPENDENT CHALLENGE 2

You have recorded several original songs and want to get feedback on your work from a friend who works in the music business. You decide to use a label template in Publisher to create a shipping label to send the CD to your friend.

a. Start Publisher, then create a new label based on the Borders template (Avery 5164).

b. Use any Business Information set to enter appropriate information, including your name, choose any color scheme that you like, then close the Format Publication task pane.

c. Save the publication as **Personal Shipping Label** to the drive and folder where you store your Data Files.

d. Edit the mailing address information at 2" H / 2" V, using a fictitious name and address.

Advanced Challenge Exercise

- Create a DVD label using the Mosaic CD/DVD template (Avery 8931). (*Hint*: Choose the first instance of Mosaic (Avery 8931). There are two in the CD/DVD category.)
- Save the publication as **CD-DVD Label ACE**.
- Add actual or fictitious information to the label placeholders, but use Your Name as the Performer's Name.
- Delete any unnecessary objects, add artwork if you choose, then compare your work to Figure G-23.

e. Save and print the publication, then exit Publisher.

FIGURE G-23

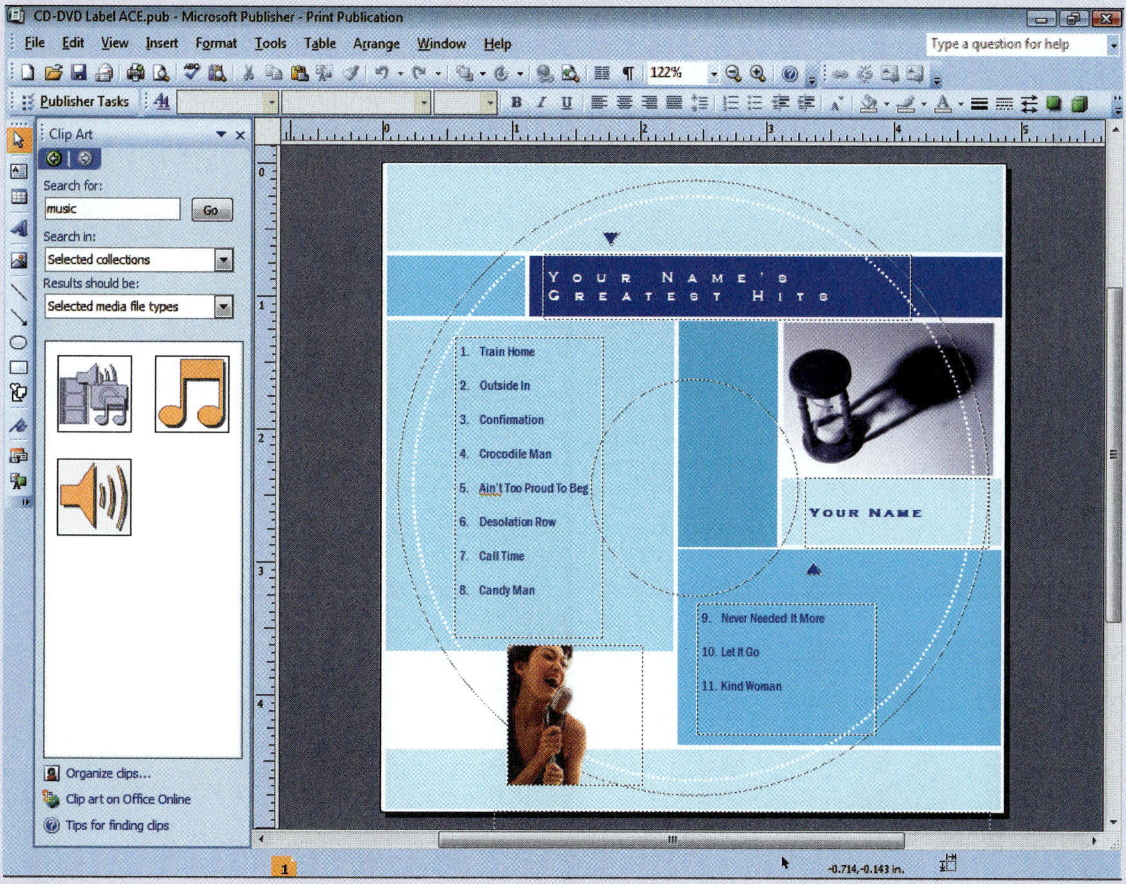

▼ INDEPENDENT CHALLENGE 3

A local elementary school asks you to design a newsletter for its staff and students. The staff and students will provide all of the stories except for one that you will write.

   a. Start Publisher, use the Publication Types list to create a new newsletter based on the Kid Stuff template in the Newsletters category.

   b. Use any Business Information set to enter appropriate information.

   c. Change the color scheme to a scheme of your choice, then close the Format Publication task pane.

   d. Save the publication as **School Newsletter** to the drive and folder where you store your Data Files.

   e. Delete pages 2 and 3. Open the Insert Page dialog box. Click the Left-hand page list arrow, then click Calendar. Click the Right-hand page list arrow, click Response Form, then click OK.

   f. Replace the newsletter title with your elementary school's name, followed by the word **News**.

   g. Make up your own headings and replace at least one story with your own original story on the topic of your choice.

   h. Edit the story in Word (if you have this program installed), then check the spelling in the publication.

   i. Add your name in the Table of Contents on the first page of the newsletter.

Advanced Challenge Exercise

   ■ Change the single master page to left-right master pages.

   ■ Add a footer to the master pages, then compare your work to the sample shown in Figure G-24.

   j. Save and print the publication, then exit Publisher.

FIGURE G-24

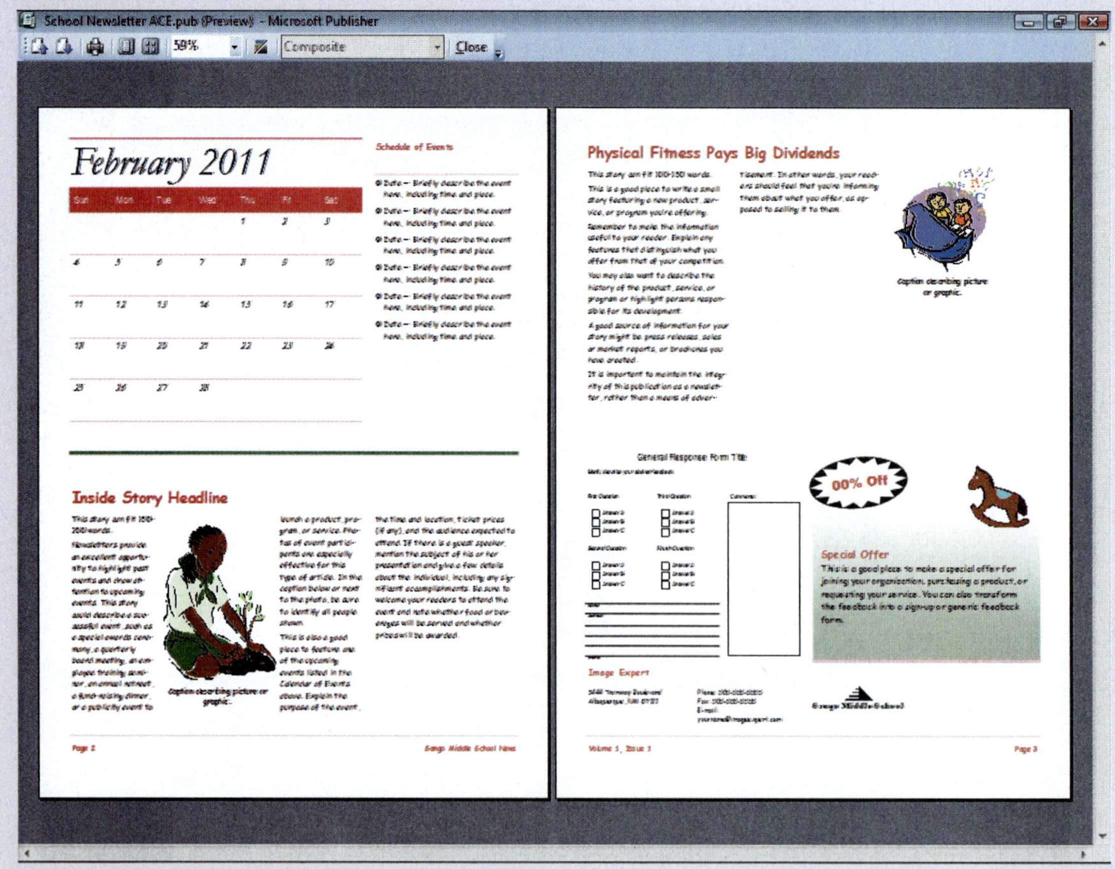

▼ REAL LIFE INDEPENDENT CHALLENGE

This Independent Challenge requires an Internet connection. You work at a computer camp during the summer and have been asked to teach a course on how to use Publisher. You decide to create a newsletter to inform the campers about the features of Publisher, and show them an example of a great publication.

a. Connect to the Internet and use your browser to go to www.microsoft.com. Find the home page for Publisher 2007.

b. Find information about Publisher's highlights and capabilities, then print out information pertaining to two topics of interest to you.

c. Start Publisher if necessary, then select a newsletter template of your choice.

d. Save the publication as **Publisher Newsletter** to the drive and folder where you store your Data Files.

e. Use the Business Information set of your choice to enter appropriate information, then delete pages so that only two pages remain.

f. Create a title for the newsletter. Use the information you found on the Microsoft Web site to compose two stories for the newsletter, a lead and secondary story. You can copy and paste information from the Web site, or write your own stories from scratch.

g. Add any clip art you feel is appropriate, then check the spelling in the publication.

h. Type your name in a text box on page 1, then compare your work to Figure G-25.

i. Save and print the publication, then exit Publisher.

FIGURE G-25

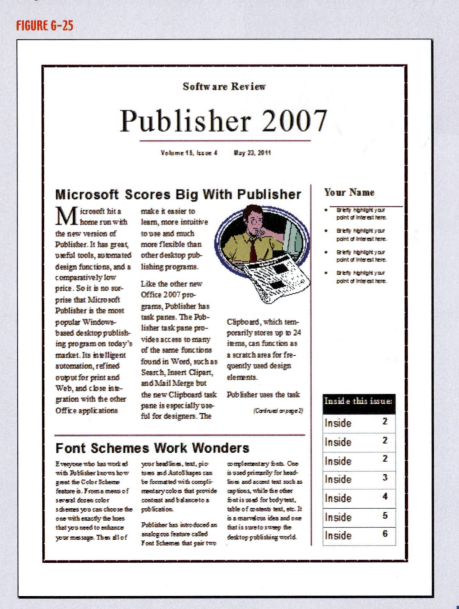

Publisher 2007

▼ VISUAL WORKSHOP

Open PUB G-8.pub from the drive and folder where you store your Data Files. Save the publication as **Rug Collection Binder**. Modify the publication so that it looks like Figure G-26. (*Hint*: You'll find the image, PUB G-9.tif, which you need to add to the master page, in the drive and folder where you store your Data Files.) Be sure to include your name where indicated. Save and print the pages. Figure G-26 is shown in Portrait orientation in Print Preview showing Multiple Pages in a 2 × 1 view.

FIGURE G-26

Using Advanced Features

Now that you have a grasp of Publisher basics, you are ready to add sophisticated design elements to your work, and get your message in the mail. Publisher makes it easy to add fancy borders to text boxes, create curved text designs, wrap text around a frame, rotate text boxes, make your work portable, and get it into the hands of your audience. Image Expert has been hired to create a brochure for Piano Bravo, a company that sells and services pianos. You have created a draft of the brochure and are making final enhancements to it. In addition to your design work, the client also wants you to send the brochure to their customers. Your contact at Piano Bravo, Emma Rose, has given you a customer database you can use to address each brochure.

OBJECTIVES

Add BorderArt

Design WordArt

Wrap text around an object

Rotate a text box

Understand mail merge

Create a mail merge

Prepare for commercial printing

Use the Pack and Go Wizard

Capstone Project: Automotive Gift
    Certificate

Adding BorderArt

Attractive borders can add pizzazz to a publication. You can add borders to any frame or text box. As with any design element, judicious use creates a smart, professional look; overuse distracts from the message. **BorderArt** lets you choose from a wide variety of decorative borders that come with Publisher. You can add a border to a text box using the BorderArt dialog box. In this dialog box, you can choose a border style and modify the border's appearance. You want to add an eye-catching, imaginative border design to the first page of the brochure.

STEPS

1. **Start Publisher, open PUB H-1.pub from the drive and folder where you store your Data Files, then save it as Piano Brochure**

2. **Close the task pane, then click the text box containing the text "Piano Bravo" at 8" H / 1" V**
   In order to modify a frame or object, you must first select it. Compare your screen to Figure H-1.

3. **Press [F9], right-click the text box, click Format Text Box, click the Colors and Lines tab if necessary, then click BorderArt**
   The BorderArt dialog box opens. Borders can be simple lines of varying thickness or color, or they can be more elaborate designs that will help reinforce the theme of your document.

4. **Scroll through the Available Borders list, then click Music Notes**
   Figure H-2 shows the BorderArt dialog box with the Music Notes border selected. Available borders are listed in alphabetical order. When you click a border, the sample appears in the Preview box.

QUICK TIP

To remove existing BorderArt from a selected text box, open the Format Text Box dialog box, select the Color and Lines tab, click BorderArt, click None, then click OK.

5. **Click the Always apply at default size check box to deselect it, then click OK**

6. **Select the contents of the Weight text box, type 12, then click OK**
   The BorderArt pattern appears on the edge of the text box, as shown in Figure H-3.

7. **Press [F9], then click the Save button 💾 on the Standard toolbar**

Creating custom BorderArt

In addition to choosing a border style in the BorderArt dialog box, you can create your own custom borders using almost any simple clip art or graphic image. To do so, open the BorderArt dialog box, then click the Create Custom button. You can choose from images in the Clip Gallery, or elsewhere on your computer. You can even create BorderArt from images you created. Click the Select Picture button, locate the image, click the image, click OK, choose a name for your border, then click OK.

FIGURE H-1: Text box selected

Piano Brochure.pub - Microsoft Publisher - Print Publication
The Benefits of Childhood Music Education
Piano Bravo
We make you look great!

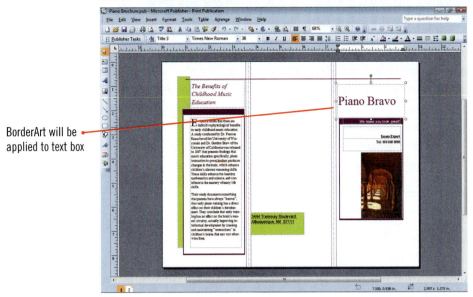

BorderArt will be applied to text box

FIGURE H-2: BorderArt dialog box

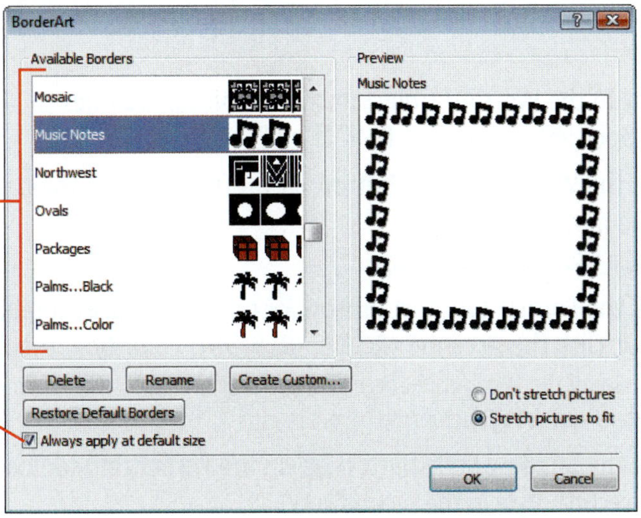

BorderArt
Available Borders
Mosaic
Music Notes
Northwest
Ovals
Packages
Palms...Black
Palms...Color
Preview
Music Notes
Delete
Rename
Create Custom...
Restore Default Borders
Always apply at default size
Don't stretch pictures
Stretch pictures to fit
OK
Cancel

Available borders appear here

Deselect checkbox to change the size of the border

FIGURE H-3: BorderArt added to text box

Piano Brochure.pub - Microsoft Publisher - Print Publication
Piano Bravo
We make you look great!
Image Expert
Tel: 555 555 5555

BorderArt added

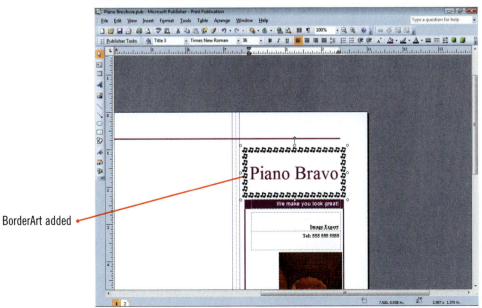

Designing WordArt

You have probably seen text that is curved, or in a specific shape, such as a circle or semi-circle. You can create this effect in Publisher by using **WordArt**. WordArt gives you a wide variety of text styles and effects from which to choose. You can transform text into all kinds of shapes, you can add shadows and patterns, and you can change text color. ▇▇▇▇▇ You want to add WordArt to the right panel of page 2 to identify the store that will be the back cover of the flyer. You want to emphasize the curve of the piano in the image at the bottom of the panel, so you decide to change the shape of the WordArt once you've inserted it, so that the text curves in a way to complement the piano's shape.

STEPS

1. **Click the Page 2 icon 2 on the status bar, then click the Insert WordArt button 4 on the Objects toolbar**

   The WordArt Gallery displays 30 WordArt styles.

2. **Click the first box in the fifth row of the WordArt Gallery, as shown in Figure H-4**

3. **Click OK, type Piano Bravo in the Edit WordArt Text dialog box, click the Size list arrow, click 28, then click OK**

   The Piano Bravo WordArt object and the WordArt toolbar appear on the screen. See a description of the WordArt toolbar buttons in Table H-1.

4. **Point to the WordArt object until the pointer changes to ⬩, then drag the object so that its upper-left corner is at 8¼" H / ½" V**

5. **Click the WordArt Shape button A on the WordArt toolbar, then click Wave1 (the fifth shape in the third row)**

   The text takes on a "wavy" shape.

6. **Click the Format WordArt button 🖎 on the WordArt toolbar, click the Fill Color list arrow, click the Accent 1 (RGB (119, 8, 90)) color box, then click OK**

   The color of the WordArt has been changed to match the color scheme in use. It creates a focal point that draws the reader's eye across the page.

7. **Click the Shadow Style button 🔲 on the Formatting toolbar, then click Shadow Style 4 (the second style in the second row)**

   The shadows appear in the text design. This addition improves the design by adding an illusion of depth.

8. **Click anywhere on the scratch area**

   The WordArt is deselected and the WordArt toolbar closes. Compare your page to Figure H-5.

9. **Click the Save button 🔲 on the Standard toolbar**

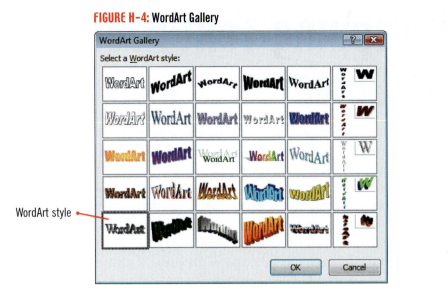

WordArt style

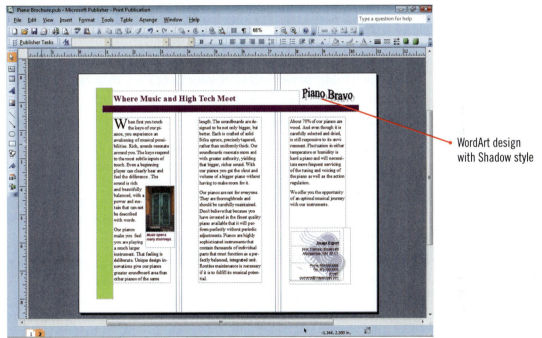

WordArt design
with Shadow style

TABLE H-1: WordArt toolbar buttons

button	name	description
	Insert WordArt	Opens WordArt Gallery
Edit Text...	Edit Text	Opens Edit WordArt Text dialog box for modifying text in the current WordArt object
	WordArt Gallery	Displays available WordArt styles
	Format WordArt	Opens the Format WordArt dialog box for modifying the current WordArt object
	WordArt Shape	Opens a palette of available WordArt shapes for changing the current WordArt object
	Text Wrapping	Opens a list of text wrapping options for the current WordArt object
	WordArt Same Letter Heights	Makes all letter heights equal
	WordArt Vertical Text	Places text on the vertical axis
	WordArt Alignment	Opens a list of options for modifying text alignment in the current WordArt object
	WordArt Character Spacing	Allows you to change the character spacing within the current WordArt object

Wrapping Text Around an Object

The careful integration of an image with text creates a polished look, and can contribute to your overall design. One way to integrate text and images is to wrap text around an object. **Wrapping** text reshapes a text box (or just the flow of text in a text box) so it conforms to the shape of a nearby image or other object. Depending on an object's width, wrapped text can appear at the top and bottom, or along the sides, of the frame surrounding the object. You like what you have done so far, but you want to experiment with adding another image of a piano to page 2. You think that adding an object to the lower-left corner of the publication would create a new focal point, and wrapping text around an image could guide the reader's eyes across the page. The image of a piano will reinforce the subject matter of the brochure and direct the reader's eyes up and to the right.

STEPS

1. **Press [F9] if necessary, right-click the photograph at 3" H / 4½" V, then click Delete Object**
    The image disappears, and the text fills that space.

2. **Click Insert on the menu bar, point to Picture, click From File, click PUB H-2.tif from the drive and folder where you store your Data Files, then click Insert**
    The attractive piano image is placed on the page.

3. **Right-click the picture, click Format Picture, then click the Layout tab**

4. **Select the contents of the Horizontal text box in the Position on page section, type 1.25, select the contents of the Vertical text box in the Position on page section, type 5.5, then click OK**

    The picture frame is inserted into the text box and the default text wrapping style, Square, is applied, as shown in Figure H-7. The image takes up so much space inside the connected text boxes that some text in the third text box doesn't fit.

QUICK TIP

Review text carefully after wrapping it to remove any awkward-looking hyphenation or isolated gaps of white space.

5. **Right-click the picture, click Format Picture, click the Layout tab, click Tight in the Wrapping Style section of the dialog box, then click OK**

    Text is tightly wrapped around the image and slants upward along the lines of the image, as shown in Figure H-8. You don't see any problems with hyphenation, and the text that was in overflow is now inside the text box.

6. **Click the Save button 💾 on the Standard toolbar**

Design Matters

Editing wrap points

You can fine-tune the way text wraps around a detailed object by editing the **wrap points**, the sizing handles that surround the object. To edit these points, select the image, click Arrange on the menu bar, point to Text Wrapping, then click Edit Wrap Points. The handles appear around the image. You can drag the handles in order to fix specific areas and you can also add or delete handles by pressing and holding [Ctrl] as you click an existing handle (to delete) or an empty spot on the selection border (to add). In Figure H-6, the handles surrounding the image can be moved to create an interesting effect.

FIGURE H-6: Text wrapped around points surrounding image

A piano is a wonderful addition to any home. It is a beautiful piece of furniture in its own right and some pianos appreciate n value. But think of the contribution music can make in your life and in your relationships with others. A piano can serve as a gather- ing place, as well as a place of solitude and medi- cation. Think of it as fine art you can use to make more art. It's an unending source of enjoyment.

If you have children, you should be aware that studies have shown that exposure to music, and particularly musical training, has a lifelong effect. A musical background can

FIGURE H-7: Image inserted in text box

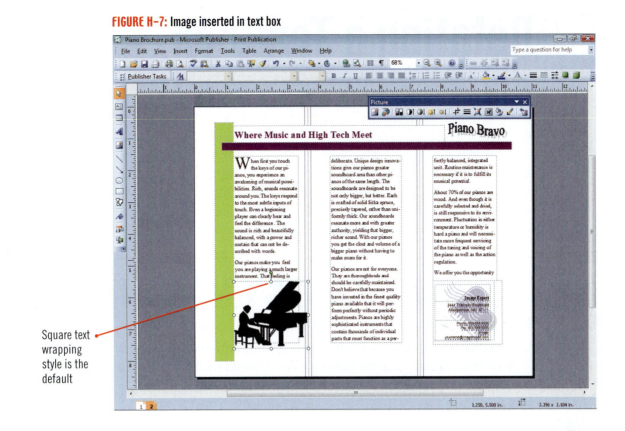

Square text wrapping style is the default

FIGURE H-8: Text wrapped to image

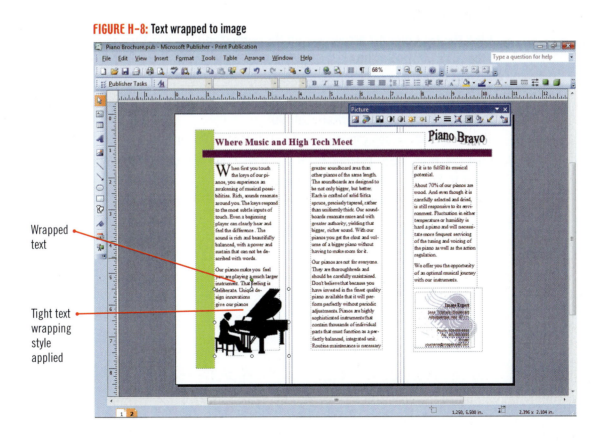

Wrapped text

Tight text wrapping style applied

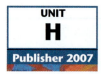

Rotating a Text Box

You can rotate a text box to create interesting effects, or to reorient text for a specific purpose, such as folding a publication. By rotating text in selected text boxes, you can ensure that all text in the publication will be easy to read depending on its placement in the final, folded publication. You want to rotate a text box in the brochure to draw attention to important promotional text. You also want to rotate the recipient's address and client's return address text boxes so they are "right side up" when the brochure is complete and folded for mailing. You want to use a rotated text box on the bottom of the first panel to add important text. First, you will create a text box, enter the promotional message, then rotate it into position on the page. Then, you'll create and rotate text boxes for the store's return address and the recipient's address. These new text boxes will appear in the middle panel of the brochure.

STEPS

1. Click the Page 1 icon, click the Text Box button 🔲 on the Objects toolbar, then drag to create a text box from 7¾" H / 7¼" V to 10¼" H / 7¾" V

2. Press [F9], if necessary, then type In-Store Piano Lessons

QUICK TIP

The promotional text should be brief but prominent; it is a visual analogy to a sound bite.

3. Press [Ctrl][A], click the Font list arrow on the Formatting toolbar, scroll if necessary and click Arial Narrow, click the Font Size list arrow on the Formatting toolbar, click 18, click the Bold button 🔲, click the Center button 🔲, then press [Esc]

   Compare your screen to Figure H-9.

QUICK TIP

You can drag the text box into different positions and use the green rotation handle to fine-tune the positioning.

4. Right-click the text box, click Format Text Box, click the Size tab, make sure that the height of the box is 0.5" and the width is 2.5", select the contents of the Rotation text box, type –20, then click OK

   The text box is rotated –20°.

5. Click the Fill Color list arrow 🔲 on the Formatting toolbar, then click the Accent 2 (RGB (184, 219, 77)) color box

   This text is more noticeable with the added fill color.

6. Press [F9], click the text box at 5" H / 6½" V, click Arrange on the menu bar, point to Rotate or Flip, then click Rotate Left 90°

   The return address is now correctly placed and oriented for printing.

7. Click 🔲, then drag ╋ from 4½" H / 3" V to 7" H / 4½" V, click Arrange on the menu bar, point to Rotate or Flip, then click Rotate Left 90°

   Compare your work to Figure H-10.

8. Click the Save button 🔲 on the Standard toolbar

FIGURE H-9: Completed text in text box

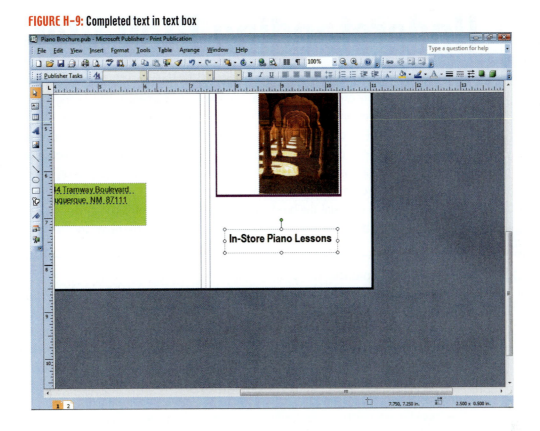

FIGURE H-10: Rotated text boxes

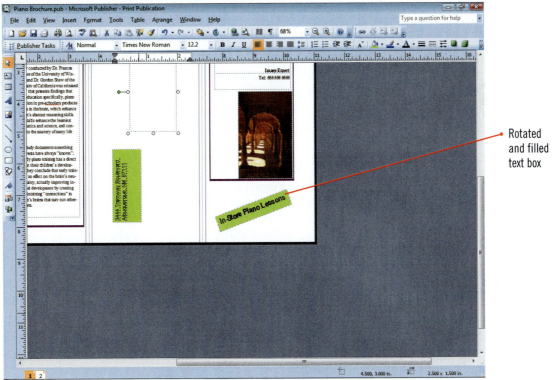

Rotated
and filled
text box

Understanding Mail Merge

A **mail merge** blends a publication that contains generic information with a data source that contains unique pieces of information. For example, a gift certificate could contain generic text regarding the store's location and details about the gift, and unique text, such as the first and last names of each recipient. The unique text comes from a data source. In Publisher, this feature is called **mail merge**. In a mail merge, two documents are combined, resulting in a set of customized versions of the publication. Figure H-11 shows an overview of a mail merge. Types of publications that can be customized include sales literature, postcards, greeting and invitation cards, catalogs, award certificates, gift certificates, and labels. You know that once the publication is complete, Piano Bravo will want the brochure personalized with information it has collected about potential customers. Before you begin the mail merge process, you consider all the necessary steps.

DETAILS

QUICK TIP

You can use the following Microsoft products to create a source: Publisher, Excel, Access, or Outlook.

- ### Select the recipients

    A **data source** is a file that contains information about the recipients. It is made up of fields organized into records. A **field** is a category of information—such as last name, first name, address, state, or zip code. A **record** is a set of information about an individual or an item—for example, a person's complete address. **Data source files** can come from several programs, but you will most likely use a database, a spreadsheet, a Microsoft Outlook contact list, or a table from a word processing program.

    If you don't have a data source file from another program, or prefer to create a new one, you can create one using Publisher. The Mail Merge task pane guides you through the main steps: creating or connecting to a recipient list, creating the merged publication, and preparing the merged publication. The Mail Merge task pane offers choices as to the type of information you can collect for the data source file, and even lets you add your own fields. Some commonly used mail merge information fields are address, city, zip code, country, e-mail address, and home phone. The Catalog Merge command makes it possible to quickly create directories and product catalogs by automatically filling pages with text and images from a product database or list. A product list is merged into a desired format in a three-step process. To begin, click Tools on the menu bar, point to Mailings and Catalogs, then click Catalog Merge.

- ### Create the publication

    A Publisher publication contains the generic information that appears in every merged publication. In the mail merge process, you insert a text box or a table frame that will contain the merge fields, where the unique information about the recipient is placed inside the publication. For example, you can insert the person's name in the Greeting line so that it will read "Dear John Smith." With the Mail Merge task pane, it is easy to go back and edit the fields until you get exactly the publication you want.

- ### Consider Options

    Using the mail merge capabilities, you can filter and sort a subset of records. **Filtering** allows you to print, preview, or merge a portion of qualifying records. **Sorting** allows you to change the order in which the merged publications are printed or viewed. You can sort and filter records using the Mail Merge Recipients dialog box.

- ### Preview the publications

    The ability to preview the merged publications allows you to look over the output before it is printed to catch any mistakes without wasting paper. This is particularly important since printing and mailing publications can be expensive. Paper, inks, envelopes, and even bulk postal rates are costly. Assuming all your merge fields are correct, there are a variety of ways you can preview your work without printing: Using the Preview window in the Insert Address Block dialog box, the Preview recipient area of the Mail Merge task pane, the Print Preview link in the Mail Merge task pane, once you've created merged publications, or the Preview window in the Print dialog box.

- ### Print the publication

    Publisher's Mail Merge task pane uses dialog boxes to guide you through printing your publications.

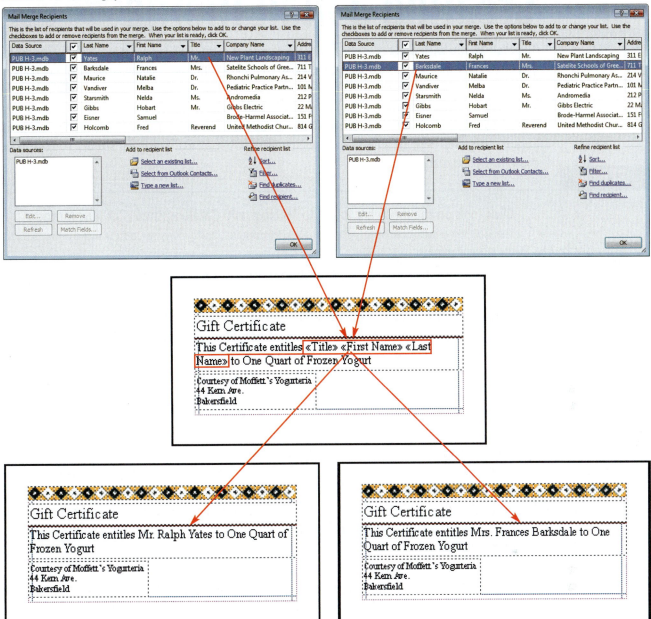

Design Matters

Catching costly errors

There are several types of spelling errors that demand your attention. The most obvious is the danger of misspelled words in a publication. Such errors make your company seem unprofessional. Another important spelling error is the misspelling of a person's name. Errors in people's names and titles can offend them. A simple misspelling or a misuse of Mrs. or Ms. may annoy potential clients to the point that they will not do business with your company. When in doubt, find a way to verify a potential misspelling: it pays off. Bulk mailings are often a one-way communication and you may never know that a recipient was offended.

Creating a Mail Merge

The **Mail Merge task pane** is an effective tool for creating personalized publications. This feature guides you through the merging process and allows you to customize both your data source and your publication. It unites the power of the database and the functionality of the desktop publishing program. 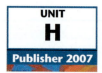 Emma Rose, your contact at Piano Bravo, has provided you with a data source containing a small group of customers. You want to test the merge on this smaller group before creating a merge document for their entire customer base. You want the merged address information to appear in the recipient text box you created in the middle panel of the second page.

STEPS

1. **Click Tools on the menu bar, point to Mailings and Catalogs, then click Mail Merge**

   The Mail Merge task pane opens, displaying a brief introduction to merging, and the first in three steps in the merging process.

2. **Make sure the Use an existing list option button is selected, then click Next: Create or connect to a recipient list**

3. **Navigate to the drive and folder where you store your Data Files, click Pub H-3.mdb, click Open in the Select Data Source dialog box, then click OK in the Mail Merge Recipients dialog box**

QUICK TIP

Clicking the address block link ensures that the address information is correctly placed when the merged publication is generated.

4. **Click the text box at 5½" H / 4" V to select it, if necessary, click the Address block link on the Mail Merge task pane, adjust the settings in the Insert Address Block dialog box so they match the settings shown in Figure H-12, then click OK**

   The Insert Address Block dialog box provides a wide variety of ways to insert the recipient's name in the address block, and shows a preview of how it will look. On your screen, the address block field appears in the text box. It is difficult to read on the screen because it is rotated 90 degrees, but when the publications are printed and folded, the recipient's address will be in just the right spot for mailing.

TROUBLE

If you added extra spaces to either the Title or Name fields, the spaces will appear in the text box, and your name and title will be shown with the extra spaces.

5. **Click Edit recipient list in the Mail Merge task pane, click the first entry in the Mail Merge Recipients dialog box if necessary, click PUB H-3.mdb in the Data sources box, then click Edit**

   Compare your screen to Figure H-13.

6. **Replace the first three fields in this record with your preferred title and your first and last names, click OK, click Yes to save your changes, then click OK to close the Mail Merge Recipients dialog box**

   Your name and title appear in the text box on the brochure. Compare your screen to Figure H-14.

TROUBLE

If you find any mistakes in the mail merge, use the link to the Previous task pane to go back and correct the mistakes. If necessary, print the pages again using the Test button.

7. **Click Next: Create merged publications at the bottom of the Mail Merge task pane, click Print in the Mail Merge task pane, make sure that the correct printer is selected, then click Test in the Print dialog box**

   Examine your publication.

8. **Click Cancel to close the Print dialog box, click the Close button on the Mail Merge task pane, then click the Save button 🖫 on the Standard toolbar**

FIGURE H-12: Insert Address Block dialog box

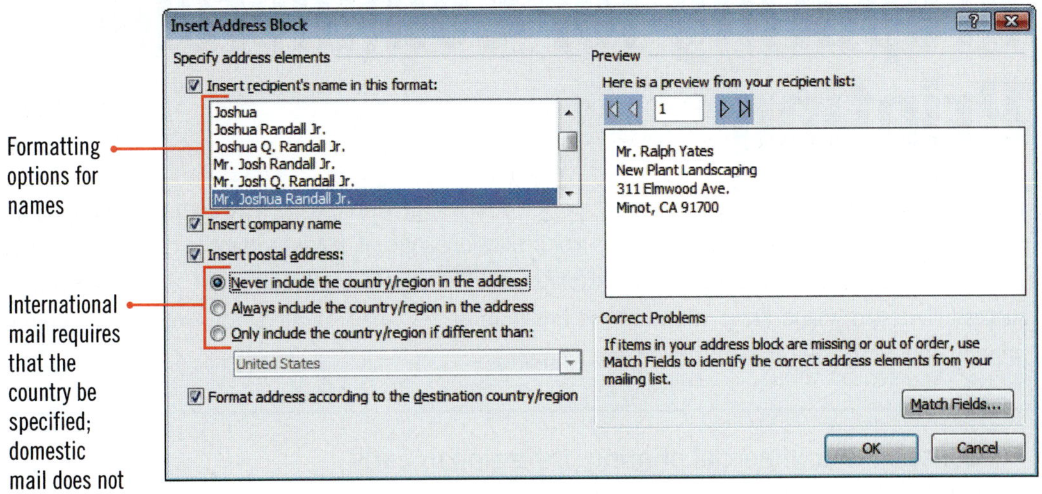

Formatting options for names

International mail requires that the country be specified; domestic mail does not

FIGURE H-13: Edit Data Source dialog box

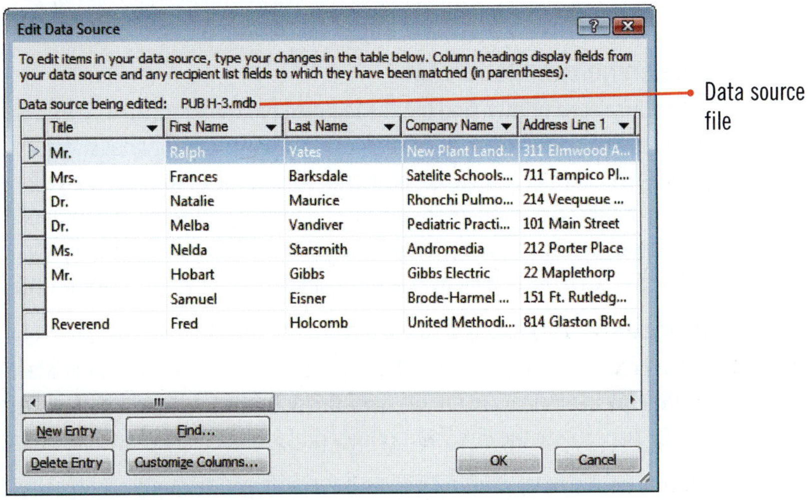

Data source file

FIGURE H-14: Preview of the Mail Merge

Move back and forth between task panes

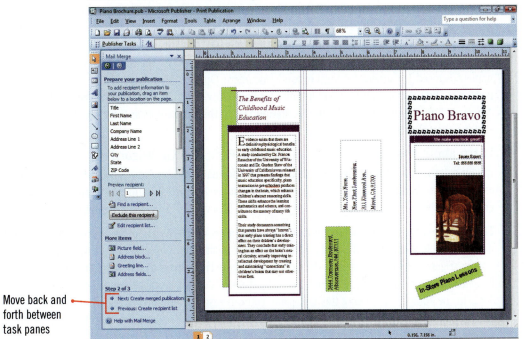

Preparing for Commercial Printing

Once your publication is completed, you can print it yourself, or send the files to a commercial printer for bulk printing with high-quality options and results. For professional output, it is important to consult with the printer during the design process to save time and expense.  You know that once the project is complete and successfully tested, Piano Bravo will want the brochure professionally printed. You examine the commercial printing options so you can start making arrangements.

- ### Consult the commercial printing professionals early

  Cost is important. You will need to know about quantity, quality, paper stock, binding, folding, trimming, and deadlines so that you can determine a budget and schedule. Ask your printer for recommendations on ways to reduce costs. For example, updating your graphics by doing your own scanning, or creating your own art files instead of relying on the printer's art services may reduce expenses.

- ### Determine the file format

  Once you select a printer, find out the required hand-off format. The **hand-off format** is the final format the printer receives. Publisher can create files in the PostScript or Publisher formats. You can also prepare your files in the CMYK format (composite postscript files in the cyan-magenta-yellow-black format), which many commercial printers prefer. There are advantages to using the Publisher format, but this option may also limit your commercial printing options. You also need to know if your printer prefers to accept transferred files on disks, flash drives, CDs, by e-mail, by posting to an ftp site, or through some other means.

- ### Explore the PostScript file format

  If your commercial printer doesn't accept Publisher files, or uses only Macintosh computers, you can use the **PostScript** file format. To do this, **you must install a PostScript printer on your computer,** then follow the steps to use the PostScript printer driver. Figure H-15 shows the Save As PostScript dialog box.

  Ask your commercial printing service if it wants you to apply any specific print settings, then save the publication in the PostScript format. Be aware that these files can become quite large. Try saving to your hard drive, then copying to a large capacity media, such as a thumb drive.

  Your printer may ask you for a CMYK PostScript file. CMYK, which stands for Cyan Magenta Yellow Black, is a color model used by many commercial printers. You can save a composite CMYK PostScript file by clicking Save As on the File menu, supplying a name for the file, clicking the Save as type list arrow, clicking PostScript, then clicking Save. Click the Properties button, then click the Advanced button. Under printer name Advanced Document Settings, expand Document Options, then expand PostScript Options. In the PostScript Output Option list, select Optimize for Portability, then click OK. On the Printer Details tab, click Advanced Printer Setup, then click the Separation tab. In the Print colors as list, click one of the composite options, then click OK.

- ### Learn about the Publisher format and the Pack and Go Wizard

  If your commercial printing service accepts Publisher format hand-off files, you can take advantage of several important features. The Publisher format is accessible with the Pack and Go Wizard, and verifies linked graphics, embeds TrueType fonts, and will pack all the files your printing service might need.

  The printing service can use Publisher format to do **pre-press work**. As part of this process, the printer can verify the availability of fonts and linked graphics, make color corrections or separations, and set the final printing options. Figure H-16 shows the Fonts dialog box, and Figure H-17 shows the Graphics Manager task pane. (The Graphics Manager is accessed in the Tools menu; the Fonts dialog box is available as part of Commercial Printing Tools in the Tools menu.) Using this task pane, you can easily determine the names, file types, and sizes of graphic objects in a publication. Each of these features gives your printing service important information about elements that make up your publication, and any potential problems.

FIGURE H-15: Save As PostScript dialog box

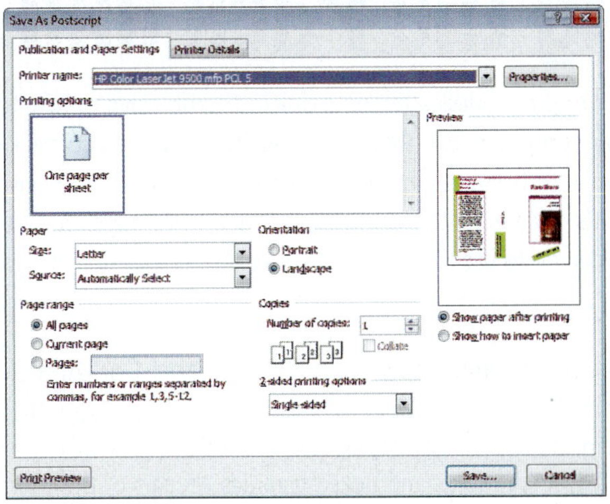

FIGURE H-16: Fonts dialog box

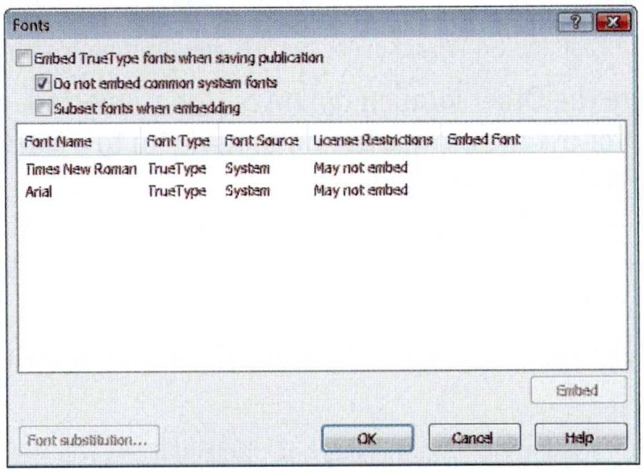

FIGURE H-17: Graphics Manager task pane

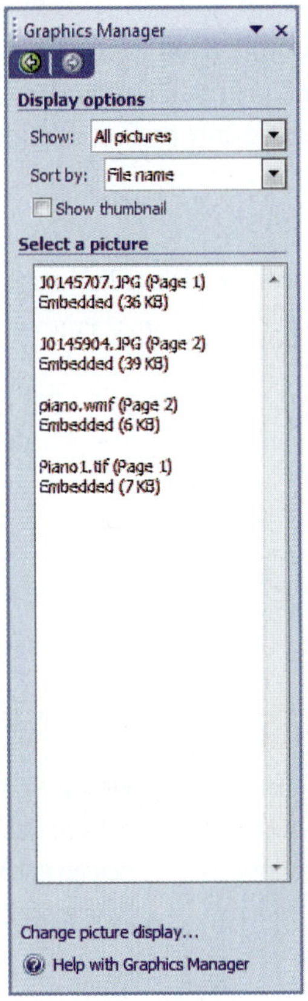

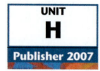

Using the Pack and Go Wizard

You may need to put a publication on a disk or thumb drive to take to a commercial printing service, or to use at another computer. The **Pack and Go Wizard** lets you package all the fonts and graphic images needed to work with your publication elsewhere. You have arranged to have the Piano Bravo brochure printed by a commercial printing service. They have requested that you provide the file on a flash drive, so you decide to use the Pack and Go Wizard to transfer the publication.

1. **Click File on the menu bar, point to Pack and Go, then click Take to Another Computer**
   The Pack and Go Wizard dialog box opens, as shown in Figure H-18. The first Pack and Go Wizard dialog box explains the advantages of using the wizard. The items included in the packaged publication file include embedded TrueType fonts and linked graphics. As part of the packing process, the wizard also prints the publication.

2. **Click Next**
   The second Pack and Go Wizard dialog box lets you determine where you want the packaged files.

3. **Make sure the Other location option button is selected, insert a flash drive in an empty USB port or use the Browse button to navigate to a location where you want to store this file, click OK, then click Next**
   The third Pack and Go Wizard dialog box lets you decide what attributes to include, as shown in Figure H-19. You can embed TrueType fonts, include linked graphics, and create links for embedded graphics, or you can deselect any of these options, if necessary.

4. **Click any unselected checkboxes in the third Pack and Go Wizard dialog box**

5. **Click Next**
   The fourth Pack and Go Wizard dialog box displays. It lets you know the options you've selected, and the file-naming scheme it will use.

6. **Click Finish**
   As the Pack and Go Wizard works, you'll see that as the files are completed, several processes take place. The files are compressed and your publication (Piano Brochure.pub) is saved as Piano Brochure.zip. Once the publication has been successfully packed, the final Pack and Go Wizard dialog box opens, as shown in Figure H-20.

7. **Click OK**
   As part of the packaging process, the Wizard prints the publication.

8. **Click File on the menu bar, then click Exit**

Creating an E-mail Merge

When you send a lot of e-mail messages that are nearly all identical, but contain some unique information, you can use the E-Mail Merge feature to create individually customized messages that contain personalized notes. You use this feature by creating or connecting to a recipient list, preparing a publication, then creating the merged publication. When you prepare the publication, you create the text that you want in every version of the message. When you create the merged publication, you can preview the individual messages and make specific changes.

FIGURE H-18: First Pack and Go Wizard dialog box

Pack and Go Wizard

Pack your files to take to another computer

The wizard will prepare your publication to take to another computer.
You can use the wizard to:

Embed fonts.
Include linked graphics.

< Back   Next >   Cancel   Finish

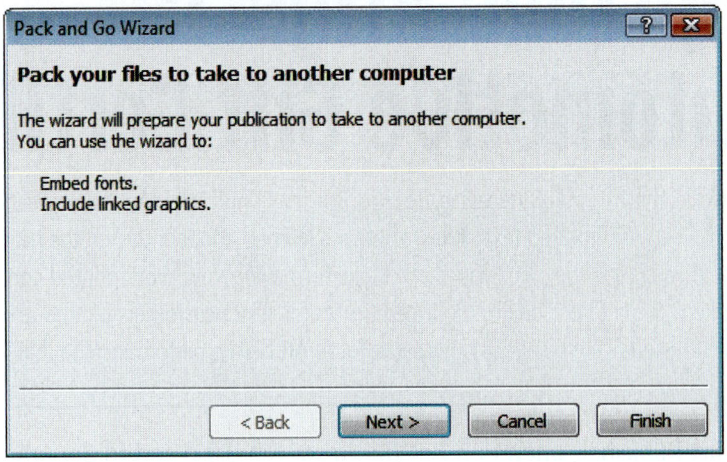

FIGURE H-19: Third Pack and Go Wizard dialog box

Pack and Go Wizard

Include fonts and graphics

Pack and Go can include linked graphics and fonts used in your publication.

If you're taking the files to a commercial printing service, the wizard can also create links for graphics you've embedded.

☐ Embed TrueType fonts

☑ Include linked graphics

☐ Create links for embedded graphics

< Back   Next >   Cancel   Finish

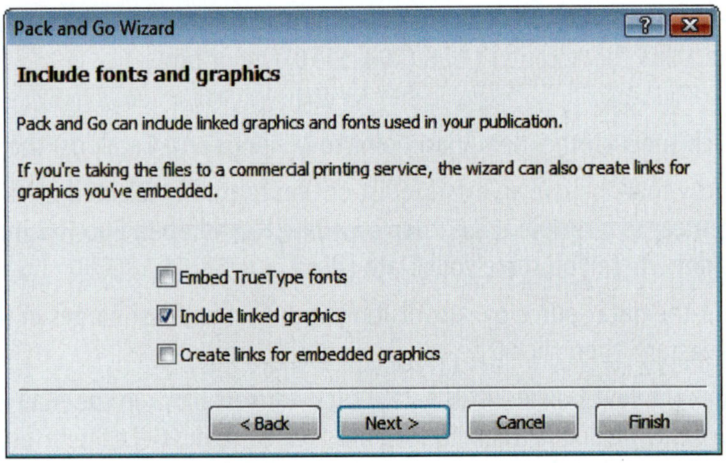

FIGURE H-20: Final Pack and Go Wizard dialog box

Pack and Go Wizard

Your publication is successfully packed

The wizard copied your packed file into the directory you selected.

If you make changes to your publication, use the Pack and Go Wizard again.

OK

Capstone Project: Automotive Gift Certificate

You have learned the skills necessary to add BorderArt and WordArt to publications. You have wrapped text around objects and rotated text boxes. You have learned about and used the Mail Merge feature and the Pack and Go Wizard, and the steps you should take for having your work printed commercially. You have been asked to create personalized gift certificates for select customers of an automotive service. You decide to enhance the certificate by adding thematic BorderArt before performing the mail merge.

1. Start Publisher, open Pub H-4.pub from the drive and folder where you store your Data Files, then save it as Automotive Gift Certificate

2. Type a new expiration date in the "Expires:" text box, right-click the text box whose top-left corner is at 4½" H / 1½" V, click Format Text Box, click the BorderArt button, then click the Coupon Cutout Dashes option

3. Click the Always apply at default size check box to deselect it, click OK, change the Line weight to 11 pt, click OK, click the Line Color list arrow 🖌▾ on the Formatting toolbar, then click the Accent 1 (RGB (204, 51, 0)) color box

   The BorderArt pattern appears on the edge of the text box, as shown in Figure H-21.

4. Click Tools on the menu bar, point to Mailings and Catalogs, then click Mail Merge

5. Verify that the Use an existing list option button is selected, click Next: Create or connect to a recipient list, then navigate to and open Pub H-3.mdb from the drive and folder where you store your Data Files.

6. Edit the data source by substituting your first and last names in the first record if necessary, then click OK

7. Click the text box at 2½" H / 2" V, click Address block in the Mail Merge task pane, make sure the 'Joshua Randall Jr.' format is selected, deselect the Insert company name, and Insert postal address check boxes, then click OK

8. Click Next: Create merged publications in the task pane

9. Click Print in the Create merged publications section of the task pane, make sure that the correct printer is selected, then click Test

   Compare your publication to Figure H-22.

10. Click Cancel, close the task pane, click the Save button 🖫 on the Standard toolbar, then exit Publisher

FIGURE H-21: BorderArt applied to text box

FIGURE H-22: Test publication

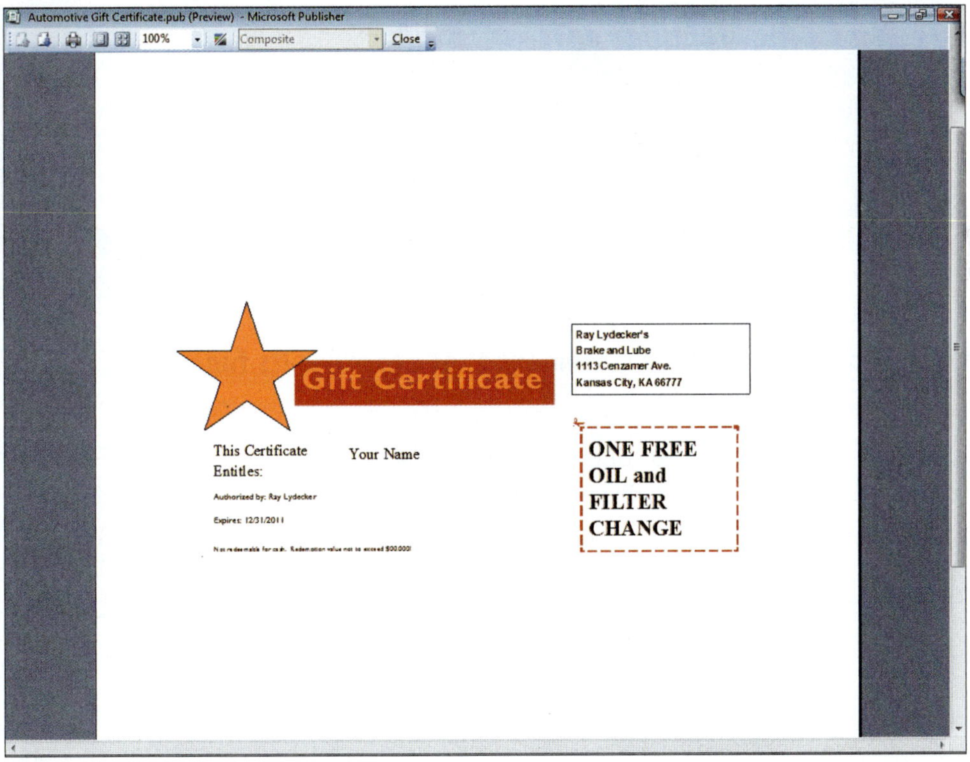

Practice

▼ CONCEPTS REVIEW

Label each of the elements in the Publisher window shown in Figure H-23.

FIGURE H-23

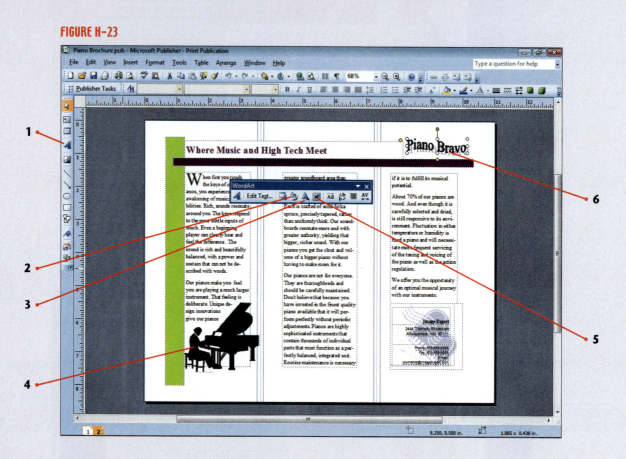

Match each of the buttons with the statement that describes its function.

7.
8.
9.
10.
11.
12.

a. Displays WordArt Gallery
b. Displays WordArt shapes
c. Formats WordArt
d. Edits wrap points
e. Changes line color
f. Inserts WordArt

Select the best answer from the list of choices.

13. **Which feature blends two information sources together?**
    - **a.** File Blender
    - **b.** Mail Marriage
    - **c.** Mail Merge
    - **d.** WordArt

14. **A file that contains information about the recipients of a mail merge is called a:**
    - **a.** Field.
    - **b.** Record.
    - **c.** Data source.
    - **d.** Blend source.

15. **Which button is used to insert WordArt?**

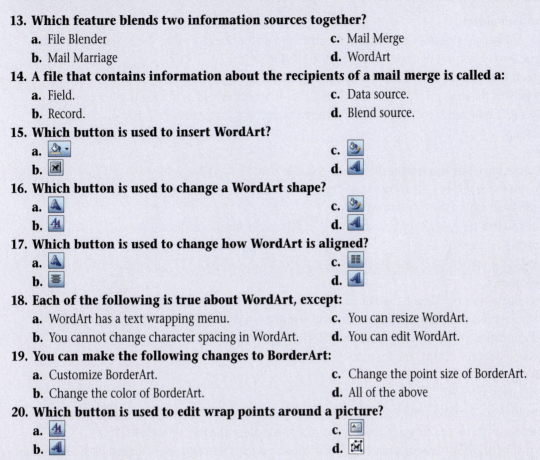

16. **Which button is used to change a WordArt shape?**

17. **Which button is used to change how WordArt is aligned?**

18. **Each of the following is true about WordArt, except:**
    - **a.** WordArt has a text wrapping menu.
    - **b.** You cannot change character spacing in WordArt.
    - **c.** You can resize WordArt.
    - **d.** You can edit WordArt.

19. **You can make the following changes to BorderArt:**
    - **a.** Customize BorderArt.
    - **b.** Change the color of BorderArt.
    - **c.** Change the point size of BorderArt.
    - **d.** All of the above

20. **Which button is used to edit wrap points around a picture?**

▼ SKILLS REVIEW

Throughout these exercises, use the Zoom feature where necessary to work with the publication more easily.

1. **Add BorderArt.**
   - **a.** Start Publisher.
   - **b.** Open PUB H-5.pub from the drive and folder where you store your Data Files, then save it as **Gym Flyer**.
   - **c.** Right-click the blue text box at 1" H / 2" V, click Format Text Box, then click BorderArt.
   - **d.** Scroll through the list of available borders, then click Hearts.
   - **e.** Click the Always apply at default size check box to deselect it, then click OK.
   - **f.** Change the line weight to 15 pt, then click OK.
   - **g.** Save your work.

2. **Design WordArt.**
   - **a.** Click the Insert WordArt button on the Objects toolbar, then click the second box in the second row of the WordArt Gallery.
   - **b.** Click OK, type **We Want You Back!** in the Text text box.
   - **c.** Change the font size to 36 if necessary, make the text bold, then click OK.
   - **d.** Reposition the WordArt so that its top-left corner is at 2" H / 1½" V.
   - **e.** Apply the Double Wave 1 WordArt shape (the seventh shape in the third row).
   - **f.** Add the Accent 2 (Gold) fill color to the WordArt.
   - **g.** Save your work.

3. Wrap text around an object.

   a. Create an AutoShape using the Heart shape (first column, sixth row) on the Objects toolbar. The top-left corner of the heart should be at 1½" H / 5" V, and its dimensions should be 2½" H × 2½" V.

   b. Click Arrange on the menu bar, point to Text Wrapping, then click Edit Wrap Points.

   c. Experiment by moving the wrap points to alter the shape of the wrapped text, then click the Undo button.

   d. Use the Fill Color list arrow and More Fill Colors to fill the heart with any shade of red you choose.

   e. Save the publication.

4. Rotate a text box.

   a. Draw a new text box anywhere that has the dimensions 1¾" H × ½" V.

   b. Type **We Miss You** in the text box, then change the font size to 20.

   c. Click the Bring to Front button on the Standard toolbar.

   d. Place the text box so that the top-left corner is at 1¾" H / 5¾" V (superimposed over the heart).

   e. Rotate the text box 25 degrees.

   f. Save your work.

5. Understand mail merge.

   a. Imagine that you are the owner of a health club. You are always looking for ways to communicate more effectively with your customers and your distributors. Given these goals, what kind of mail merge documents might you want to create?

   b. What types of information might be in the data source files for your company?

   c. What programs would you be likely to use to create these data source files?

6. Create a Mail Merge.

   a. Display the Mail Merge task pane.

   b. Select PUB H-3.mdb from the drive and folder where you store your Data Files as the data source, confirm that your first and last names and preferred title are in the first record, or make these changes, then click OK.

   c. Click the text box at 1½" H / 3" V to select it, press [F9], put the insertion point at the beginning of the text, then use the Insert Address Block dialog box to choose the Joshua Randall Jr. format and also to choose to never include the country region. (Deselect the Insert company name and Insert postal address check boxes.)

   d. Click Next: Create merged publications.

   e. Click Print in the Create merged publications section of the task pane, make sure that the correct printer is selected, then print a test. Click Cancel in the Print dialog box.

   f. Save your work.

7. Prepare for commercial printing.

   a. Use the Web and your favorite search engine to research commercial printers and their requirements. Print at least one page that you find for a commercial printer.

   b. Make a list of requirements/suggestions from a commercial printer, or underline/highlight them on the Web page you printed.

8. Use the Pack and Go Wizard.

   a. Open the Pack and Go Wizard to take files to a commercial printing service.

   b. Use a blank flash drive, thumb drive, or other blank removable device, if necessary.

   c. Answer **Next** to each of the Wizard dialog boxes, then click Finish in the last dialog box.

   d. Close the publication.

   e. Exit Publisher.

▼ INDEPENDENT CHALLENGE 1

As office manager for your company, you decide to make customized monthly calendars for the employees.

a. Start Publisher and use the Publication Types list to create a calendar using the Layers design.

b. Use the Business Information set of your choice to add appropriate information, and the color scheme of your choice.

c. Save the publication as **Monthly Calendar** to the drive and folder where you store your Data Files.

d. Add BorderArt of your choice, sized to 16 pt around the text box containing the month and year.

e. Use the WordArt feature to create vertical text that reads **Go Team**. (*Hint*: The right side of the WordArt Gallery contains several vertical text templates.) Change the font size to 40 pt.

f. Superimpose the WordArt over the filled text box to the left of the calendar.

g. Modify the fill color of the WordArt to Accent 1.

h. Type your name in the text box located at 2" H / 1½" V.

i. Delete the organization /logo placeholder if necssary, save and print the publication, then exit Publisher.

▼ INDEPENDENT CHALLENGE 2

The Believe It or Not Bookstore asks you to design a postcard announcing an upcoming book-signing event.

a. Start Publisher and use the Publication Types list to create a schedule using the Schedule template in the Event Postcards section of the Publication Types list.

b. Use the Business Information set of your choice to add appropriate information, and the color scheme of your choice.

c. Save the publication as **Believe It or Not Postcard** to the drive and folder where you store your Data Files.

d. Add BorderArt around the Activities text box.

e. Modify the text at 2" H / 2" V with your own text.

f. Delete the object at 1" H / 1¾" V.

g. Delete the contents of the Activities text box.

h. Write appropriate text in the text box and add an image.

i. Add your name as the contact person.

j. Change any text as necessary to fit the theme of a book signing at the Believe It or Not Bookstore. Make up a suitable event title.

▼ INDEPENDENT CHALLENGE 2 (CONTINUED)

Advanced Challenge Exercises

- ■ Edit the image in the center panel so it has multiple handles. (You can add wrap points if you choose.)
- ■ Move the object to illustrate the effect of the multiple handles. Compare your publication to Figure H-24.

k. Save and print the publication, then exit Publisher.

FIGURE H-24

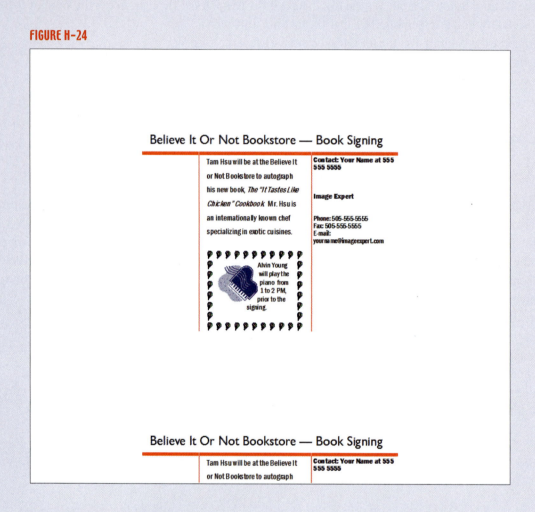

▼ INDEPENDENT CHALLENGE 3

Your Publisher skills convince you that you can open your own design shop, Design Center. First, you'll need business cards. You will use mail merge to personalize the cards for your employees and yourself.

a. Start Publisher, then choose a design in the Blank Sizes Business Cards category of the Publication Types list.

b. Use the Business Information set of your choice to add appropriate information, and add any color scheme you like.

c. Save the publication as **Design Center Business Card** to the drive and folder where you store your Data Files.

d. Open the Mail Merge task pane, then select PUB H-3.mdb from the drive and folder where you store your Data Files as the data source.

e. Insert fields for your first and last name where you want them to appear on your business card, and add a logo, title, and business name.

f. Preview the business card to make sure that your name appears. Make any necessary corrections.

g. Use the Print dialog box to test print your business card.

h. Save the publication and exit Publisher.

▼ REAL LIFE INDEPENDENT CHALLENGE

A friend is celebrating her five-year wedding anniversary and has asked you to create the cover of her anniversary party invitations. To do this, you'll use a Publisher template and BorderArt.

a. Start Publisher, then choose a template design in the Invitation Cards category of the Publication Types list.

b. Use the Business Information Set of your choice to add appropriate information, and use any color scheme.

c. Save the publication as **Wedding Anniversary Invitation**.

d. Add attractive BorderArt to a text box on the cover of the invitation using any available style and size.

e. Create appropriate text for the cover, using your own name in the text. (You will add your friend's name once she approves the invitation.)

Advanced Challenge Exercises

- Change the BorderArt to a custom border using a piece of clip art.
- Add the same piece of clip art to the cover of the invitation.
- Recolor the clip art. (*Hint*: Right-click the object, then click Format Picture.) Compare your publication to Figure H-25.

f. Save your work and print the publication, then exit Publisher.

FIGURE H-25

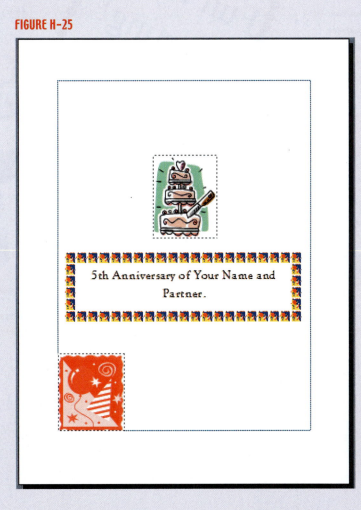

5th Anniversary of Your Name and Partner.

Use the Publication Types list to create an Accessory Bar Informational Brochure as the initial design of a brochure for Rif's Toy Shop. Save this publication as **Toy Shop Brochure** to the drive and folder where you store your Data Files. Use Figure H-26 as a guide. The BorderArt around the text box at 9" H / 1½" V has a zigzag pattern. The style for the "Specializing In Model Airplanes" text comes from the WordArt Gallery—experiment to find the right style. Replace the email address with your email address. Save and print the first page.

FIGURE H-26

Working Efficiently

Files You Will Need

PUB I-1.docx
PUB I-2.pub
PUB I-3.pub
PUB I-4.docx
PUB I-5.pub
PUB I-6.pub
PUB I-7.pub
PUB I-8.docx
PUB I-9.docx

Both choosing the right tool for the right job and choosing to do tasks in the best order help you to increase your effectiveness. Understanding how to integrate Publisher with other Office programs and peripheral devices means that you can join their strengths and work around their limitations. Learning how to use additional features, such as AutoCorrect and Speech Recognition, can speed up your work. AutoCorrect automatically fixes your typing errors as you type. Speech recognition software lets you create text and initiate commands vocally. Image Expert is holding a two-day computer-training course for its employees. The goals of the training sessions are to introduce the employees to efficient methods of working with Publisher and other Microsoft applications, as well as to use peripheral devices to enhance and speed up their work. You have been asked to organize and create course materials for this event.

OBJECTIVES

Integrate with Office programs

Import a Word document

Use AutoCorrect

Use digital images

Embed and link objects

Use Design Checker

Understand speech recognition

Capstone Project: Dinner Invitation

Integrating with Office Programs

All Microsoft Office programs are designed to work together. Because the Office programs have a similar look and feel, your familiarity with one program can make it easier to use others. Another advantage of using Office programs is that you can easily transfer information or objects created in one program to another. One of the goals of the training course is to familiarize employees with business productivity software, and advise them on which programs are best suited to individual jobs. To make the training interactive, you decide to ask co-workers familiar with specific programs to speak about how they use them at Image Expert.

DETAILS

- ### Microsoft Word

  Almost everyone at Image Magic uses Word, a **word processing** program, to create letters, memos, reports, and stories. But not everyone is as familiar with Publisher as you are. You plan to educate employees about how they can import a Word document, such as the one shown in Figure I-1, into a publication, in order to take advantage of some features in Word, such as grammar checking and word count, which aren't available in Publisher.

- ### Microsoft Excel

  Many employees use Excel, an **electronic spreadsheet** program that automatically calculates and analyzes data and creates powerful charts. A **chart** is a graphical representation of data. Ricardo Fernandez, Image Expert's office manager, uses Excel to create budgets and financial statements, and to track customer billing and invoices. Figure I-2 shows an Excel worksheet with data and a chart. This chart is also shown in Figure I-3, after it was pasted into a publication in Publisher.

- ### Microsoft PowerPoint

  When they need to present information to a group of people, employees create professional visual presentations using PowerPoint. A **presentation** is a series of projected slides and/or handouts that a speaker refers to while delivering information. Together, Publisher and PowerPoint can make for an impressive and cohesive presentation using a slide show from PowerPoint and supporting documents from Publisher, which share similar fonts and colors. Maria Abbot, Image Expert's president, will use PowerPoint to create a slide show summarizing the company's growth and financial performance; she will give the presentation during the training session, and later at an annual meeting of investors, creditors, and clients.

- ### Microsoft Access

  Complex data can be organized, tracked, and updated using an Access database. A **database** is a collection of related information that is organized into tables, records, and fields. Information in a database can be sorted and retrieved in a variety of ways, and then used to make business decisions. Access databases can be used as a data source for Publisher mail merges. Nancy Garrott, Image Expert's marketing manager, uses Access to create and maintain a customer information database. She shares this information with the accounting department so it does not have to re-enter information about new customers and sales.

- ### Microsoft Outlook

  All employees use the Outlook **personal information manager** to keep track of business and personal contacts and to schedule appointments. Outlook contact lists can be used as data sources for mail merges in Publisher.

- ### Office tools

  All Office programs include **online collaboration**, the ability to share information over the Internet. Employees can schedule online meetings and have discussions over the World Wide Web. **Speech Recognition** lets them enter data and give commands verbally using a computer microphone. You can use the Research task pane to reference online information from reference sources such as the Encarta Dictionary, Thesaurus, eLibrary, Factiva Search, and MSN Search.

FIGURE I-1: Word document

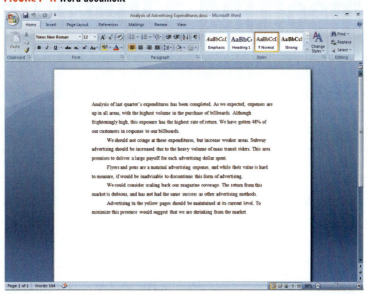

FIGURE I-2: Excel worksheet containing a chart

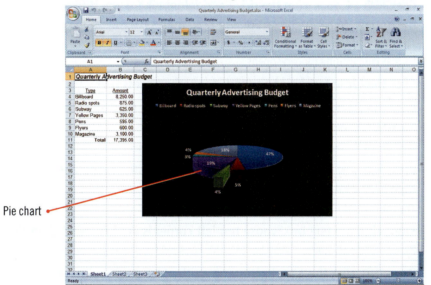

Pie chart

FIGURE I-3: Excel chart and Word story in publication

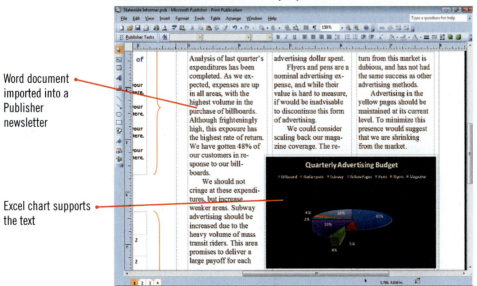

Word document imported into a Publisher newsletter

Excel chart supports the text

Importing a Word Document

You have already imported Word documents into text boxes. You have also edited a Publisher story in Word and returned it to Publisher. Publisher also lets you import Word documents directly into a publication, where you can automatically add design elements to ensure that all of your documents have similar designs and maintain the same look and feel. It also provides an easy way to enhance an unformatted Word document. You want to include a book review in the pre-course materials. This publication will be distributed one week before the training session and will be designed to raise questions about job effectiveness and to spark discussion.

STEPS

TROUBLE
If you get a warning box that you need a converter, contact your instructor or technical support person.

1. **Start Publisher, click Import Word Documents from the Publication Types list, then click Linear Accent**

2. **Click the Columns list arrow, click the 2 button, click the Color scheme list arrow, click Wildflower, as shown in Figure I-4, then click Create**
   The Import Word Document dialog box opens.

3. **Navigate to the location where you store your Data Files, as shown in Figure I-5**

4. **Click PUB I-1.docx from the drive and folder where you store your Data Files, click OK in the Import Word Document dialog box, then save the publication as Book Review**
   The Word document is imported into a Publisher text box and the Word Import Options section of the Format Publication task pane opens.

5. **Click the Close button on the task pane, then press [F9]**

6. **Click the Document Title placeholder text, then type Sources of Power: How People Make Decisions**
   The title of the book review is inserted, but it looks too small.

7. **Press [Ctrl][A] to select the text, click Format on the menu bar, point to AutoFit Text, then click Best Fit**
   The font size of the title is now larger.

8. **Right-click the text box whose top-left corner is at 1" H / ½" V, then click Delete Object**
   Page numbers are not necessary because this is a single-page publication. Compare your page to Figure 1-6.

9. **Press [F9], click the Save button 🖫 on the Standard toolbar, then close the publication**

FIGURE I-4: Import Word Documents window

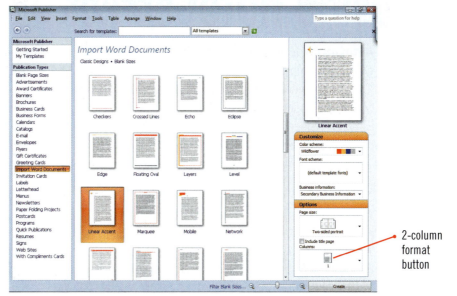

2-column format button

FIGURE I-5: Import Word Document dialog box

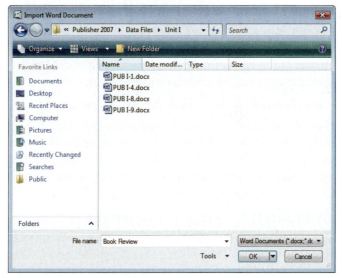

FIGURE I-6: Imported Word document

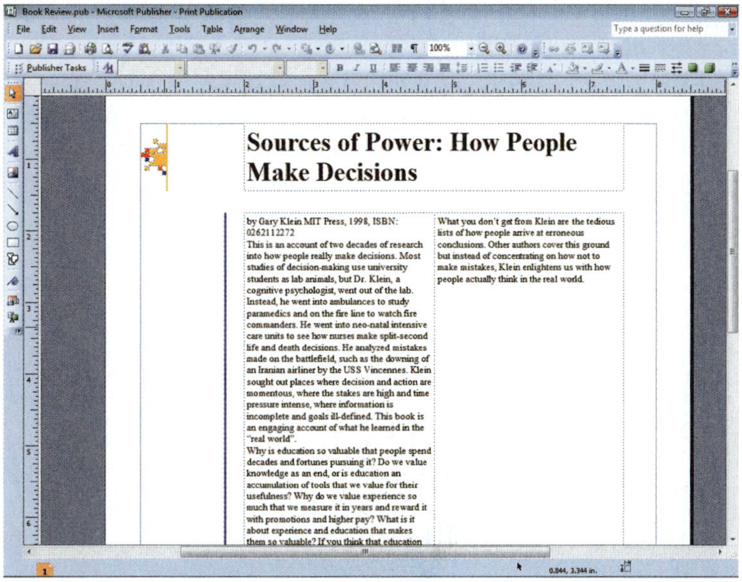

Using AutoCorrect

The **AutoCorrect** feature can detect and correct misspelled words, typos, and other common errors as you type. For example, if you type "yuo" followed by a space, AutoCorrect replaces the incorrect word with "you." In addition, AutoCorrect lets you quickly insert text, graphics, or symbols. For example, you can type "(tm)" to insert "(tm)", or customize AutoCorrect to automatically replace abbreviations such as "potus" with President of the United States. You want to change the AutoCorrect settings to speed up your work and help avoid spelling errors as you generate training materials for the course. You review how AutoCorrect works and how it can be modified.

DETAILS

- ### Add to or change AutoCorrect entries

  AutoCorrect uses AutoCorrect entries, a list of commonly misspelled words and typos, to detect misusages and automatically correct them. It also contains some common symbols, such as ©, that can be substituted for specific keystrokes. You can easily add your own custom AutoCorrect entries or remove unwanted ones by clicking Tools on the menu bar, then clicking AutoCorrect Options. You can make additions or changes to AutoCorrect in the AutoCorrect: English (United States) dialog box. You can add an entry to AutoCorrect by typing the text you want replaced in the Replace text box, and the text that will replace it in the With text box. Once you create your entry, click Add, and the new AutoCorrect entry will be in effect. Figure I-7 shows a new entry added to AutoCorrect. You can delete an AutoCorrect entry by clicking the entry you want to delete, then clicking Delete. You can also use AutoCorrect to format as you type. By clicking the AutoFormat As You Type tab in the AutoCorrect dialog box, shown in Figure I-8, you can set this feature to automatically apply bullets and numbers to lists of text.

- ### Use AutoCorrect to correct capitalization errors

  AutoCorrect recognizes words that are commonly capitalized and corrects them when they are entered incorrectly. For example, the first word in a sentence, or the days of the week, are recognized and corrected if they are not capitalized. AutoCorrect also recognizes when the first two letters of a word have been capitalized incorrectly and makes the second letter lowercase. You can also add names or words that you want capitalized or in lowercase to the AutoCorrect entries.

- ### Use AutoCorrect to correct spelling errors

  AutoCorrect works differently than the Publisher Spell Checker. The Spell Checker does not automatically correct all of your spelling errors. After it identifies potential misspellings, it underlines the words with a red wavy line. As you edit your publication, you can decide whether the underlined words are truly misspelled. AutoCorrect, on the other hand, makes spelling corrections automatically. With AutoCorrect, you enter your common misspellings and the proper replacement spellings. It then identifies the misspellings and makes the replacements as you type.

- ### Prevent AutoCorrect from making specific corrections

  To modify AutoCorrect, you can turn options on and off, or edit the AutoCorrect entries. For the AutoCorrect capitalization and Spelling Checker options, you can also create an exceptions list that specifies which words should not be changed. For example, you can prevent AutoCorrect from capitalizing a word that you want to appear in lowercase for stylistic reasons.

FIGURE I-7: Entry added in AutoCorrect: English (United States) dialog box

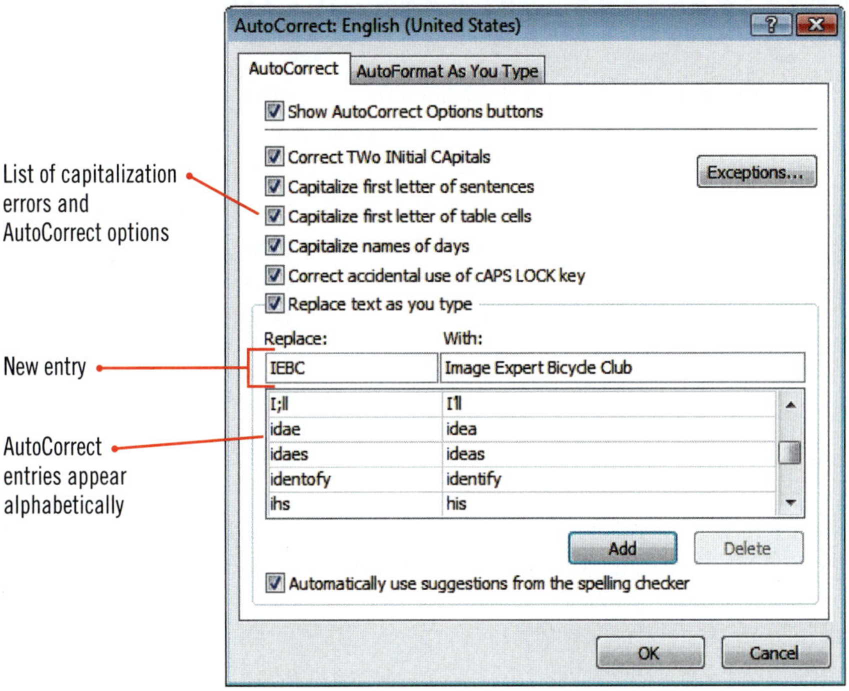

List of capitalization
errors and
AutoCorrect options

New entry

AutoCorrect
entries appear
alphabetically

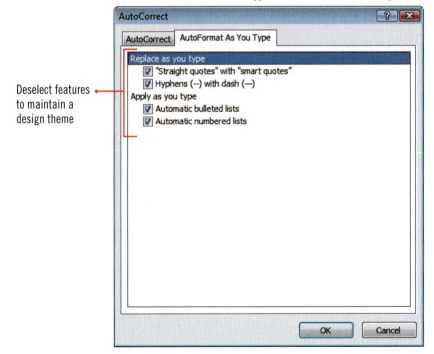

FIGURE I-8: AutoFormat As You Type tab in the AutoCorrect dialog box

Deselect features
to maintain a
design theme

Design Matters

Using tools wisely

AutoCorrect is a powerful tool. However, like all tools, it is important to recognize appropriate uses and limitations. There may be occasions when, for design or literary reasons, you want to turn off AutoCorrect features. Consider how the works of Mark Twain, James Joyce, e. e.Cummings, Lewis Carroll, and other English-speaking authors would have been altered by the tools found in software products. Knowing how and when to use a tool is vital. Knowing when and how to dispense with a tool is important, too.

Using Digital Images

Publisher is a powerful program because of its ability to handle both text and graphics. As your publications become targeted to a specific audience, your choice of graphic images will become targeted as well. Instead of relying on digital images created by others, you may wish to create your own. A **digital image** is a picture in an electronic file. The two most common methods of creating digital images are using a scanner and using a digital camera. You want the training materials to foster a sense of inclusion and help all employees get to know each other. You decide to ask each employee to provide a favorite photo for you to scan, or to pose for a photograph that you will take with a digital camera.

DETAILS

- ### Types of scanners

  There are many kinds of scanners in use today, each with advantages and disadvantages. By far, the most popular scanners are the flatbed and sheetfed variety. Some common features to both types are that they come with their own software that must be loaded on the computer, and they must be connected to a computer. Most scanners come with **optical character recognition** (**OCR**) software for scanning and translating text documents. To scan an image into Publisher, you click Insert on the menu bar, point to Picture, then click From Scanner or Camera. The Insert Picture from Scanner or Camera dialog box opens, and the installed scanner appears, as shown in Figure I-9.

  - ### Using a flatbed scanner

    A **flatbed scanner** has a flat surface from which the image is scanned, and it is the best type for creating digital images from photos and printed materials. To scan an item, you place it face down on the scanner's glass surface, just as you would on a copy machine. Since you can remove the scanner's lid, you can scan large objects, such as books, because you can place the object face down on the glass. The biggest disadvantage of a flatbed scanner is that it takes up space on your desk because of its large flat glass surface.

  - ### Using a sheetfed scanner

    The biggest advantage of a **sheetfed scanner** is its size. Commonly the size of a portable printer, it takes up little space on a crowded desktop. Instead of placing a document on a flat piece of glass, you feed the document into the scanning system using rollers. This limits sheetfed scanners to scanning single sheets of paper, which makes scanning a page from a book or other bulky object impossible. Most sheetfed scanners are more adept at scanning text than photos.

- ### Digital cameras

  A **digital camera** does not require film; it stores images on a memory device. Pictures are stored on the device until they are transferred to another storage medium or are deleted. The memory device can then be used again to take and store more images. The number of pictures a camera can save depends on the **resolution** (the density of **pixels**, or color dots) and the capacity of the memory device. Generally, the higher the resolution, the fewer pictures can be stored.

  Once you take the pictures that you want, you must download them using a software program that comes with the digital camera. As with scanners, the software program must be installed on your computer to download the pictures. In addition, you need a way to transfer the images from the camera to the computer. Some cameras use a memory card to transfer the images, while some connect to a computer using a cable. In Windows Vista, you can organize your images in the Windows Photo Gallery, as shown in Figure I-10.

- ### Copyright laws

  Images that you take with your own camera are your property to use as you want. However, images from other sources, including magazines, books, and the Internet, are the **intellectual property** of others and may be copyrighted and have limitations placed on their use. Permission for you to use an image may be granted by the copyright holder; sometimes permission is received just by asking, and other times you may be required to pay a fee. It is your legal and ethical responsibility to only use images that belong to you or that you have permission to use.

FIGURE I-9: Insert Picture from Scanner or Camera dialog box

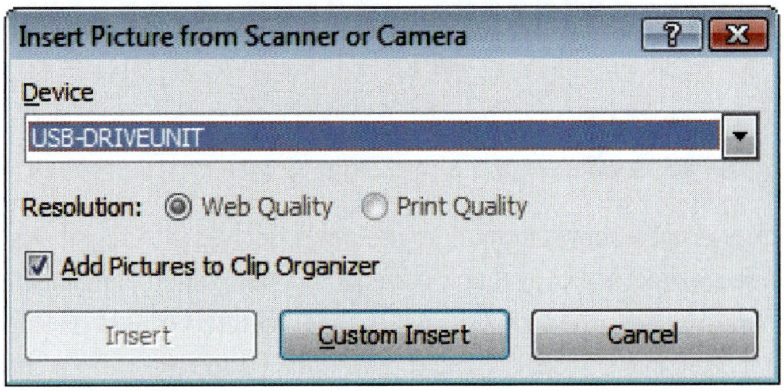

FIGURE I-10: Windows Photo Gallery

Design Matters

Studying color

Color is one of the most difficult areas of design to master, for a variety of reasons. Color perceptions and descriptions are subjective since the human eye can detect several million hues. Adding to that complexity is the limitation of language to deal meaningfully with so many shades of color. Also, between five to eight percent of males have some defect of color vision (females are much less affected because color-blindness is a male dominant trait). Considering the limitations of language and perception, a good way to study color is by using a color wheel. **Color wheels** teach color relationships by organizing colors in a circle so you can visualize how they relate to each other.

Embedding and Linking Objects

You can link or embed objects from other programs, such as pictures, charts, and tables, into a publication. An **embedded object** is a copy that is pasted into a publication. It maintains no ties to the original, so that if the original is modified, the copy does not change. A **linked object** is a copy that is connected to the original. When the original is modified, the copy is updated to reflect those changes. For example, you might want to include an Excel chart that shows quarterly sales in promotional literature for potential investors or informational literature for employees. If you link the chart instead of simply embedding it, then the chart in the publication will be updated whenever new data is entered into the Excel workbook. As part of the training literature, you want to include a chart of Image Expert's growth in a publication that documents the history of the company. Because you anticipate using the publication in the future with only minor changes, you want to explore different ways of importing the chart from Excel.

DETAILS

- ### Embedded objects

    An **embedded object** is created in another program and copied to a publication in Publisher. The **source file** contains the original information, and the **destination file** is the recipient of the information. There is no connection between the two programs, so if you modify the information in the source file, the information in the destination file does not change.

    The advantages of embedding are permanence and portability. You do not have to worry that a source file will be deleted, moved, or renamed, which would render the link between the files useless, or that its contents or formatting will change. Because the object is contained within your publication, it will stay the same unless you change it. An embedded object can always be edited using its original program by double-clicking it, but once the editing is done, the connection is again severed. To embed an object in any Office program, click the object, then click the Copy button 🖺 on the Standard toolbar. You can embed the object by clicking the Paste button 🖺 on the Standard toolbar, or by clicking the copied item on the Office Clipboard, as shown in Figure I-11.

    The disadvantages of embedding an object are that it increases the size of the publication, and if any changes are made to the source file, they are not updated in the destination file.

- ### Linked objects

    A **linked object** has a connection to the original object. When the object is updated in the source file, it is automatically updated in the publication (the destination file).

    Linking has two advantages over embedding. First, the publication file is smaller because it contains only links to the objects, not the objects themselves. Second, if changes are made to the source objects, they are automatically reflected in the publication when you view the objects. You can link an object in any Office program by clicking the object to select it, then clicking the Copy button 🖺 on the Standard toolbar. Once the object is copied, click Edit on the menu bar, then click Paste Special. The Paste Special dialog box opens, showing the source of the copied data. Click the Paste Link option button, as shown in Figure I-12, then click OK.

    The disadvantages are that the contents may change and those changes will not be reflected in the surrounding text; the formatting may change and be disruptive to your design; and if you move, delete, or rename the source file, the link is broken.

FIGURE I-11: Objects in the Clipboard task pane

Object is from Microsoft Office Access

Object is from Microsoft Office Excel

Object is from Microsoft Office Word

Object is from Microsoft Office PowerPoint

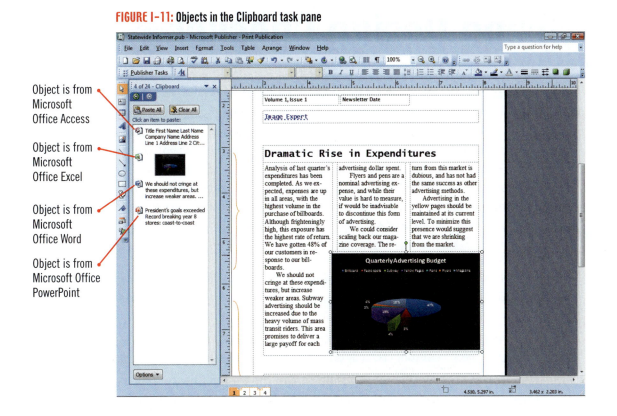

FIGURE I-12: Paste Special dialog box

Paste Link option button

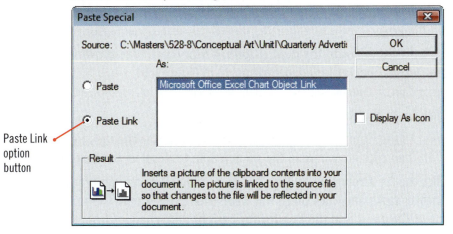

Using Publisher E-mail

Publisher contains hundreds of E-mail templates that can be used to create electronic publications such as a letter, an announcement of an event or featured product, a product list, or a newsletter. These publications are found in the Publication Types list when you open a new publication and are designed to contain hyperlinks. If you use Microsoft Office Outlook Express (version 5.0 or later) or Windows Mail, you can send a single publication page as the body of an e-mail message. You can use any of the provided templates to keep your e-mail messages consistent with your publication designs.

Using Design Checker

In most publications, there are multiple text and graphic elements, making it easy to miss design problems in a casual review. You can use the Design Checker to objectively review your publication and identify potential general design problems, commercial printing issues, Web site design issues, and e-mail text problems. **Design Checker** looks for errors in layout, alerts you, and suggests changes, but it does not fix the problems automatically. There may be times when your design choices may cause you to reject the Design Checker suggestions, but often it can help find areas of your publication that you can improve. You created a flyer containing intentional errors that can be used to dramatize the capabilities of the Design Checker feature. You want to use this publication so others can see how Design Checker works.

STEPS

1. **Open PUB I-2.pub from the drive and folder where you store your Data Files, then save it as Training Flyer**

   The flyer appears on the screen. It has two areas of color on the page.

2. **Click Tools on the menu bar, then click Design Checker**

   The Design Checker task pane opens. By default, it will check all pages, as well as the master page.

3. **Click Design Checker Options at the bottom of the Design Checker task pane, click the Checks tab, read all the selected features that Design Checker can examine, then make sure all your checkboxes contain a checkmark**

   See Figure I-13.

4. **Click OK in the Design Checker Options dialog box**

   The errors found by the Design Checker do not have to be addressed or fixed in any particular order. Design Checker finds that part of the e-mail address went into the overflow area. Design Checker makes suggestions about possible remedies in the task pane. Several errors are listed in the task pane. The first error listed reads "Page has space below top margin." In order to go to a specific item listed in the task pane, you have to position the pointer over the item, then click the list arrow that appears to the right of the item.

   > **TROUBLE**
   > Design Checker results may vary with different printer installations.

5. **Click the list arrow to the right of item 2: Story with text in overflow area (Page 1) on the Design Checker task pane, as shown in Figure I-14**

   Design Checker finds that the text box in the lower-left corner has a text-overflow, as shown in Figure I-14.

6. **Click Go to this Item**

7. **Point to the right border of the text until the pointer changes to ↔, drag the border to 3" H, then click anywhere in the scratch area to deselect the text box**

8. **Click the list arrow next to Page has space below top margin (Page 1) on the Design Checker task pane, click Go to this Item, then press ↑ until the selected objects are at the top of the page, and the icon for the current item changes from red to green in the task pane.**

   There are no more items in the Design Checker task pane.

9. **Make sure Your Name displays in the e-mail address in the lower-left text box, click the Print button 🖨 on the Standard toolbar, click the Save button 💾 on the Standard toolbar, then exit Publisher**

FIGURE I-13: Design Checker Options dialog box

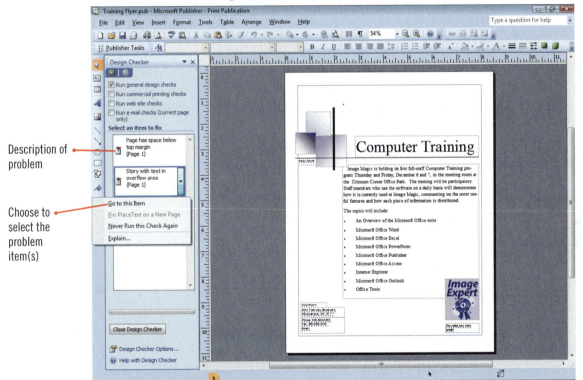

FIGURE I-14: Results of the Design Checker

Description of problem

Choose to select the problem item(s)

Design Matters

Working with Design Checker

Design Checker is a good and valuable tool, but it is crucial to recognize its limitations. For example, Design Checker does not recognize WordArt as text; instead, it considers it an object, and does not recognize it when it is placed on an otherwise empty text box. It does not recognize color clashes, or insufficient white space in a publication. You can work around these limitations by visually inspecting a publication in addition to running Design Checker. In addition, there may be occasions when you wish to ignore the Design Checker suggestions in order to achieve a design goal. For example, you may want to change the proportions of an image to create an interesting visual effect, or simply to fill a space.

Understanding Speech Recognition

Speech recognition is an emerging technology that translates spoken language into computer commands or text. It is a technology available in Windows Vista. When you talk into a microphone connected to a computer, your words are converted into a text file by a software package. You have heard a lot about speech recognition technology. You think a brief overview of the technology would interest employees at the training session and foster discussion about improving work practices at Image Expert. You consider some key issues related to speech recognition that you want to bring up at the training session.

DETAILS

- ### Installation

  Installation of the Speech Recognition component may require some additional hardware, such as a microphone, and requires answering some simple questions in several dialog boxes.

- ### Training sessions

  To set up Speech Recognition on your computer, open the Control Panel, click Ease of Access, then click Start speech recognition. The first time you start the Speech Recognition feature the Welcome to Speech Recognition dialog box opens, as shown in Figure I-15. Training involves reading a series of paragraphs into your computer's microphone. Figure I-16 shows an explanatory dialog box that lets you set up the type of microphone you want to use and appears before the training session. The training sessions teach the software's speech module to recognize your voice, and teach you the correct speed and clarity that are understandable to the program, as shown in Figure I-17. Training sessions can be completed more than once, and repetition results in improved performance of the Speech Recognition module.

- ### Using Speech Recognition

  Once the Speech Recognition component is installed in Windows Vista, it is available for all Office applications and can be turned on by clicking the Start button, then clicking Windows Speech Recognition. With Speech Recognition turned on, the Speech Recognition bar appears at the top of the screen.

Choosing a microphone

Many newer computers come with a microphone already installed, allowing you to easily use the speech recognition feature. If your computer did not come with this accessory, use the Web to research manufacturers and styles, and to learn which models work best with your system. Connect to the Internet, then use your browser and your favorite search engine to search on "PC microphones" or "PC sound systems."

FIGURE I-15: Set up Speech Recognition dialog box

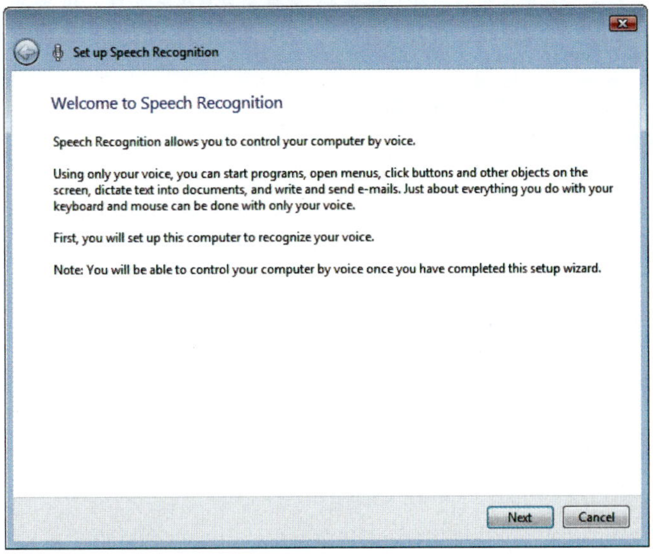

FIGURE I-16: Selecting the type of microphone you would like to use

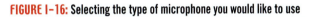

FIGURE I-17: Adjusting the microphone volume

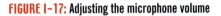

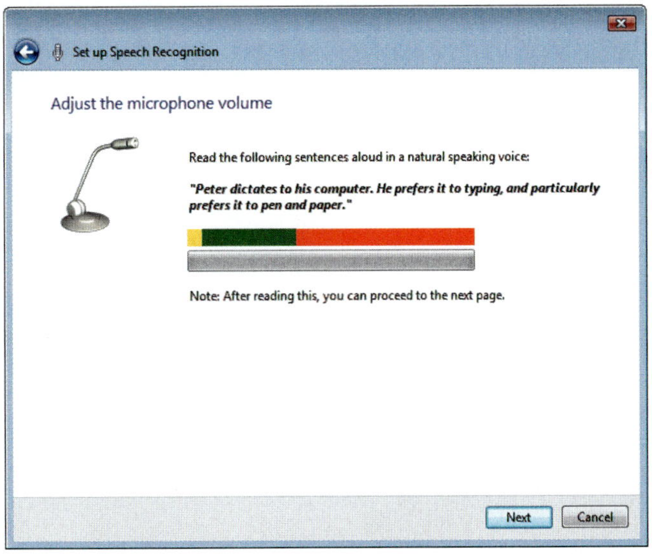

Capstone Project: Dinner Invitation

You have learned the skills necessary to transform Word documents into publications. You have learned about and used Design Checker. You have also learned about using alternative input devices: scanners, digital cameras, and speech recognition, as well as linking and embedding objects. The president is inviting the staff of Image Expert to a formal dinner. The invitations will be engraved so you want them to be perfect when you hand the file over to the printer. You decide to use the Design Checker.

STEPS

1. **Start Publisher, open PUB I-3.pub from the drive and folder where you store your Data Files, then save it as Dinner Invitation**

   The invitation appears on the screen with two elements of color alongside the text at the top and bottom.

2. **Click Tools on the menu bar, then click Design Checker**

   The Design Checker task pane opens, as shown in Figure I-18. By default, it will check all pages, as well as the master page.

3. **Click the Object has no line or fill (Page 1) list arrow, then click Fix: Delete Object**

   The first item in the task pane has been checked off and is no longer displayed in the publication.

4. **Click the Page has space below top margin (Page 1) list arrow, then click again to close it**

   Design Checker finds that there is more than 1 inch of blank space at the top of page 1. This white space is intentional since it allows you to personalize the invitations with a quick note of thanks to each employee, recognizing their hard work.

5. **Click the Page has space below top margin (Page 2) list arrow, click Go to this Item, then drag the selected objects to the top of the page**

   The remaining items in the Design Checker task pane are not troublesome to you.

6. **Scroll so page 3 is visible, then delete the extra spaces between the words "some" and "business"**

   Compare your work to Figure I-19.

7. **Click the Save button 💾 on the Standard toolbar, then exit Publisher**

   Examine your printed page. If you find any mistakes, go back and correct the mistakes. If necessary, print the pages again.

FIGURE I-18: Design Checker task pane

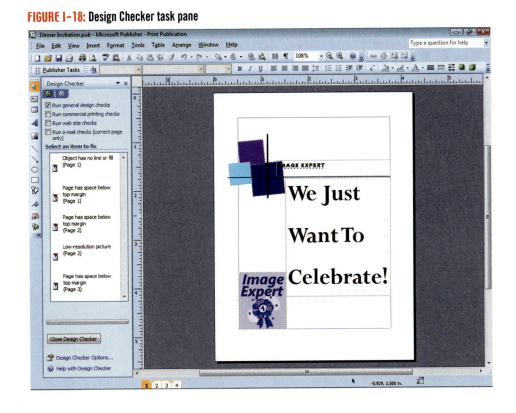

FIGURE I-19: Completed Dinner Invitation

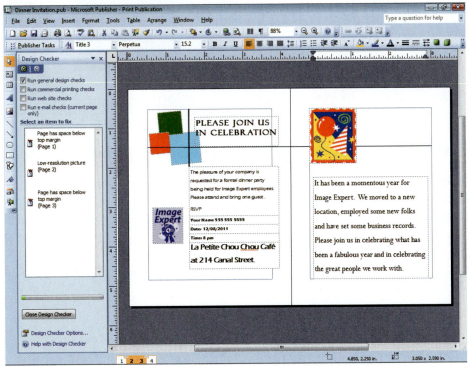

Practice

If you have a SAM user profile, you may have access to hands-on instruction, practice, and assessment of the skills covered in this unit. Log in to your SAM account (http://sam2007.course.com/) to launch any assigned training activities or exams that relate to the skills covered in this unit.

▼ CONCEPTS REVIEW

Label each of the programs that created the Office Clipboard contents shown in Figure I-20.

FIGURE I-20

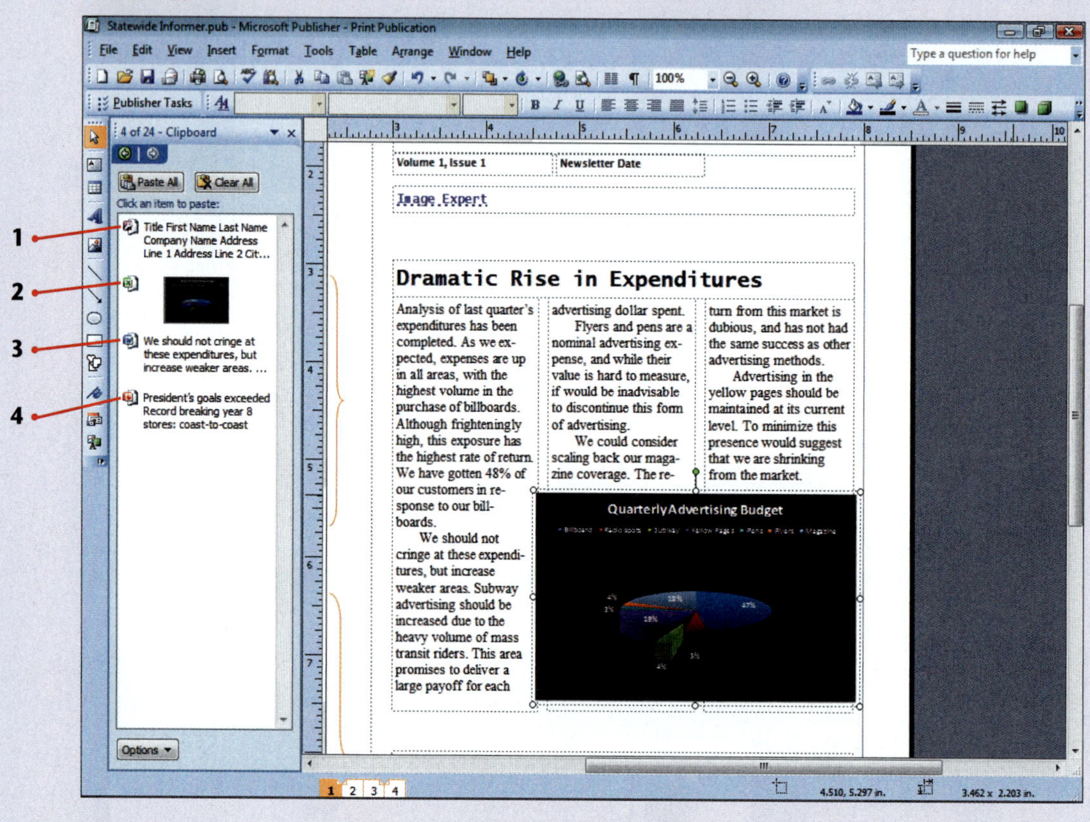

Match each of the features with the statement that describes its function or attribute.

5. **Embedded object**
6. **Design Checker**
7. **Digital cameras**
8. **AutoCorrect entries**
9. **Linked object**
10. **Flatbed scanner**

a. Creates images free of copyright restrictions
b. List of common misspellings
c. Finds problems such as an object in non-printing areas of the page
d. Maintains a connection to the source file
e. Must be double-clicked for editing
f. Transforms images or text into electronic files

Select the best answer from the list of choices.

11. Design Checker can check for:
    a. Text in the overflow area.
    b. Blank pages.
    c. Subject verb agreement.
    d. Clashing colors.

12. You can use a copyrighted image in a publication if:
    a. You ask permission of the copyright holder.
    b. You copy it from the World Wide Web.
    c. You credit the copyright owner in a footnote.
    d. You receive written permission from the copyright holder.

13. You can use Microsoft Excel to:
    a. Create presentations.
    b. Create charts.
    c. Write e-mails.
    d. All of the above

14. Which Microsoft product can you use to organize data into tables, records, and fields?
    a. Access
    b. Excel
    c. Outlook
    d. PowerPoint

15. AutoCorrect is used to do everything listed below, except:
    a. Correct misspelled words.
    b. Find and correct typos.
    c. Correct errors in capitalization.
    d. Correct layout and design errors.

16. An embedded object:
    a. Can never be updated.
    b. Is updated automatically.
    c. Is updated by double-clicking on the object.
    d. Has to be removed from the publication for updating.

17. You can use Design Checker to:
    a. Correct misspelled words.
    b. Find and correct typos.
    c. Correct errors in capitalization.
    d. Correct layout and design errors.

18. Which Microsoft product can you use to exchange e-mail across the Internet?
    a. Access
    b. Outlook Express or Windows Mail
    c. Excel
    d. PowerPoint

19. A linked object:
    a. Can never be updated.
    b. Is updated when the source file is changed.
    c. Is updated by double-clicking on the object.
    d. Has to be removed from the publication for updating.

20. **Each of the following is true, except:**
   a. Word documents can be imported directly into Publisher.
   b. Word can be used to edit stories written in Publisher.
   c. Stories written in Word are created in text boxes by default.
   d. One reason to import Word documents into Publisher publications is to maintain design consistency by adding design elements.

21. **To detect and correct misspellings, AutoCorrect uses:**
   a. A list of AutoCorrect entries.
   b. The main dictionary.
   c. The custom dictionary.
   d. A thesaurus.

▼ SKILLS REVIEW

1. **Integrate with Office programs.**
   a. You work for a chain of restaurants and are responsible for creating menus, advertisements, business plans, and monthly special flyers. List at least three ways in which you could integrate Office programs to create these materials on a regular basis.
   b. You work for a non-profit organization dedicated to pet adoptions. What tasks could you perform using Office programs?
   c. You work for a small, family-owned plumbing company. How could you use Office products to make this business more efficient?

2. **Import a Word document.**
   a. Start Publisher, then create a new publication using the Bars template in the Import Word Documents category in the Publication Types list.
   b. Choose 2 columns, the color scheme of your choice, then click Create.
   c. In the Import Word Document dialog box, select PUB I-4.docx in the drive and folder where you store your Data Files, click OK, then save the publication as **Astronomy Story**.
   d. Close the task pane, then press [F9].
   e. Replace the Document Title placeholder text with **Enjoying Astronomy Correctly**.
   f. Change the title font size to 18 point.
   g. Click the Save button on the Standard toolbar, then close the file, but do not exit Publisher.

3. **Use AutoCorrect.**
   a. Examine the list of default AutoCorrect entries. Are there any entries missing that you think you will need?
   b. Will any of the default entries cause problems in your everyday use?

4. **Use digital images.**
   a. Find two images, then scan them.
   b. Open a new, blank publication, then save it as **Scanning Practice** in the drive and folder where you store your Data Files. Insert the two images, place your name somewhere on the page as well as the title 'Scanning Practice', print the page, then save and close the file.

5. **Embed and link objects.**
   a. Think of a real-world situation in which linking an object, such as financial data, would be advantageous. One example might be a book distributor working with several warehouses across the country. How could linking help to keep inventory reports in this sort of business up to date?

6. **Use Design Checker.**
   a. Open PUB I-5.pub from the drive and folder where you store your Data Files, then save it as **New IE Newsletter**.
   b. Start Design Checker.
   c. Ignore the items **Object encroaches nonprinting region (Page 1)** and **Object partially off page (Page 1)** if they appear in the list.
   d. Fix items 3 and 4 that say **Object is not visible (Page 1)**.

e. Fix the remaining problems by either deleting empty text boxes, moving objects, scaling objects proportionally or bringing objects forward. (Your results using the Design Checker may vary.)

f. Print page 1 of the publication.

g. Save the publication and exit Publisher.

7. Understand speech recognition.

a. If you have a microphone and speakers attached to your computer and you completed the Speech Recognition training in the lesson, make a list of two simple tasks in which you could use the speech recognition feature. (*Hint:* You could create a text box, then use the speech recognition feature to fill it. Or, you could select a text box, then use the speech recognition feature to open the Format Text Box dialog box.)

b. Write down what tasks you accomplished, then try each task and rate the feature's effectiveness.

▼ INDEPENDENT CHALLENGE 1

As the office manager for your local Chamber of Commerce, you decide to spend time working with employees to improve their skills. One of the employees needs help with a postcard announcing an upcoming event. You will use Design Checker to find and fix problems.

a. Start Publisher, then open the file PUB I-6.pub from the drive and folder where you store your Data Files.

b. Save the publication as **Potluck Supper Postcard**.

c. Use Design Checker to find and correct any problems.

d. Adjust the text point size so that all of the text is visible and no words are hyphenated.

Advanced Challenge Exercises

- Scan artwork appropriate to this publication.
- Place the artwork in the publication.
- Make any necessary adjustments such as cropping, or changing the way the text wraps around the image, then compare your work to Figure I-21.

e. Include **your name** in the e-mail address.

f. Save and print the publication, then exit Publisher.

FIGURE I-21

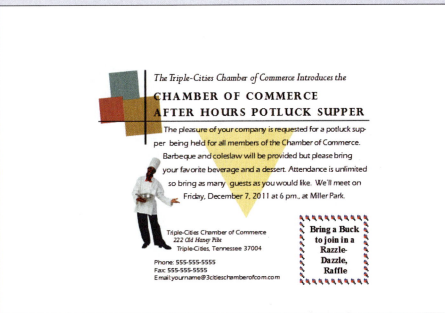

▼ INDEPENDENT CHALLENGE 2

Some friends from an art school are giving a party with the theme "Bad Taste in Your Face". You agreed to make a flyer in the worst taste you can imagine to announce the party.

a. Start Publisher, then open the file PUB I-7.pub from the drive and folder where you store your Data Files.

b. Save the publication as **Party Flyer**.

c. Use Design Checker to find and correct any problems it identifies in the flyer.

d. Correct any text spacing problems not found by Design Checker.

e. Correct any typos or misspellings.

f. Substitute your name for the e-mail address.

g. Save and print the publication, then exit Publisher.

▼ INDEPENDENT CHALLENGE 3

You have been researching the topic of color psychology in preparation for a talk you are giving to graphic designers later this month. You wrote up a summary of your notes in a Microsoft Word document, and have decided that you want to provide a hard copy of the summary to people attending the talk. You decide to import the document into Publisher so that you can create a sharp-looking publication to hand out to attendees.

a. Start Publisher, then click Import Word Documents in the Publication Types list.

b. Click the Blocks template, then click Create.

c. In the Import Word Document dialog box, open the file PUB I-8.docx from the drive and folder where you store your Data Files, click OK, then save the publication as **Color Psychology Story**.

d. Close the task pane, then press [F9].

e. If necessary, adjust the spacing between paragraphs and change the font size of the imported text to 12, then delete the page number text box.

f. Click the Document Title placeholder text, right-align it, type **The Psychology of Color, by**, then type **your name**.

g. Select the text, click the Font Size list arrow on the Formatting toolbar, then click 20.

FIGURE I-22

Advanced Challenge Exercises

- Change the number of columns to 2.
- Create shapes for some of the colors mentioned in the publication, then arrange and group them.
- Compare your publication to Figure I-22.

h. Save and print the publication, then exit Publisher.

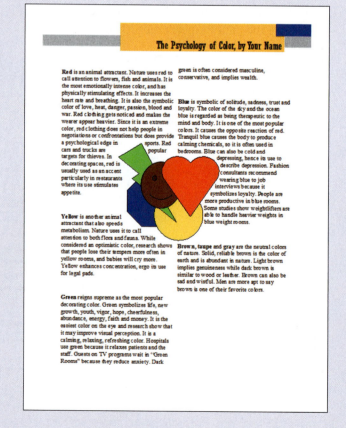

▼ REAL LIFE INDEPENDENT CHALLENGE

This Independent Challenge requires an Internet connection. You consider yourself artistic with good instincts about design, but wish you knew more about colors and how to choose them. Use your browser and search engine to explore articles about color wheels on the World Wide Web. Create a brief description of color wheels in Word, then import it into Publisher.

a. Connect to the Internet, then use your browser and favorite search engine to explore the term "color wheel."

b. Find out the key features and benefits of color wheels and print out any information that will help you write a brief Word document about the subject.

c. Use the information you gathered online to write a short Word document about color wheels, then save it as **Color Wheel Story** to the drive and folder where you store your Data Files.

d. Use the Publication Types list to pick the Word document template of your choice in Publisher.

e. Import your Word document into Publisher.

f. If possible, find an image of a color wheel and insert it into the publication.

g. Save the publication as **About the Color Wheel** to the drive and folder where you store your Data Files.

h. Change the title to **About the Color Wheel, by**, then type **your name**.

i. Select the one-sided printing option.

j. Save and print the publication, compare it to Figure I-23, then exit Publisher.

FIGURE I-23

About The Color Wheel, by Your Name

The **Color Wheel** shows how colors are related. It is laid out so that any two primary colors (red, yellow, blue) are separated by the secondary colors (orange, violet, purple and green) which are made by combining two primary colors.

Primary Colors are basic and cannot be mixed from other elements. They are analogous to prime numbers in mathematics. You can mix two primaries to get a **Secondary Color**. Each Secondary Color on the Color Wheel is bounded by two primaries. Those are the components that you mix to get that Secondary Color.

Color complements are color opposites. These colors contrast each other in the most extreme way possible. They help to make each color seem more active.

All light travels as waves. Color complements have drastically different wavelengths and, consequently, cause some perception problems for a viewer if they are placed close to each other in a design or in art. The cones and rods of the eye cannot separate the information, so we sometimes detect a quivering or optical distortion when two complements are used near each other.

▼ VISUAL WORKSHOP

Use the Publication Types list to create the Studio publication (found in the Import Word Documents category). This is the initial design of a story you are importing from Word. Import the file PUB I-9.docx into the publication, save the publication as **Presenting Designs**. Use Figure I-24 as a guide for enhancing the publication and including or removing additional elements such as your name. Move any of the objects on the page to make the publication easier to read, and use the Best Fit AutoFit feature. The clip art shown in the sample can be found by searching, using "meeting" as the keyword (it is j0233018.wmf). Save and print the first page.

FIGURE I-24

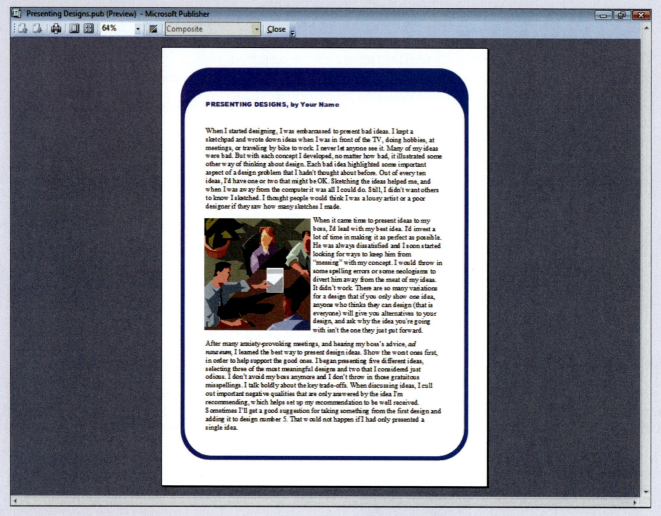

Creating Web Documents

Files You Will Need:

PUB J-1.tif

PUB J-2.docx

PUB J-3.pub

PUB J-4.tif

PUB J-5.tif

Publisher has Web capabilities and graphics tools that make it easy to create multi-page Web sites. You can create professional-looking sites with attractive backgrounds, useful navigation bars, and interesting links. You can test a finished site with a browser, and publish it to the Internet so that others can access it. Before you create a Web site, you must identify your goals and resources.  Image Expert has decided to create a company Web site and has asked you to begin planning and designing the site. The primary purpose of the Web site is to introduce potential customers to Image Expert and provide contact information.

OBJECTIVES

Plan a Web site

Design a Web site

Create a Web site

Add hyperlinks

Modify a Web page background

Test a Web site

Publish a Web site

Convert a publication to a
Web page

Capstone Project: Personal
Web Site

Planning a Web Site

The steps in planning a Web site are similar to planning a paper publication, but with some important differences. You must begin by considering how much time, money, and expertise are available for your Web site. Because of the dynamic nature of a Web site, it may require more resources than a typical paper publication. For example, paper publications are a form of one-way communication, where the reader does not interact with the document. Web sites, on the other hand, must be interactive, so that readers can navigate the site, use hyperlinks, and provide information or ask questions. Another difference is that Web sites must be maintained and their content updated to attract multiple visits. You think about the key questions necessary to plan a Web site.

DETAILS

- ### What are the constraints?

  Time, money, expertise, and competing needs are the limiting factors in most enterprises. Being aware of budgetary, scheduling, and technical limits may influence your selection of a target audience and consequently, your design. A few of the things you should consider before designing a Web site are shown in Figure J-1. Image Expert has only a limited budget for the initial Web site, and wants it published as soon as possible. You will be the primary designer of the site, though the company may hire someone later to maintain and expand the site so that it can be used for customer service activities, such as order tracking.

- ### Who is the target audience?

  The Internet makes it difficult to identify who is actually visiting your site because anyone can access it, but you can take steps to reach your target audience. The more narrowly you can define the characteristics of your ideal audience, the more you can tailor the content, design, and access to your Web site so that the site appeals to them. This may influence your choice of design elements, the amount of text you include on each page, and the degree of interactivity in the site. Image Expert has a profile of its current average client and designs its Web site according to that profile's tastes.

- ### What is the desired effect of the Web site?

  Are you trying to sell something, persuade, teach, motivate, inform, or solicit a contribution of time or money? Deciding what effect you want is the first step to obtaining it. The answers to those questions will help you decide whether the site should give technical support, or be a clearinghouse of information, an electronic catalog, or another type of site. Visitors to the Image Expert site will want to know the benefits of becoming a customer, and may want to see links to existing clients.

- ### What response do you want?

  Do you intend the site to simply provide information, or do you want feedback? If you want people to interact with your site, what structure should the feedback take? Do you want to solicit and register people for attendance at an event? Do you want e-mail inquiries for additional information, such as a catalog? Do you want multiple visits to your Web site? If you plan to collect money, do you want to collect credit card information? How will you deal with tariffs and taxes and other barriers to international trade? Your answers to these questions will help you to reexamine and reevaluate the constraints and the desired effect of your Web site. Image Expert plans to install a customer survey as part of its future Web site. This will make the site more interactive, and encourage feedback from clients.

- ### What will you do with the responses?

  If you offer people a product in exchange for money, or offer some free service such as additional information by mail, or an e-mail response, you must be able to deliver on your offer. If you don't have enough merchandise or other materials prepared for a timely response, you risk alienating customers and potential customers who show interest in your products or services. If you don't have adequate resources to deal with the potential responses your Web site will generate, then you should adjust your goals accordingly. It is the goal of Image Expert to respond to all e-mail inquiries within 24 hours.

Web Site Planning Constraints

- Budget limitations
- Limiting technologies
- Staffing needs (current and future requirements)
- Development staff (programmers, designers, etc.)
- Maintenance staff (e-mail responses)
- Security issues (prevention of hacking)
- Privacy issues (guarding clients' personal information)
- Web site transactions (credit cards, order processing)
- Customer service issues (pre-sales questions, customer support, warranties, returns, etc.)
- Foreign language services

Planning and customer service

One of the most problematic areas of planning is customer service. Even with earnest research efforts to try to anticipate the need for your product or service, the marketplace determines the actual demand for a product or a service. Underestimating this demand can lead to outstripped supply. Overestimating demand can lead to idle capacity, underutilized workers, and eventually, perhaps, layoffs and/or bankruptcy. When developing a Web site, carefully consider the developmental and maintenance costs. Unless there is value in a return visit, either to purchase additional product, or read updated content, the number of visits to a site will drop off. Changing content requires an investment of time and energy on the part of developers and management. You must plan for direct contact with visitors to your site too. While e-mail responses can be standardized and automated to respond to customer needs, someone has to make sure that the responses are timely and accurately answer the customers' questions. If you do not satisfy your customers' needs, someone else will.

Designing a Web Site

Before creating a Web site, it's a good idea to decide on the design of the site, including how you want elements to appear on the pages. Although you'll probably make many modifications to your initial design over time, a master design with a list of required elements can help you work more effectively. The elements may include a logo, colors, font selections, and other items that support you or your business's identity. As you plan the content of the Image Expert Web site, you want to present the company in the best possible light. To accomplish this, you want to incorporate success stories and accolades from credible outside sources.

DETAILS

- ### Create an outline or a sketch

  The first step in preparing a Web site is to prepare an outline. The outline should include a list of the elements to place on each page. Information you might want to have on a page includes: a title, introductory paragraph, contact information, links to other sites and other pages, and graphic images. For the Image Expert Web site, you have decided to create four pages. You want the primary page, or **home page**, to briefly describe Image Expert, including what they can do for customers and how they can be contacted. You also want a page for the company's success stories, or **testimonials**, in the form of a list of satisfied clients and some of their comments. And you want to include a page promoting an upcoming design clinic.

- ### Decide on a navigation structure

  Before you work on the Web site, you should consider the number of pages for the site and how they will be linked together. Each page should be linked to the home page, and it should be easy for a reader to jump from page to page. Figure J-2 illustrates a typical Web site navigation structure.

- ### Add links to other sites

  In addition to linking associated pages within your site, you can also provide helpful links to other Web locations of interest to your readers. If you have a page that lists Image Expert's clients, you might include links to the clients' Web sites. By including your clients on your corporate Web site, they become ambassadors for your company. These links also serve to promote your corporate clients. While there is no legal requirement to ask permission to link to another site, it is a good idea to seek the cooperation of clients, and keep them updated on how you represent their interests.

QUICK TIP

GIF stands for Graphics Interchange Format.

- ### Add graphics, backgrounds, and design elements

  A few well-placed graphic images can enhance your Web site by breaking up blocks of text and making your pages more attractive. You can use all types of clip art files on your pages, and Publisher provides **animated GIFs**—images with movement—for Web page use on the Clip Art and Media Home Page of the Microsoft Office Online Web site. Using one of the many backgrounds available on the Background task pane can make your pages eye-catching. The Design Gallery contains a variety of elements designed specifically for Web pages, such as navigation bars. The Web Site Options section of the Format Publication task pane lets you quickly add response forms and navigation bars to your Web pages.

- ### Critically examine the page

  Because Publisher shows you exactly how your page looks by letting you view it in a browser, you can monitor your progress as you work. Figure J-3 shows the sample Image Expert home page, and Figure J-4 shows the design clinic page. Pages 2, 3, and 4 are linked to the home page, and the vertical navigation bar is present on each page, making it easy for a reader to jump to any page on the site. It's a good idea to occasionally step back and imagine that you're seeing your work for the first time. Ask yourself if you find the pages easy to read and navigate. See if the pages look attractive.

- ### Preview the Web site and test the links

  If your pages include links to other Web sites, make sure that the links are correct. Periodically check the links to make sure that they work as intended. There is software available that can test links automatically, but you must still manually test them to make sure that the content on the sites to which you are linking is still relevant and appropriate.

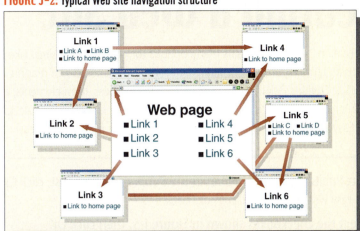

Navigation bar to
pages on the site

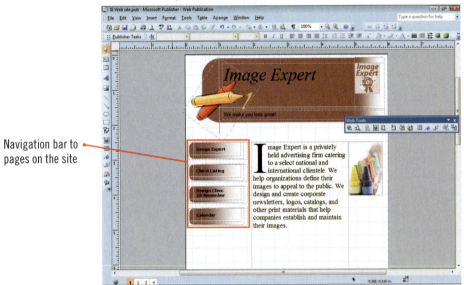

Link returns to
home page

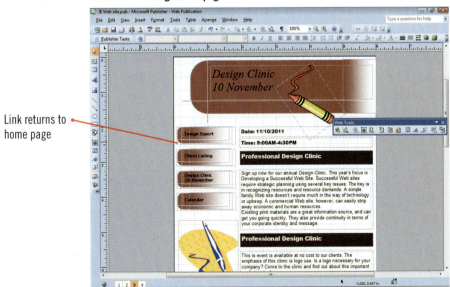

Publisher 2007

Creating a Web Site

The Publication Types list contains many options for creating Web sites. Like other publications, Web sites created using templates have coordinated colors and placeholders for graphic images and text. Additionally, the Web Site Options task pane offers navigation bar choices, form elements, and background textures. You can easily create Web sites using the Easy Web Site Builder. You decide to use a Web Site template and the Easy Web Site Builder to get a quick start on your new design ideas.

STEPS

1. **Start Publisher, click Web Sites in the Publication Types list, click Crisscross, then click Create**
   The Easy Web Site Builder dialog box opens.

2. **Select the checkboxes shown in Figure J-5, then click OK**
   If you only wanted the Web site to have a single page, you would leave all the checkboxes deselected.

3. **Click Color Schemes in the Format Publication task pane, then click Trek**

4. **Save the publication as IE Web Site to the drive and folder where you store your Data Files**

5. **Click anywhere in the publication, press [F9], right-click the picture of the pasta dish, in the upper-right corner of the page, point to Change Picture, click From File, then click PUB J-1.tif from the drive and folder where you store your Data Files, click Insert, then press [Esc]**
   The Image Expert logo replaces the picture placeholder on the page.

6. **Right-click the logo image, click Format Picture, click the Picture tab if necessary, click Recolor, click the Color list arrow, click the third box from the left, click OK, click OK, then press [Esc]**
   The Image Expert logo is recolored using the active color scheme.

QUICK TIP
The unit of measurement in Web page rulers is in **pixels**. Tick marks are in increments of 8 pixels.

7. **Click the Picture Frame button 🖼 on the Objects toolbar, click Empty Picture Frame, then drag ╋ below the navigation bar from 16 H / 384 V to 176 H / 544 V click 🖼, click Clip Art, type paint cans in the Search for text box in the Clip Art task pane, search in All Collections, then click Go**
   Verify that the Photographs checkbox in the Results should be list is checked.

TROUBLE
If this image is not available, choose a similar image.

8. **Point to the clip art image shown in Figure J-6, click the list arrow, then click Insert on the menu**
   The empty picture frame is filled with the image of the paint cans.

9. **Right-click the text frame at 384 H / 288 V, point to Change Text, click Text File, click PUB J-2.docx from the drive and folder where you store your Data Files, then click OK**
   The document file replaces the placeholder text.

TROUBLE
A warning box appears when you add a drop cap if the insertion point is not in the paragraph.

10. **Click anywhere *within* the paragraph, click Format on the menu bar, click Drop Cap, click the first choice on the left in the second row, click OK, then click the Save button 🖫 on the Standard toolbar**
    Compare your page to Figure J-7.

FIGURE J-5: Easy Web Site Builder dialog box

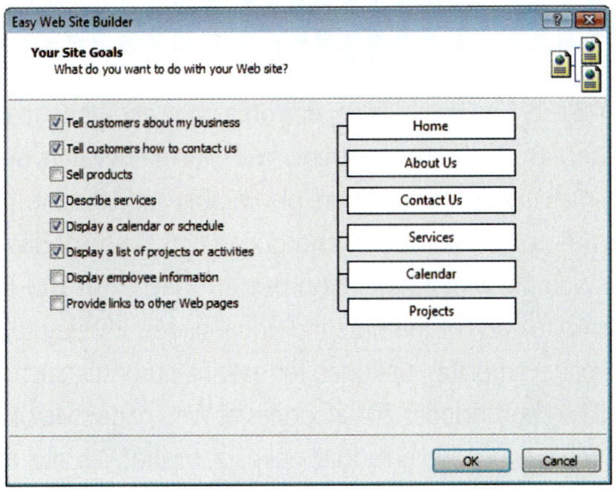

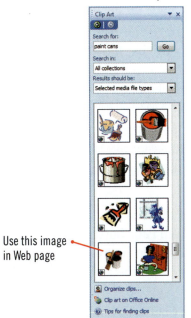

FIGURE J-6: Clip Art task pane

Use this image
in Web page

FIGURE J-7: Home page with image and text replaced

Drop cap

Text file inserted
in Web page

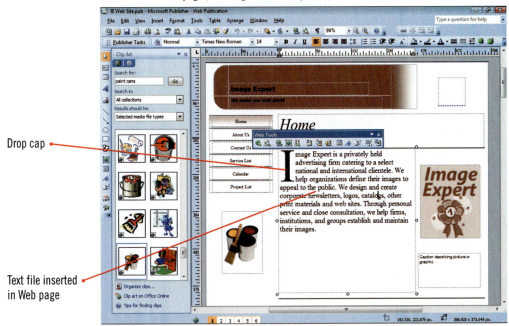

Adding Hyperlinks

You use a hyperlink each time you click an area on a page and jump to another Web site. **Hyperlinks**, or **links**, are electronic connections to locations within a Web site or elsewhere on the Internet. Links are included on Web pages to make the reader's experience more pleasurable and efficient. You can create links to your own or other Web pages, Web sites, e-mail addresses, and documents on a specific computer. Publisher automatically links pages added to a Web site with a navigation bar. A **navigation bar** is a row or column of buttons on a Web page containing links to each of the site's individual pages. It's easy to add pages to a Web site. You can even choose from Web page templates, designed for specific purposes, such as adding a resume page or a form. The Insert Web Page dialog box includes 20 categories of Web page styles, such as Photos, Product List/Resume, and Services. 🎨 You want to add an additional page to the Web site, and include a link to a client's Web site.

STEPS

1. **Close the task pane, click Insert on the menu bar, then click Page**

   The Insert Web Page dialog box opens, as shown in Figure J-9. You can choose from a variety of page styles.

2. **Click Related Links, make sure that the Add hyperlink to navigation bars check box is selected, then click OK**

   The newly inserted page 2 is now the current page, and the default heading is "Related Links". There is now a new entry at the bottom of the navigation bar whose heading is identical to the current page title.

3. **Click the text Web site or page name 1, press [F9], then type Course Technology**

   The company name, Course Technology, appears.

4. **Select the text Course Technology, then click the Insert Hyperlink button 🖳 on the Web Tools toolbar**

   The Insert Hyperlink dialog box opens.

5. **Click the Existing File or Web Page button if necessary, type http://www.course.com in the Address text box as shown in Figure J-10, then click OK**

   The selected Course Technology text is now a hyperlink, indicated by its change in color and its underline formatting applied.

6. **Click the text beneath the Course Technology link, type A publisher of high-quality technology textbooks and other electronic training materials., then press [Esc] twice**

7. **Click the Save button 🖫 on the Standard toolbar**

   Compare your page to Figure J-11.

Modifying a navigation bar

You can modify the text and order of pages within a navigation bar by clicking anywhere within the bar, then clicking the Click to edit options for this Navigation Bar button 🖎 which displays once the navigation bar is selected. The Navigation Bar Properties dialog box opens, as shown in Figure J-8. Click the name of the page you want to move in the Links list, then click the Add Link, Remove Link, Modify Link or Move Up and Move Down buttons, as necessary.

FIGURE J–8: Navigation Bar Properties dialog box

Navigation Bar Properties	
Name:	
Main Navigation Bar	
Links:	
Home	Add Link...
About Us	
Contact Us	Remove Link
Service List	
Calendar	Modify Link...
Project List	
Related Links	Move Up
	Move Down

☑ Update this navigation bar with links to new pages that are added to this publication.

OK   Cancel   Help

URL address for the link

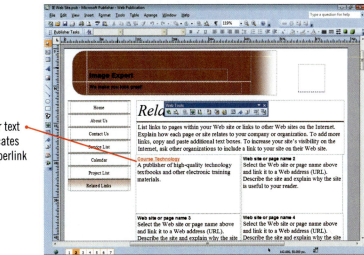

Color text indicates a hyperlink

Publisher 2007

Adding a hyperlink to an e-mail address

By adding a hyperlink to an e-mail address, you can make it easy for your readers to keep in touch. Because the Internet is a fairly impersonal medium, this kind of contact with readers can be invaluable. It can lead you to new ideas, and new sources of content, and expand your network. Complaints can be particularly valuable because they help you identify problems that might otherwise escape notice. To establish a hyperlink to an e-mail address, first select the text that you want to be the link, open the Insert Hyperlink dialog box by clicking the Insert Hyperlink button on the Web Tools toolbar, click E-mail Address, then enter a valid address in the E-mail address text box. You can confirm that the hyperlink is attached to the selected text by placing your pointer over the hyperlink. When you do this, a ScreenTip displays.

Modifying a Web Page Background

The background of the pages on a Web site can be modified to have different colors and textures, or no texture at all. The addition of carefully chosen background colors and textures enhances a Web site's design by adding visual interest and an illusion of depth. You can easily modify the background colors and textures individually on each page, or on all the pages, using Master Page view or using a button on the Web Tools toolbar. You want to modify the background texture so that it has a pattern, but still allows the text to be easily readable.

STEPS

1. **Click the page 1 icon on the status bar**
   You will use a button on the Web Tools toolbar to change the background of the current page.

2. **Click the Background button on the Web Tools toolbar**
   The Background task pane is displayed.

3. **Click the first box on the left in the sixth row, as shown in Figure J-13**
   Page 1 has a light beige, textured background that will add visual interest and an illusion of depth when the design elements are visible.

4. **Click the Save button on the Standard toolbar, then compare your screen to Figure J-14**

Design Matters

Creating a custom color scheme

You can create your own custom color schemes, just like those included in the Publisher Color Scheme list. Custom color schemes include main, accent, and hyperlink colors, as well as background textures. You create a custom color scheme by making selections in the Color Schemes task pane. Click Create a new color scheme at the bottom of the Color Schemes task pane. Name the custom color scheme in the Create New Color Scheme dialog box, shown in Figure J-12. You can now change the color scheme selections. Click the list arrows for any of the Scheme colors in the New column, then click a color from the palette. When all your selections are made, you can name the scheme by clicking the Save Scheme button, typing a name for the scheme, then clicking OK twice.

FIGURE J-12: Create New Color Scheme dialog box

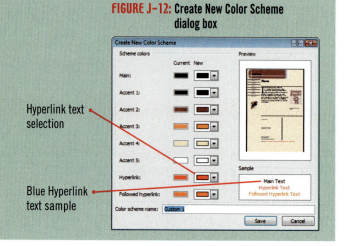

Hyperlink text selection

Blue Hyperlink text sample

FIGURE J-13: Background task pane

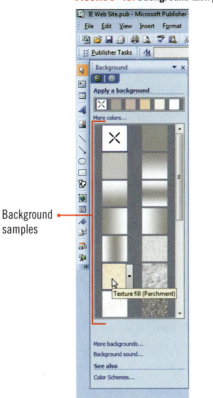

Background
samples

FIGURE J-14: Web page background texture modified

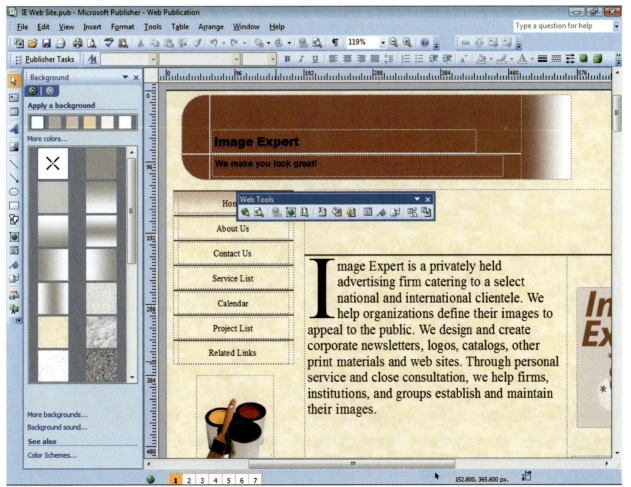

Testing a Web Site

On a Web site, the potential for embarrassment caused by typos, misspellings, and awkward or poor design is worldwide. It is important to test and critique your Web site before publishing it to the Internet. Careful examination of the publication, first using Design Checker, and then the Web Page Preview feature, can help you identify and correct errors before they become public. ▰▰▰▰ You want to preview the publication in Internet Explorer.

1. **If the Web Tools toolbar is not open, click View on the menu bar, point to Toolbars, then click Web Tools**

2. **Connect to the Internet, if necessary**

    If you are unsure how to connect to the Internet, contact your instructor or technical support person. If you are unable to connect to the Internet, skip Step 5.

    TROUBLE
    Your page may look different depending upon which browser is installed.

3. **Click the Web Page Preview button 🔍 on the Web Tools toolbar**

    The first page of the Web site opens in your browser, as shown in Figure J-15.

4. **Click Related Links on the navigation bar**

    Page 2 of the IE Web site appears on the browser screen, as shown in Figure J-16.

    TROUBLE
    You will not be able to test the hyperlink if you cannot connect to the Internet.

5. **Click the Course Technology link**

    The Course Technology Web site now appears on the browser screen.

6. **Click the Close button on the browser window**

7. **Click the Save button 💾 on the Standard toolbar in the Publisher window, then close the publication**

Renaming a Web page

The name of each page displays when you position the pointer over the page icon at the bottom of the screen. This name is generated automatically when you create the page, so it may not be to your liking. You can change the name of the page by right-clicking the page icon, then clicking Rename. Type the new name in the Page title text box in the Web Page Options dialog box, then click OK.

FIGURE J-15: Web Page preview of Page 1

FIGURE J-16: Web Page preview of Related Links page

Hyperlink to Course
Technology Web site

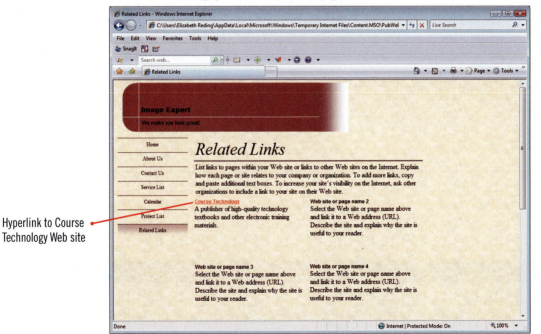

Publishing a Web Site

Once your Web site is finished, you will want to publish it to the Internet so that others can see it. Publisher offers several ways to do this. The following instructions are for Windows Vista. Before you can publish a Web site to the Internet, you must subscribe to a Web hosting service. This service will provide you with Internet access, storage space on a Web server, and a **Uniform Resource Locator (URL)**. Once the Image Expert Web site is complete, it will need to be published to the Internet. You research the steps required to do this so that you will be familiar with the procedure.

STEPS

Read below to understand how to publish a Web site, but *do not* complete the instructions at this time.

- **Finding a Web hosting service**

  The first step in publishing a Web site is to find a Web hosting provider. The Web page shown in Figure J-17 is a good place to start if you need assistance. Note the URL in the Address text box on the page. Once your ISP has provided you with a URL, click File on the menu bar, then click Publish to the Web. Click OK to close the warning box if necessary, then supply a file name (if saving locally) or the URL for the network server where you want to save your Web site in the Publish to the Web dialog box, as shown in Figure J-18, then deliver your file(s) to your ISP.

- **Saving the publication as a Web page**

  To save the publication as a Web page, you must use the Publish to the Web Page dialog box, which is available by clicking Publish to the Web on the File menu or clicking the Publish to the Web button on the Web Tools toolbar. Open the location you want, double-click the folder in which you want your files published, then click Save.

- **Publishing to the Web incrementally**

  Once your site is ready to be uploaded to the Web, you can publish it. Later, as you make changes to your files, you can publish incrementally to the Web. This means that you won't have to republish each file, just the ones that have been updated. You can change the incremental option by clicking Tools on the menu bar, then clicking Options. Click the Web tab in the Options dialog box, select the Enable incremental publish to the Web check box, then click OK.

Design Matters

Adding design elements

There are a wide variety of design elements for Web pages, which can be found on the Microsoft Office Clip Art and Media Web site, including some that create movement and sound. Animated GIFs and sound clips will not be visible or heard within Publisher. They are only displayed or played with a browser. You can attract attention by creating moving images or using an animated GIF. The **Graphics Interchange Format (GIF)** is commonly used on the Web because of its small file size, which makes it quick to download.

Additionally, you can add sounds to your Web pages so that people with sound-capable computers will be able to hear them when the page opens. You can install most commonly used sound formats by clicking Tools on the menu bar, then clicking Web Page Options. Click the Browse button located near the bottom of the Web Page Options dialog box, then navigate to the location of a specific sound on your computer.

FIGURE J-17: Web Hosting Services Web Site

FIGURE J-18: Publish to the Web dialog box

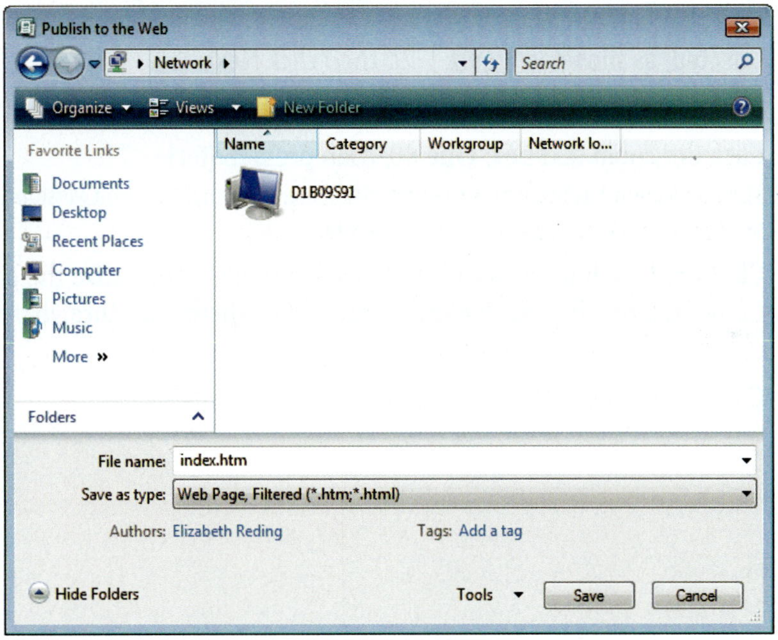

Increasing Web site traffic

The key to a successful Internet site is its accessibility to all Web users. After all, if no one sees your site, the caliber of its design is irrelevant. At minimum, you want to contact interested parties by e-mail to let them know of your site. You also want to register your Web site with several **search engines**, special Web sites that search for and report on information found on the Internet. Because many search engines compile their indices using keywords, the descriptive reference words found on a page, it is important to include those words. Additionally, there are several listing services on the Internet that will make submissions to the search engines, and provide information on maximizing the amount of traffic to your site.

Converting a Publication to a Web Page

By using existing documents in a Web site, you can increase your site's usefulness to a reader, and make additional use of your written work. Using Publisher, it is easy to convert a publication, such as a newsletter or brochure, to a Web page. Once a publication is converted to a Web site, you can modify the design and create your own hyperlinks. In the future, you plan to convert several Image Expert publications to Web pages, including a new information brochure on the company. You decide to start creating the brochure, and then use this work-in-progress to test the conversion process.

STEPS

1. Click **File** on the menu bar, click **New**, then click **Brochures** in the Publication Types list
2. Click **Borders** in the Informational section of Classic Designs, then click **Create**
   The brochure is created and appears on the screen.

> **QUICK TIP**
> You can switch to the Color Schemes task pane to find out which color scheme is currently in use.

3. Apply the **Tidepool color scheme**, then save the publication as **Brochure Conversion** to the drive and folder where you store your Data Files
4. Click the **text frame** at **9" H / 5" V**, type **Image Expert Brochure**, then press **[Esc]** twice
5. Click **File** on the menu bar, click **Convert to Web Publication**, then verify that the **Yes, save my print publication and then convert it to a Web publication option button** is selected, as shown in Figure J-19, then click **Next**
6. Verify that the **No, do not add a navigation bar option button** is selected, then click **Finish**
7. Click the **Zoom text box**, type **60**, then press **[Enter]**
   The publication has been converted to a Web site. Although the print version of this publication has been saved, the Web version has not yet been saved.
8. Click the **Save button** on the Standard toolbar, then save the publication as **Converted Brochure** to the drive and folder where you store your Data Files
   Compare your screen to Figure J-20.
9. Click **File** on the menu bar, then click **Exit**

Using Web mode

Once a print publication is converted to a Web publication, you are using the Web mode. The Web mode includes the Web Tools toolbar, which contains commonly used tools for making changes and additions to hyperlinks and navigation bars. The Web mode specifically tailors Web publications for optimal effectiveness when viewed in a browser. You can view your publication in your installed browser by clicking the

Web Page Preview button on the Web Tools toolbar. By clicking the Page button (to the far right of the tabs), then clicking Edit with Microsoft Office Word, you can edit the browser document using all the tools available in Microsoft Word (assuming this program is installed on your computer).

FIGURE J-19: Convert to Web Publication dialog box

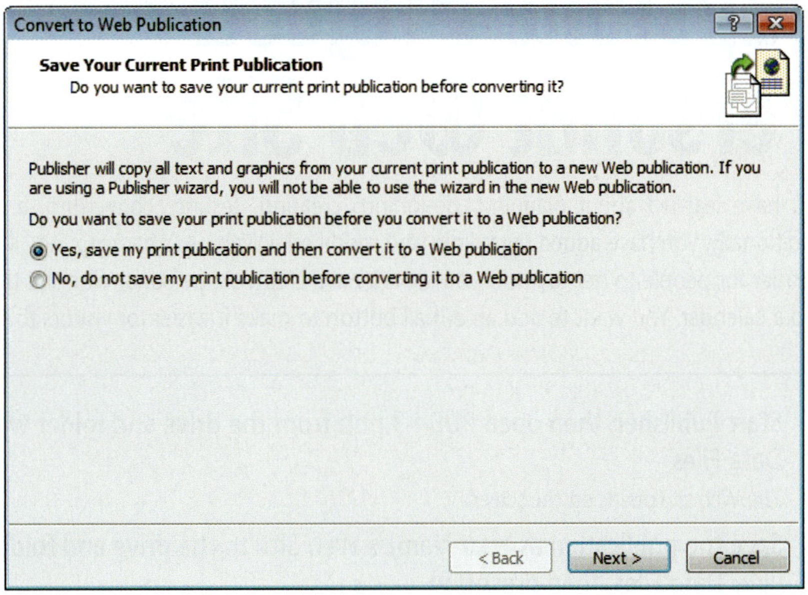

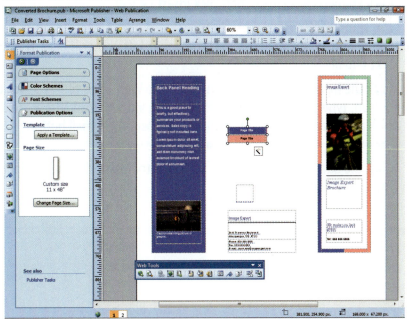

FIGURE J-20: Web site after conversion from a brochure

Publisher 2007

Converting a Web site to a print publication

You can also convert a Publisher-designed Web site into a brochure or newsletter. Once the Web site you want to convert is open, click File on the menu bar, then click Convert to Print Publication, select the Yes, save my Web publication and then convert it to a print publication option button, then click Finish.

Capstone Project: Personal Web Site

You have learned about planning, designing, creating, testing, converting, and publishing Web sites. Additionally, you have added hyperlinks and modified a Web site's background. You want to make it easier for people to get to know you so you have created a personal Web site that contains your resume and a calendar. You want to add an e-mail button to make it easier for visitors to the page to contact you.

1. **Start Publisher, then open PUB J-3.pub from the drive and folder where you store your Data Files**

   The Web site opens on the screen.

2. **Save the publication as Your Name's Web Site to the drive and folder where you store your Data Files, then press [F9]**

   The Design Gallery contains many design elements specifically created for use on Web sites.

3. **Click the Design Gallery Object button on the Objects toolbar, then click Buttons in the Categories list**

   You can easily find a variety of design elements specifically made for insertion on Web pages, as shown in Figure J-21.

4. **Click Framed Oval Email, then click Insert Object**

   The button is inserted onto the Web page.

5. **Using drag the object so that the upper-left corner is at ½" H / 4½" V, then click the text E-mail**

6. **Click the Insert Hyperlink button on the Web Tools toolbar, click the E-mail Address button, type yourname@imageexpert.com in the E-mail address text box, click OK, then click anywhere on the scratch area to deselect the E-mail button**

   The e-mail hyperlink is created. Compare your page to Figure J-22.

7. **Click the Save button on the Standard toolbar, print the first page of the Web site, then close Publisher**

FIGURE J-21: Buttons category in the Design Gallery

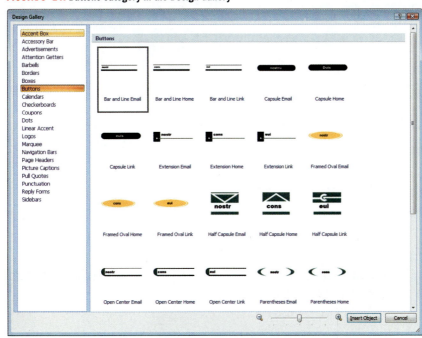

FIGURE J-22: Text box added to Web site

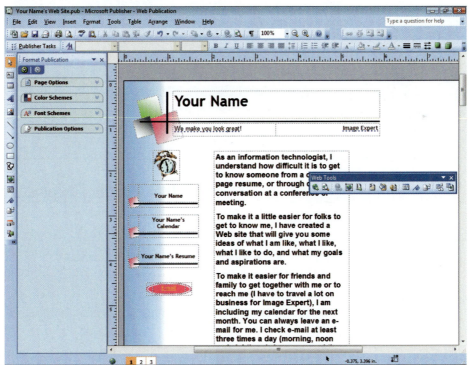

Practice

▼ CONCEPTS REVIEW

Label each of the elements in the Publisher window shown in Figure J-23.

FIGURE J-23

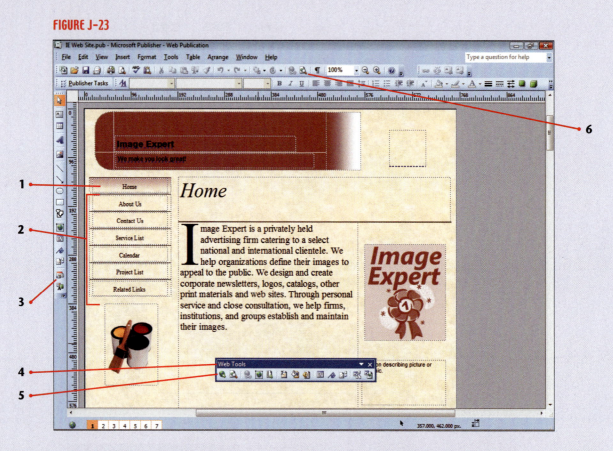

Match each of the buttons or terms with the statement that describes its function.

7. 🔍

8. **Animated GIF**

9. **Navigation bar**

10. 🖼

11. **Internet Service Provider**

12. 🖼

a. Image with movement

b. Displays page in browser

c. Provider of Internet access and Web site services

d. Creates a hyperlink

e. Contains Web design elements

f. Buttons on a Web page containing links to other Web pages in the same Web site

Select the best answer from the list of choices.

13. **Which button would you use to add a hyperlink to a page?**
    a.
    b.
    c.
    d.

14. **Which button can you use to add a Design Gallery element to a page?**
    a.
    b.
    c.
    d.

15. **Each of the following is true about a navigation bar, except:**
    a. Publisher creates one automatically as part of a Web site.
    b. It can contain an animated GIF.
    c. It can be horizontal or vertical in design.
    d. It is automatically updated when a page is added.

16. **You can modify a Web page's background texture using the:**
    a. File menu.
    b. Edit menu.
    c. Web Tools toolbar
    d. All the above

17. **Which of the following can be hyperlinks on a Web page?**
    a. Other Web sites
    b. E-mail addresses
    c. Web pages on your own Web site
    d. All of the above

18. **GIF stands for:**
    a. Great Image Format.
    b. Graphics Interchange Format.
    c. Good Image Format.
    d. None of the above

19. **Add sound clips to a Web page using the:**
    a. Objects toolbar.
    b. Tools menu
    c. Format menu.
    d. Programs menu.

20. **Which statement about hyperlinks is true?**
    a. You can add a hyperlink to any object.
    b. The only object to which you can add a hyperlink is an animated GIF.
    c. You cannot add a hyperlink to a text frame.
    d. A hyperlink cannot be used with e-mail.

21. **Which statement is true about animated GIFs?**
    a. They only display movement in a browser.
    b. They display movement in Publisher and a browser.
    c. They cannot be added to the Clip Gallery.
    d. They are available for a fee from Microsoft Design Gallery.

▼ SKILLS REVIEW

Throughout these exercises, use the Zoom feature when necessary to adjust your view of the page.

1. **Planning a Web site.**
   a. You own Ladders By Mail, a small business that sells a wide variety of ladders to individuals and other businesses. You specialize in high-quality ladders for indoor and outdoor use, and in timely shipment and delivery. You are planning a Web site for Ladders By Mail. What are your constraints?
   b. Who is your target audience?
   c. Do you want your Web site to be interactive? If so, what type of interaction do you think will be effective in attracting potential customers?

2. **Designing a Web site.**
   a. Make a list of the type of information you want to display and the number of pages that will be required.
   b. Make preliminary sketches of the pages that will be required.

3. **Create a Web site.**
   a. Start Publisher.
   b. Use the Publication Types list and the Web Sites category to create a Web site for Ladders By Mail. Select the Bubbles template and do not select any checkboxes in the Easy Web Site Builder dialog box. Use the Secondary Business Information Set and the Citrus color scheme.
   c. Save the file as **Ladders By Mail Web Site** to the drive and folder where you store your Data Files.
   d. Replace the Home Page Title text at 288 H / 64 V with **Ladders By Mail**.
   e. Replace the text in the frame at 96 H / 16 V with **Your Name, Owner**.
   f. Replace the logo text (at 672 H / 48 V) with the company name, then save your work.

4. **Add hyperlinks.**
   a. Insert a Related Links page after the home page. (*Hint*: Make sure that the hyperlink is added to the Web navigation bar.)
   b. Change the title on page 2 at 288 H / 160 V and on the navigation bar to **Happy Customers**.
   c. Click the Web site or page name 1 text, then type **Microsoft Corporation**.
   d. Select the Microsoft Corporation text, then click the Insert Hyperlink button on the Web Tools toolbar.
   e. Make sure that the Existing File or Web Page button is selected, enter the Internet address **http://www.microsoft.com**, then click OK.
   f. Save your work.

5. **Modify a Web page background.**
   a. Open the Master Page, display the Background task pane, click More backgrounds, then click the Texture tab in the Fill Effects dialog box.
   b. Click the Blue tissue paper texture, the first sample in the fifth row.
   c. Click OK.
   d. Return to Normal view.
   e. Save your work.

6. **Test a Web site.**
   a. Display the Design Checker task pane, make a note of any errors other than alternative text and space below margins, then close the Design Checker.
   b. Click the Web Page Preview button on the Web Tools toolbar.
   c. Click Happy Customers on the navigation bar on page 1.
   d. Click Microsoft Corporation. (*Hint*: If you are not connected to the Internet, you will not be able to view the Microsoft Web site. Skip Steps d and e.)
   e. Close the browser.
   f. Print the current page.
   g. Save and close the Web site publication.

7. Publishing a Web site.

   a. Using your own ISP as an example, investigate the procedure you would use to publish the Web site for Ladders By Mail.

   b. Find out if your ISP has any hosting fees or space limitations.

8. Convert a publication to a Web page.

   a. Use the Publication Types list to create a brochure for Ladders By Mail. Select the Bubbles template in Classic Designs, use the Secondary Business Information Set (using appropriate names, etc.), then apply the Citrus color scheme and change the logo text to reflect the company name.

   b. Save the file as **Ladders By Mail Brochure** to the drive and folder where you store your Data Files.

   c. Click Convert to Web Publication on the File menu, making sure that you save the print publication before the conversion, and add a navigation bar.

   d. Make sure Your Name displays in the email address at the bottom of the center panel on page 1.

   e. Save the file as **Ladder Brochure Conversion** to the drive and folder where you store your Data Files.

   f. Move the navigation bar to the top of the center panel on page 1, then save your work and print page 1 of the Web site.

   g. Close the publication.

   h. Exit Publisher.

▼ INDEPENDENT CHALLENGE 1

You are the proud owner of a very successful rare comic book store in Binghamton, NY. You decide to expand your store, Comix Alive, by designing a Web site. This way, you will be able to retain all the university student customers who leave town after graduation.

   a. Start Publisher, create a new Web site based on the Blocks template.

   b. Your Web site should contain only the home page.

   c. Use the Business Information Set of your choice, an appropriate slogan for the store, and the Floral color scheme.

   d. Save the publication as **Comix Alive Web Site** to the drive and folder where you store your Data Files.

   e. Change the title of the home page to **Your Name's Comix Alive**.

   f. Insert a Related Links page after the home page.

   g. Select the Web site or page name 1 text listed on page 2.

   h. Create a hyperlink to any comic book site. Use your favorite search engine to find a site.

   i. Save the publication, print the first page of the publication, then exit Publisher.

▼ INDEPENDENT CHALLENGE 2

Your family asks you to create a newsletter that can be distributed to everybody, and you know that a request for a Web site isn't far behind. Thinking ahead, you want to prepare a simple mock-up of a family newsletter, convert it to a Web site, then suggest it to the family at your next gathering.

a. Start Publisher, then use any newsletter template to create a new publication, accepting all the defaults.

b. Use the Business Information Set of your choice to enter appropriate information, customize all information, such as newsletter and logo text, then change the color scheme to one of your choice.

c. Save the publication as **Family Newsletter** to the drive and folder where you store your Data Files.

d. Make modifications you feel are necessary to give family members a feel for the newsletter, but make sure that the newsletter masthead contains your last name. (For example, the masthead might be "Your Name's Family News.")

e. Place your name in one of the headlines on page 1.

f. Save your work and print the first page of the newsletter.

g. Convert the publication to a Web site.

h. Save the converted publication as **Family Web Site** to the drive and folder where you store your Data Files.

Advanced Challenge Exercises

■ Use the Design Gallery Object button to add a Web button on the home page.

■ Create a hyperlink to the Web button that allows a user to send e-mail to you.

■ Rename pages 2 and 3 as **Page 2** and **Page 3**.

i. Save the Web site, print the home page, then exit Publisher.

▼ INDEPENDENT CHALLENGE 3

You are creating a Web site for Jackie's Joke Shop, a novelty store. The company's management team is not technologically sophisticated but they believe they need a Web site to be competitive in their local market. You need to plan and then create the Web site.

a. Write down a list of key questions that management should consider before pursuing their planning process.

b. Sketch out two Web site plans. One plan involves creating a Web site describing the shop, and showing their location, phone number and an e-mail link at minimal cost. The other option is more involved. In addition to informing potential customers about Jackie's, it would, at moderate cost, let them sell a limited number of items over the Internet.

c. Make a recommendation of which plan they should choose. Support your recommendation in terms that will be understandable given your client's limited knowledge of technology.

d. Based on your recommendation, use Publisher to create a Web site using the design and style of your choice.

e. Save the publication as **Joke Shop Web Site** in the drive and folder where you store your Data Files.

f. Include your name, address and phone number in the Web site.

g. Save the Web site, print the home page, then exit Publisher.

▼ REAL LIFE INDEPENDENT CHALLENGE

This Challenge requires an Internet connection.

You have seen how dynamic Web sites look when they contain animated GIFs, or other sources of animation. But you have probably also seen Web sites that go overboard in gimmicky and silly design stunts that distract from their message. In this exercise you are asked to use your own judgment about what is good design.

a. Connect to the Internet and use your favorite search engine to search on **good Web site design** or **best of the Web**, then locate two examples of well-designed Web sites.

b. Start Publisher. Create a flyer. Use the Business Information Set of your choice to enter appropriate information, customize any information such as a company name or logo text, then apply the color scheme of your choice. Save the publication as **Best Web Site Design Flyer**.

c. Describe the Web sites you chose in the flyer and list the sites by their URL.

d. Modify the flyer to include your name.

e. Describe what could be done to improve those Web sites.

Advanced Challenge Exercise

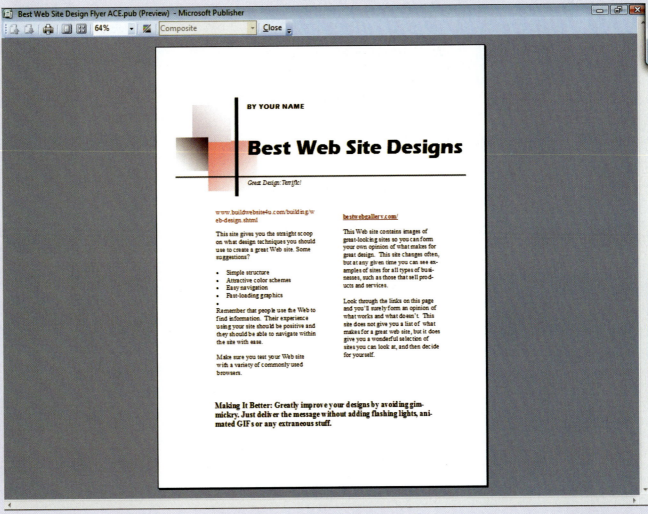

■ Using the URLs you entered in Step c, create hyperlinks to the sites.

f. Print the flyer, as shown in Figure J-24, exit the browser, then exit Publisher.

FIGURE J-24

▼ VISUAL WORKSHOP

Use the Publication Types list to create the Southwest Web site. Save the Web site to the drive and folder where you store your Data Files as **Ultimate Traveler Web Site**. Use the Olive color scheme, add two additional story pages (Colorado Adventures and New Mexico Adventures), and change the background to Canvas. Insert the images PUB J-4.tif and PUB J-5.tif (found in the drive and folder where you store your Data Files) into the home page. Replace any text, and resize and rearrange any elements, using Figure J-25 as a guide. Include your name in a text box on page one, then print page one.

FIGURE J-25

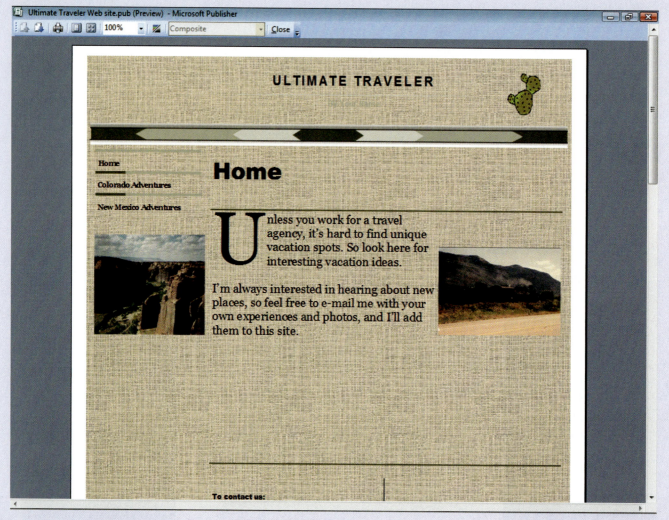

Glossary

Align To arrange two or more items along an edge.

Animated GIFs An image with movement; commonly used in Web pages.

Asymmetrical balance Balance of elements on the page that achieves a more dynamic and informal appearance than symmetrical balance.

AutoCorrect A feature that automatically corrects misspellings and grammar errors as you type.

AutoFit A feature that automatically resizes type and manipulates text to fit within a text box.

Autoflow A feature that automatically places text that does not fit in a text box into the next available text box.

AutoShapes Ready-made design elements, including lines, connectors, basic shapes, flowchart elements, stars and banners, and callouts.

Balance Symmetrical arrangement of design elements on a page.

Baseline guides A set of layout guides that automatically align text to the baseline, and add equal line spacing so the text appears balanced along columns.

Booklet A multi-page publication that is folded or bound.

Border The edge or boundary line of an object.

BorderArt Decorative borders that come with or can be created using Publisher for placement around most objects.

Bring to front Command that places the currently selected object in front, or on top, of other objects.

Browser A program that locates and displays data from sources on the Internet, such as Web pages, and other networks.

Bulleted list Used to illustrate items that can occur in any order or that are of equal importance.

Business Information Sets An unlimited number of distinct sets of information that can be used to store frequently used information such as names, addresses, and phone numbers, which can be placed automatically in publications.

Camera-ready artwork Graphic illustrations that have been fully prepared for the printing of a publication.

Catalog A publication that presents a list or display of items.

Chart A graphic representation of numerical information.

Clip art Electronic artwork available for use on a computer.

Clipboard Temporary holding area in Windows into which as many as 24 objects can be copied and pasted.

Color schemes Coordinated sets of matched and complementary colors that may be applied to a publication.

Color wheels Circular illustrations where primary and intermediate colors are arranged so that related colors are next to each other and complementary colors are opposite.

Continued on/Continued from notices Text that tells on what page a story is continued on or from, and automatically updates if the story is moved.

Copyfitting To make text fit into a space within a publication.

Crop To conceal portions of an image.

Data source Files in which names, addresses, and other contact information is stored to be used in a mail merge.

Data source files Files that can come from several programs that are used in a mail merge.

Database A collection of information arranged for easy search and retrieval.

Design The layout and choice of colors, fonts, and artwork that enhance a publication.

Design Checker A feature that searches publications for specific layout problems.

Design Gallery A collection of formatted elements, such as pull quotes, sidebars, and logos, that can be added to an existing publication.

Design Gallery Objects Objects created by the Design Gallery that contain text or graphic images that can be edited for size, shape, and content.

Desktop publishing program A program that lets you combine text and graphics, as well as worksheets and charts created in other programs, to produce typeset-quality documents for output on a computer printer, or for commercial printing.

Destination file The file into which an object is embedded or linked.

Digital camera A camera that captures and stores images as digital electronic information instead of on photographic film.

Digital image A pictorial representation generated, stored, or displayed electronically.

Drag and drop Moving or copying technique in which an object, or a copy of an object, is dragged to a new location.

Drawing tools Toolbox buttons that let you create geometric designs.

Drop cap A formatting feature that lets you change the size and appearance of a paragraph's initial character.

Electronic spreadsheet Software in which data is arranged in rows and columns and mathematical operations and charting functions are performed.

Embedded object An object created in a source file that is inserted in a destination document. The object then becomes part of the destination file.

Field An element of a database record that contains one piece of information, such as a zip code or first name.

Fill To add a color, pattern, or texture to a design element.

Fill color The hue added to shade a design element.

Filtering Allows you to print, preview, or merge a portion of qualifying records in a mail merge.

Flatbed scanner A type of digital scanner that has a sheet of glass where the page is place to be scanned. The optical sensor then passes along the glass.

Flip To rotate an object 180 degrees horizontally or vertically using a toolbar button.

Font schemes Coordinated sets of matched and complementary fonts that may be applied to a publication.

Footer Text that repeats on the bottom of each page.

Foreground The section of a publication where non-repeating information is placed, such as textboxes or images.

Formatting toolbar Buttons on a toolbar that change the appearance of objects within a publication.

Frame An object in a publication containing a photographic image, a table, or any combination of these.

GIF (Graphics Interchange Format) A commonly used file format for graphics used in Web pages due to its small size; displayed by most browsers without the use of additional programs.

Graphic image A piece of artwork in electronic form.

Group Selection of multiple images that can be moved or resized as a single unit.

Grouping To turn several objects into one, which is an easy way to move multiple items.

Handles Small hollow circles displayed around the perimeter of a selected object.

Hand-off format The final digital electronic format of a publication that is conveyed to a commercial printer.

Header Text that repeats on the top of each page.

Help Feature that gives you immediate access to definitions, explanations, and useful tips on working in Publisher.

Home page The first page, or primary page, in a Web site.

Horizontal ruler Measuring guide that appears above the publication window.

Hyperlink A connection, either text or an object, in a document that, when clicked, connects with another page or object. Hyperlinks connect Web pages together on the Internet. Also called a link.

Intellectual property Digital materials, including images, magazines, books, and other material available on the Internet, that may be copyrighted and have limitations placed on their use. Permission is required for the use of such materials.

Kerning A form of character formatting that adjusts the spacing between character pairs.

Keywords Words used to search for specific pages, objects, or images within applications.

Layer To change the position of objects in relation to one another so that one appears to be on top of or in back of another.

Layout guides Horizontal and vertical lines positioned on a publication's Master Page and visible on all pages to help you accurately position objects.

Leaders Dots, dashes, or lines in a row that make it easier to read a table of contents or other information by guiding the eye across the page.

Link *See* Hyperlink.

Linked object An object created in a source file that is shared in a destination file. The object retains its connection to the source file.

Logo Distinctive shape, symbol, or color that visibly identifies a company or product.

Mail merge A feature that combines a destination document, such as a personalized brochure, with a data source, such as an Excel or Access file containing names and addresses, using an interactive set of dialog boxes that guides the user in creating a mail merge.

Mail Merge task pane Tool that guides you through the merging process and allows you to customize your data source and your publication.

Margin guides Lines that repeat on each page, separating the margins from the other design elements.

Margins White space between the edge of design element and the edge of a page.

Mask An object designed to hide a specific area so that the final result looks seamless.

Master page The section of a publication where objects are placed so that they are reproduced on every page.

Masthead The banner at the beginning of a newsletter with its name, volume, issue, and date, which remains consistently formatted from issue to issue.

Matte A colorful shape positioned behind an object to make it stand out.

Measurement toolbar Toolbar that lets you more precisely move, resize, or adjust objects.

Menu bar Contains menus from which you choose Publisher commands.

Microsoft Clip Organizer The artwork organizer in Publisher.

Microsoft Office Online A Microsoft Web site that continually offers new downloadable resources for creating publications.

Mirrored guides Layout guides and margins on left and right facing pages that appear to be mirror images.

Mirrored image A type of two-page layout where either page appears as if viewed in a mirror, with right and left reversed.

Navigation Bar A row of buttons on a Web page containing links to information on the site's subpages.

Nudge To move a selected object a defined distance by pressing an arrow key.

Numbered list Used to list items that occur in a particular sequence.

Object An element such as a table, text box, geometric shape, clip art, and picture frame that can be resized, moved, joined, or layered.

Object shadow Gives an object the illusion of depth by adding a shadow behind it.

Objects toolbar Contains buttons used to create and enhance publication objects.

Office Collections The artwork library shared by all Microsoft Office applications.

Online collaboration Participants working together on a project across the Internet.

Optical center The point around which objects on the page are balanced, approximately 3/8" from the top of the page.

Optical Character Recognition (OCR) A software application that transforms scanned images of text into digital electronic documents.

Orientation Direction in which paper is printed.

Pack and Go Wizard Feature that compacts all the files (fonts, graphics, and essential design elements) needed by a commercial printing service onto your choice of media.

Page navigation icons Located at the bottom of the workspace, one page icon displays for each page in the publication. You click a navigation icon to go to a specific page.

Page numbers The numbers assigned in sequence to pages of text in a publication.

Personal Information Manager A program that keeps track of business and personal contacts and schedules appointments.

Pixel The fundamental unit of an image on a television screen, computer monitor, or similar display.

Placeholders Design elements provided by Publisher that you can replace with your own information to customize a publication.

Point size The measurement of the height of a character. 1/72 of an inch equals one point.

Postscript file A page description format developed by Adobe Systems that is widely supported by both hardware and software vendors.

Pour To move text that will not fit in a text box to an empty text box.

Pre-press work Process in which a commercial printer verifies the availability of fonts and linked graphics, makes color corrections or separations, and sets the final printing options.

Presentation A series of projected slides and/or handouts that a speaker refers to while delivering information.

Print Create output from a publication into paper form.

Print Preview A feature that lets you see exactly how the publication will look when printed.

Proof print Approximation of how your final printed publication will look.

Publication A document created in Publisher.

Publication Types list A section of the Publisher window that includes a list of categories for publication types, such as newsletters.

Pull quote A short statement extracted from a story and set aside from the body of the text.

Record A group of related fields, such as the name, address, and title of a customer.

Resolution A measure of the fineness of detail that can be distinguished in an image.

Response Form A printed or electronic arrangement of blanks for the insertion of information that invites a reply.

Reversed text Format text so that it appears in white on a dark background.

Rotate Changes the position of an object in degrees from a horizontal plane.

Rotation An object's position measured in degrees from a horizontal plane.

Ruler guidelines *See* Ruler guides.

Ruler guides Created in the foreground of individual pages by dragging a ruler by holding [Shift]. Also referred to as ruler guidelines.

Rulers Horizontal and vertical measurement guides located beneath the toolbars and to the left of the workspace.

Sans serif font A typeface that has no small strokes at the end of the main stroke of the character.

Scaling Formatting effect that stretches or shrinks the widths of characters.

Scanner Hardware that enables you to turn information on paper into an electronic file format.

Scratch area Area surrounding the publication page that can be used to store design elements.

Search engines Special Web sites that search for and report on information found on the Internet.

Send to back Command that places an object behind other objects.

Serif The small decorative strokes added to the end of a letter's main strokes. They help distinguish one character to another and serve as an aid to comprehension.

Serif font A typeface that has a small cross stroke at the end of the main stroke of the letter.

Sheetfed Scanner A type of digital scanner that uses rollers to pull a single sheet of paper past the optical scanning device.

Sidebar Information not central to a story in a publication, placed to the side of the regular text to create interest.

Signature A large sheet printed with four or a multiple of four pages that when folded becomes a section of a book or catalog.

Smart objects An object category in the Design Gallery that can be modified by clicking the associated Wizard button.

Snap To commands When turned on, this feature has a magnet-like effect that pulls whatever is being lined up to an object, a guide, or a ruler mark.

Sorting Allows you to change the order in which the merged publications are printed or viewed.

Source file When linking, the file that contains the information you want to share with another document. Once linked, the shared information will be updated if the source file is updated.

Speech recognition Software used to transform human speech into computer commands or text.

Spelling checker Used to check a story or publication for spelling errors.

Standard toolbar Toolbar containing buttons for common tasks, such as saving and printing.

Status bar Located at the bottom of the Publisher window; provides information relevant to the current task.

Story Text in a publication.

Style Defined set of text formatting attributes.

Style by example To name an existing set of text attributes as a style.

Symmetrical balance Objects are placed equally on either side of an imaginary vertical line.

Tab A location that the insertion point advances to when you press [Tab].

Table Arrangement of information in a grid of columns and rows.

Table AutoFormat Pre-existing designs used to quickly format an existing table.

Table of contents A sequential list of the contents and associated page numbers of a publication.

Task pane An area of the Publisher window that is used to organize design templates, color schemes, font schemes, and other layout tools in a visual gallery which appears alongside the publication.

Template A specially formatted publication with placeholder text that serves as a master for other, similar publications.

Testimonial An affirmation of an entity or product's worth by a non-involved party; a recommendation.

Text box Object in which text is typed.

Text overflow Text that does not fit within a text box.

Text wrapping The automatic placement of text around design elements.

Title bar Where the program name and the filename of the open publication appear.

Toolbars Contain buttons for frequently used Publisher commands, and are organized by subject, such as Formatting, Measurement, or Objects.

Tracking The spacing between characters.

Two-Page Spread View that enables you to see two pages at once.

Ungroup To turn one combined object into individual objects.

URL (Uniform Resource Locator) A Web page's address.

Vertical ruler Measuring guide that displays to the left of the page.

Washout A faint, lightly shaded image that appears behind other images. Also known as a watermark.

Web folder A shortcut to a location on a Web server where your pages will reside.

Web hosting service A service that will provide you with Internet access, storage space on a Web server, and a Uniform Resource Locator (URL).

White space Blank space in a publication.

Word processing program A software application used to generate and edit electronic documents.

WordArt An object containing curved or wavy text.

Workspace The area where a new or existing publication appears and its surrounding scratch area.

Wrap points The sizing handles that surround the object that are used to fine-tune the way text wraps an object.

Wrapping Text reshaped so it conforms to the shape of a nearby image or other object.

Zero point The location of zero on both the vertical and horizontal rulers that can be moved and lets you make precise measurements.

Zoom To make the page scale larger or smaller so that you can move in or away from page objects.

Index